D1091095

IN HIS OWN IMAGE:
The Supreme Court
In Richard Nixon's America

IN HIS
OWN IMAGE
The Supreme Court in
Richard Nixon's America

❦

JAMES F. SIMON

David McKay Company, Inc.

NEW YORK

FOR MY PARENTS
Natalie and Richard U. Simon

I have heard a great many people say to me "Well, I agree with your opinions on these civil rights, all right, but don't you think you are going too fast?" Of course, the answer to that is "We haven't anything to say about how fast we go." We go with the cases that come to us, and when they come to us with a question of human liberties involved in them, we either hear them and decide them, or we let them go and sweep them under the rug, only to leave them for future generations.

Chief Justice Earl Warren

It is not for nothing that one of the symbols of the law is the tortoise even though less well known to laymen than the blindfolded lady with the scales. This is why [Oliver Wendell] Holmes argued so vigorously all his life for the right of the political branches to experiment in the search for answers.

Chief Justice Warren E. Burger

CONTENTS

CHAPTER ONE

Politics and the Court

Events that shape a nation's future often occur unheralded at the time. But on June 23, 1969, a brief ceremony took place in the marbled chambers of the United States Supreme Court that journalists and judges, scholars and statesmen all knew was of historical moment. The fourteenth chief justice of the United States, Earl Warren, administered the oath of office to his successor, Warren E. Burger.

President Richard M. Nixon chose the occasion to deliver a speech, the first given by a president to the Court in the nation's history. Dressed in cutaway coat and striped trousers, the president spoke of the Court as a dual symbol of continuity and change in the nation. In praising Chief Justice Warren, Nixon said that his example, "the example of dignity, the example of integrity, the example of fairness, as the chief law official of this country, has helped to keep America on the path of continuity and change, which is so essential for our progress."

After the ceremony the two chief justices, Warren and Burger, joined the president on the courthouse steps. Against the backdrop of the huge, Corinthian columns, the three presented an imposing picture for the history books. They waved for the photographers, but the gesture was really for the nation. Here was the graphic continuity that the president had spoken of only moments before.

Despite that tidy impression, there was a surrealistic uneasiness to the scene. It was not what it appeared to be and no formal statement of unity, however forceful, could brush over that fact. The whole affair had the air of a celebration, produced, directed and celebrated by a single man: Richard Nixon. He had taken the initiative, not only appearing at the ceremony, but focusing attention on its significance. For his part, Chief Justice Warren chose to render a heartfelt and deeply personal defense of his judicial record and that of the Supreme Court under his leadership. "We have no constituency," said Warren. "We serve no majority. We serve no minority. We serve only the public interest as we see it, guided only by the Constitution and our own consciences."

Other signs of the Nixonian cast to the occasion abounded. The courtroom was packed with four hundred invited guests, almost all members or guests of the Nixon Administration or its newest appointee, Chief Justice Burger. To be sure, some of those present exemplified the stressed continuity of past with present, but they only underscored the Nixon triumph. William P. Rogers, former attorney general under President Dwight D. Eisenhower, and the new attorney general, John N. Mitchell, attended. But conspicuously absent was Ramsey Clark, Mitchell's predecessor at the Justice Department, and the man whom candidate Nixon had vowed to replace if elected.

Mrs. Nixon and Mrs. Earl Warren fell into easy conversation in the family section of the courtroom, something their husbands had been unable to do for twenty-three years. In a sense, the Nixon speech to the Court was an elaborate version of the age-old political game of burying the hatchet. For Earl Warren and Richard Nixon had never been friends, even amiable political acquaintances. The hostility between the two men began in 1946 when Nixon, a Republican candidate for Congress, faced a difficult race with Democratic incumbent Jerry Voorhis. An endorsement by the Republican governor of the state, Earl Warren, would have given the Nixon campaign an important boost. But Governor Warren, in the interest of political unity, had made it official policy not to endorse Republican candidates. Nixon won anyway and in 1950, when he was elected U.S. senator from California, it was again without Governor Warren's endorsement.

As the 1952 Republican convention neared, Senator Nixon was conspicuously controlled in his enthusiasm for the favorite son candidacy of Governor Warren. Nixon had previously polled 150,000 of his 1950 campaign workers to find out who they thought the Republican candidate should be. The results showed overwhelming support for General Eisenhower, results that were somehow leaked to the press. When the California delegation, pledged to Warren, posed for a picture after arrival at the Chicago convention, the junior senator from California was not among the photographed. Nixon's later behind-the-scenes activity to swing the California delegation to Ike was well known—and not forgotten by Earl Warren. He never spoke publicly of his dislike of Richard Nixon, for that was not his style. But he did comment once that "Nixon plays for keeps, but the keeps are all for himself." Nixon appeared self-serving even in praising Warren as he did in the 1956 presidential campaign, crediting "the *Republican* chief justice" with the desegregation decision.

The 1968 presidential race did nothing to heal the wounds. In the early state primaries Nixon made it clear that he would not spare the Court in his what's-wrong-with-America campaign. He criticized Warren Court decisions, particularly those expanding the rights of criminal suspects, and supported Title

II of the Crime Control Act, legislation that attempted to nullify the most controversial Warren Court decisions in the criminal law field.

In June 1968, Chief Justice Warren announced his resignation "solely because of age." The timing of the resignation, seven months before the inauguration of a new president, raised suspicions that Warren's resignation had been inspired by politics as much as longevity. By that time Nixon, who had already scored impressive victories in the primaries, appeared to be a shoo-in for the Republican nomination and a solid bet to become the next president of the United States. Given the Nixon campaign attacks and President Lyndon B. Johnson's admiration for the chief justice's judicial views (he called Warren the greatest chief justice in the nation's history), Warren naturally preferred to be replaced by a Johnson nominee rather than one of Richard Nixon's.

When President Johnson named Associate Justice Abe Fortas, an old friend of the president's and consistent liberal voting companion with Chief Justice Warren, the Warren Court seemed secure, for a while at least. Chief Justice Warren clearly found the Fortas nomination to his liking. When the Fortas candidacy floundered, Warren called his first press conference in three and a half years. Politely declining to answer questions of a "political" nature, the chief justice, nonetheless, defended President Johnson's right to name a new chief justice in his final months in office. If the Fortas nomination failed, Warren said, he would withdraw his resignation in the interests of the Court and the country. Unfortunately for Fortas partisans, the Chief Justice had to keep his word, remaining on the Court another term before President Nixon replaced him.

Richard Nixon's grievances with the Warren Court preceded his presidential candidacy of 1968. After he moved to New York in 1963, Nixon sometimes talked to associates about the

Court like a conservative Wall Street lawyer, which he was. For lawyer Nixon and the majority of practicing attorneys in the nation, the Warren Court's performance was unsettling. The Court seemed to Nixon to be uncharacteristically innovative, uncommonly legislative in its actions. He saw the Court as almost a fourth branch of government. It made decisions that profoundly changed American society, but unlike the other governmental institutions, the Court appeared to be beyond the recall of anybody.

By 1966, Nixon had begun to crank up a political organization to help him make another drive for the presidency. He now viewed the Court less as a lawyer and more as a politician. Gradually, the term "strict constructionist" entered the Nixon vocabulary, a flabby phrase that drew its meaning primarily from the political views of the speaker. Nixon said he wanted "strict constructionist" judges who would strictly and objectively interpret the meaning of the U.S. Constitution. But what did that mean? What, after all, could be the "strict constructionist" interpretation of the Fourteenth Amendment? What do the phrases "equal protection of the laws" and "due process of law" mean to the judge who "strictly" interprets the Constitution? If the Constitution were absolutely clear in meaning, of course, there would be no dissents. Judges would do what the late Justice Owen J. Roberts suggested more than three decades ago: lay the article of the Constitution which is invoked against the statute which is challenged to decide whether the former squares with the latter. Wiser heads had never paid much heed to the theory.

"It is a great mistake to suppose that the paper we are to propose will govern the United States," Maryland's John Mercer said in 1787. "It is the men whom it will bring into the government and interest in maintaining it." For law students who viewed the Constitution as the secular Scriptures, the first Justice John M. Harlan had some rather depressing news. "I want to say to you young gentlemen that if we don't like an act of Congress, we don't have much trouble to find grounds for declaring it unconstitutional." It was left to Justice Felix Frankfurter, a judge much admired by Richard Nixon, to put the myth of "strict construction" to rest. "The words of the Constitution are so unrestricted by their intrinsic meaning or by their history or by tradition or by prior decisions that they leave the individual justice free, if indeed they do not compel him, to gather meaning not from reading the Constitution but from reading life," wrote Frankfurter. He went on: "Members of the Court are frequently admonished by their associates not to read their economic and social views into the neutral language of the Constitution. But the process of constitutional interpretation compels the translation of policy into judgment."

Nixon, to be sure, realized the political potency of the "strict constructionist" term. To minorities and white liberals, it was a subtle denunciation of the Warren Court's expansive reading of individual rights. But Republicans had not counted on many votes from those groups anyway. The phrase appealed to conservatives and the silent majority who shared Nixon's concern that the Court had allowed the nation to become too permissive —with its criminal suspects as well as its literature. If the phrase drew the secret approval of a racist backlash, well, that was unfortunate but not a factor that would cause a change in the Nixon strategy.

In the same week that the Senate began debate on the Omnibus Crime Control and Safe Streets bill, Nixon discussed the nation's crime problem and delivered his most pointed criticism of the Warren Court. He noted that only one out of eight major crimes committed in the country resulted in punishment and that a 12 per cent chance of punishment "is not adequate to deter a man bent on a career of crime." Nixon charged that the Warren Court decisions in the criminal area were contributing factors to the tiny punishment percentage. "The *Miranda* and

Escobedo decisions [which expanded a criminal suspect's rights in the police station] of the High Court have had the effect of seriously hamstringing the peace forces in our society and strengthening the criminal forces." (The peace forces–criminal forces matchup pleased Nixon so much that it became one of his most familiar slogans during the campaign.) "From the point of view of the criminal forces," Nixon went on, "the cumulative impact of these decisions has been to set free patently guilty individuals on the basis of legal technicalities. The tragic lesson of guilty men walking free from hundreds of court-rooms across the country has not been lost on the criminal community."

Nixon's position on crime was considerably more impressive for its political appeal than its factual accuracy. First of all, measuring crime by crime statistics has always been a hazard-ous business. Major crime statistics are notoriously poor indica-tors of actual crimes committed. Many major crimes are never officially reported and, in any case, the reporting accuracy has always varied widely from area to area. Moreover, the "major crime" category itself was misleading. A major crime like car theft, for example, fattened Mr. Nixon's "major crimes com-mitted" category much more than the well-publicized rapes, robberies and homocides. But it was not the car thief that the average American was worried about nor was he really the target Mr. Nixon had in mind. A second problem with the Nixon view was its undue emphasis on the low punishment rate for major offenders. The greatest difficulty for law enforcement officials, as President Johnson's Task Force on Crime had pointed out, was not punishing the criminal but catching him in the first place. And finally, the Nixon attack on the Court's decisions that "set free patently guilty individuals" did not really tell the whole story. The confession, which was the major target of the *Escobedo* and *Miranda* decisions, was rarely the only factor that led to a conviction. As if to prove the point,

Ernest Miranda himself was retried after the Supreme Court decision which threw out his confession, and was convicted on other evidence.

Richard Nixon, of course, was conducting a political campaign, not a graduate seminar in constitutional law. His advisors concentrated on political advantage, not scholarship. One advisor, Senator Strom Thurmond of South Carolina, told Nixon two months before the Republican convention that there was no stronger issue, in the South at least, than what Governor George Wallace called that "sorry, lousy, no-account outfit," better known as the U.S. Supreme Court. Not surprisingly, then, when Nixon met with southern delegates shortly before the Miami convention, the candidate did not hide his distress at the trend of the Court nor his intention, if elected president, to appoint justices who would strictly interpret the law.

After his nomination, Nixon hammered at the theme. If elected, he told a southern television audience, he would appoint men "who will interpret the Constitution strictly and fairly and objectively." And later: "I think some of our judges have gone too far in assuming unto themselves a mandate which is not there, and that is, to put their social and economic ideas into their decisions." As president, Nixon promised, he would seek out "strict constructionists."

In the final analysis, Nixon meant that he would appoint judges who took less active and reform-minded views of the Court's constitutional role than had the justices of the Warren Court. Nixon wanted a Court majority that thought more like lawyers than statesmen. He wanted judges who would leave legislators' laws alone, even if the justices thought the laws unwise. The president surely hoped also that the new Supreme Court justices would not tamper too much with his own activities. In short, Nixon planned for a more subdued U.S. Supreme Court than the one of the Warren years, one that would go about its constitutional business with caution and deference to other branches of government and one that would leave the major national policy decisions to the president and the Congress.

Throughout American history, Presidents have encouraged the politicalization of the Supreme Court. George Washington started it all. At the time of his first appointments, Washington called the Court "the keystone of our political fabric." As if to prove his point, the Father of the Country placed six loyal Federalists on the first Supreme Court. All stood steadfastly behind Federalist doctrine that supported the broad exercise of power by the national government, especially in maintaining public order and protecting the interests of the propertied classes. They would, on the other hand, limit the power of states that interfered with broad national purposes. Washington's political instincts carried him beyond merely naming Federalist faithful to the Court: he was the first president to employ a southern strategy, naming to his first Court three northerners and three southerners.

In those days, there was no shame attached to the political appointment. Indeed, many of the Court appointees continued to perform political tasks while sitting on the bench. The first chief justice, John Jay, for example, served at the same time as the President's diplomatic representative to Great Britain. In addition, Jay ran for governor of New York twice while still chief justice; when he finally won the office, Jay indicated which office he held in higher esteem by resigning from the Court to make politics his full-time job.

Two later Washington appointees, William Paterson and Samuel Chase, made no attempt to hide their political biases while on the bench. Both presided over Alien and Sedition Act convictions of those who audaciously called Federalist leaders nasty names and frequently showed their partisanship by making pro-Federalist speeches from the bench. Chase was not content to deliver speeches; he openly and eagerly participated in political campaigns against the Jeffersonian Republicans.

Thomas Jefferson was so infuriated by the success of Presidents Washington and John Adams in appointing political loyalists who continued their allegiance on the Court that he privately referred to the Federalist-dominated Court as that "subtle corps of sappers and miners constantly working underground to undermine the foundations of our confederated fabric." Outraged by Chief Justice John Marshall's "twistifications of the law," Jefferson appointed men he thought would challenge the chief justice's judicial philosophy. But to Jefferson's chagrin, Marshall's mind proved more powerful than Republican doctrine. In fact, the Court remained secure for the Federalists for the first three decades of the nineteenth century. During that time, the Court ruled that it possessed the power to void congressional legislation, gave the Constitution's contract clause a broad interpretation and declared that a state could not tax a national bank or infringe upon the national government's broad commerce powers. The Federalist judicial monopoly broke up slowly and only through the combined appointment efforts of Presidents Andrew Jackson, Martin Van Buren and James K. Polk.

Unlike Jefferson and Jackson who complained privately about the Court, Abraham Lincoln expressed his hostility toward the Court openly. Even before his election, Lincoln castigated the Court's stand on the dominant political issue of the day: slavery. After the Dred Scott decision, which gave the Court's imprimatur to official bondage, a belligerent Lincoln said that "our judges are as honest as other men and not more so. They have, with others, the same passions for party, for power, and the privilege of their corps. . . . Their power is the more dangerous as they are in office for life, and not responsible, as the other functionaries are, to elective control." And later, Lincoln addressed the Supreme Court rhetorically. "Familiarize yourselves with the chains of bondage and you prepare your own limbs to wear them," said Lincoln. "Accustomed to trample on the rights of others, you have lost the genius of your own independence."

As president, Lincoln showed his contempt for the Court by blithely ignoring an opinion, directed at him, written by Chief Justice Roger B. Taney, author of the Dred Scott decision. The middleman in the controversy, John Merryman, a Marylander with Southern sympathies during the Civil War, was arrested for treasonous activities by Union soldiers. From prison at Fort McHenry, near Baltimore, Merryman asked Taney to issue a writ of habeas corpus that would require Fort McHenry's commander, General George Cadwalader, to show the legal basis for his detention. Although President Lincoln had suspended the writ of habeas corpus during the war, Taney proceeded with Merryman's petition. General Cadwalader, through an aide, informed the chief justice that he took orders from the president —and that Lincoln's order suspending the writ made Taney's hearing superfluous.

Taney promptly issued a contempt citation against General Cadwalader but when the court marshal arrived at Fort McHenry with the citation, he was turned away at the gates. Taney then wrote a legal opinion on the Merryman case, holding that Congress, not the president, had the exclusive power to suspend the habeas corpus writ. Therefore, Taney reasoned, both President Lincoln and General Cadwalader had acted illegally. The chief justice sent a copy of his conclusions to President Lincoln so that he might "determine what measures he will take to cause the civil process of the United States to be respected and enforced." The only measure that Lincoln took was to send a message to Congress arguing a legal conclusion contrary to that of the chief justice. After that, the president simply ignored Taney's decision and continued suspension of the writ.

When it was Lincoln's turn to appoint justices to the Supreme Court, he remembered well his words that judges have the same passions for party and power as anyone else. He chose men whose political allegiances to his policies were well documented. His appointees did not disappoint him. His first four justices helped uphold the Union blockade of Southern ports (which had been ordered without a declaration of war), and voted to invalidate a state bank tax that would have made Union financing of the war difficult. They also supported pro-Union decisions that denied Court jurisdiction of cases challenging the government's legal tender legislation (which, in effect, paid the Union's bills during the Civil War) and the military's right to arrest and try civilians in areas outside the perimeter of the war.

Lincoln's fifth and final appointment, to fill the vacancy of Chief Justice Taney, was his most politically inspired of all. He gave his reasons for appointing Salmon P. Chase, his secretary of the treasury, with disarming candor. "We wish for a chief justice," Lincoln said, "who will sustain what has been done in regard to emancipation and the legal tenders. We cannot ask a man what he will do, and if we should, and he should answer us, we should despise him for it. Therefore, we must take a man whose opinions are well known."

After the death of Lincoln and victory of the Union, the Court declared the Legal Tender Acts unconstitutional by a 4–3 vote. While those first legal tender cases were on their way to the Court, however, a Republican-controlled Congress had already laid the groundwork for reversal of the Court decision by increasing the number of Court justices to nine. Almost simultaneously with the announcement of the 4–3 decision in 1870, President Ulysses S. Grant named two Republican railroad attorneys to the newly created positions. It was generally assumed that the new appointees, whose railroad clients had largely operated on paper currency, were less than enthusiastic about the Court's decision. Not surprisingly, then, when the second wave of legal tender cases came before the Court in 1871, the new majority, including Grant's two new appointees, reversed the earlier decision and ruled that the Legal Tender Acts were again constitutional.

The hasty retreat severely hurt the prestige of the Court. The public realized more clearly than ever before that justices voted their political as well as judicial convictions. Presidents, of course, had acted on that assumption the whole of the nineteenth century and would continue to do so well into the twentieth. "I should hold myself guilty of an irreparable wrong to the nation," wrote President Theodore Roosevelt, "if I should put [on the Court] any man who was not absolutely sane and sound on the great national policies for which we stand in public life." Appraising the qualifications of one Court prospect, TR ticked off his assets: "He is right on the Negro question, he is right on the power of the federal government, he is right on the insular business, he is right about corporations, and he is right about labor."

As Lincoln had been the most determined presidential critic of the Court in the nineteenth century, so Teddy Roosevelt's fifth cousin, Franklin, would take the honors in the first half of this century. His Court-baiting, like Lincoln's, began before his election to the presidency. In his 1932 presidential campaign, Roosevelt declared that the do-nothing Republican Party controlled the Supreme Court, reflecting poorly on both institutions. He pointed an accusatory finger at his hapless opponent, President Herbert Hoover, who was quite blameless as far as the Court was concerned. Actually, Hoover's appointments to the Supreme Court were among the most scrupulously objective in American history. Benjamin N. Cardozo, a Democrat, was selected primarily for his judicial eminence on the New York Court of Appeals. To be sure, Hoover's other appointees, Chief Justice Charles Evans Hughes and Justice Owen Roberts, were Republicans and highly successful corporation lawyers to boot. But neither was inflexible in ideology, as their swing to the pro-New Deal majority in 1937 dramatically illustrated.

During the controversial 1935 and 1936 Court terms when the conservative majority was tumbling major New Deal measures, President Roosevelt remained publicly serene. Even at the zenith of his national popularity in 1936, FDR would not condemn the obstreperous Court majority. When he did finally move against the Court, he paid that venerable institution the highest compliment. Fearing public reaction to a frontal attack on the Court, Roosevelt wrapped his criticism in the sweet reason of a judicial reform message to Congress.

In his now famous speech to Congress on February 6, 1937, the president told of his anxiety about the federal court system, with overworked judges, crowded dockets and all. He thought that it would, therefore, be a fine idea if a proctor be appointed to oversee the entire federal judicial system and root out inefficiencies. And, oh yes, to infuse new vigor in the system, Roosevelt suggested that judges over seventy ought to retire or have their load halved by the addition of a younger appointee. "In this connection," said FDR, "let me say that the pending proposal to extend to the justices of the Supreme Court the same retirement privileges now available to other federal judges has my entire approval." If Congress had made FDR's proposals law, the six justices over seventy on the Court would either have had to retire or be supplemented by new colleagues whom Roosevelt would appoint.

Nobody was fooled. The *New York Herald Tribune* bellowed: "It was a French King, Louis XIV, who said, *'L'état, c'est moi'*—'I am the State.' The paper shell of American constitutionalism would continue if President Roosevelt secured the passage of the law he now demands. But it would be only a shell." Apparently realizing that he had better call a court-packing plan just that, FDR went on the radio a month later to give his reasons for the proposal to the American people. The Court, said the president, was "improperly setting itself up as a third house of the Congress—a super-legislature." And he added words that would have a familiar ring three decades later: the justices, said Roosevelt, were guilty of "reading into the Constitution words and implications which are not there and which were never intended to be there."

FDR lost that battle, but he eventually won the judicial war by the surest possible strategy: he outlasted his antagonists. Though he was president for four years before he was permitted to fill a Court vacancy, he made up for the delay in fine fashion, appointing five justices in the following four years. In each case, Roosevelt chose men whose dedication to his New Deal program could not be questioned. The president was so insistent in this policy that he even rejected the name of his own majority leader, Senator Joseph T. Robinson, for his first appointment. Although Robinson had supported every New Deal measure that FDR sent to Congress, the President still had doubts about his allegiance. Roosevelt decided that he would need several Court vacancies before he could safely appoint the majority leader. Robinson died before FDR had the chance. Once the New Deal was secure, Roosevelt became less sensitive politically in his Court appointments. For his Court appointment in 1943, Roosevelt left the investigation and choice almost exclusively to his attorney general, Francis Biddle. After the attorney general recommended Wiley B. Rutledge as a "liberal who would stand up for human rights," FDR inquired as to Rutledge's home state (Kentucky) and nodded that "he'll do." Still, Roosevelt insisted on a talk with Rutledge before he actually sent his name to the Senate for confirmation.

President John F. Kennedy considered his first Supreme Court appointments among the most difficult he would make during his administration and set a staff to work on prospects before a vacancy occurred. By 1962 the president had received

a list of six names from his advisors: Professor Paul Freund of
the Harvard Law School; Secretary of Labor Arthur J. Gold-
berg; Judge William H. Hastie of the U.S. Court of Appeals,
Third Circuit; Judge Walter B. Schaefer of the Illinois Supreme
Court; Judge Roger J. Traynor of the California Supreme
Court; and Deputy Attorney General Byron R. White.

After Justice Charles E. Whittaker's announced retirement
in the spring of 1962, Kennedy met with his advisors to discuss
a successor. Attorney General Robert F. Kennedy, fresh from
a world tour in which he was constantly confronted with questions on American racial problems, raised the name of Judge
Hastie, a black, for the Court vacancy. Before making that
choice, both Kennedys wanted to be certain that Hastie was
qualified intellectually for the job and that the Kennedy administration could politically afford to give its first Court appointment to a black. Assistant Attorney General Nicholas
deB. Katzenbach, after researching the first problem, assured
the president that Judge Hastie was professionally well qualified. But after talking to White House advisors, the Kennedys
concluded that a Hastie appointment would inevitably bring
the charge that the administration was trying to woo black
votes, an accusation that would do neither Hastie nor the
Kennedy administration any good. So, the President decided to
postpone a Hastie nomination.

Professor Freund was strongly supported by some high administration officials but just as strongly opposed by others.
Judges Schaefer and Traynor were known to the Kennedys only
by reputation. Finally, the president and his brother decided to
name men who they knew shared their own perspective on
problems. That eliminated all but White (the first appointment)
and Goldberg (the second), both members of the administration. "You wanted someone who generally agreed with you on
what role government should play in American life, what role
the individual in society should have," Robert Kennedy later

explained. "You wanted someone who, in the long run, you could believe would be doing what you thought was best. You wanted someone who agreed generally with your views of the country."

History suggests that American presidents have been most attentive to the work and personnel of the Supreme Court in periods of extreme national tension. When the United States has faced political, social or economic crises on a broad scale, presidents have felt a greater compulsion to control the Court than in calmer times. The presidents have been boldest when they believed that the public supported their view that the Court exacerbated a national crisis or was likely to do so in the future.

Washington's task was to build a nation, but his institutional blueprint, the Constitution, had not provided precise language to define the relationships among the three branches of the federal government. Without violating the spirit of the document, Washington did all within in his power to make two of the three branches—the executive and judiciary—view the nation's destiny from a common vantage point. His method was the appointment; his hope—fulfilled, as it turned out—was that the leaders of the Court would share his Federalist convictions.

Lincoln's challenge was to bind the Union, not build it. But the stakes were equally high and Lincoln blamed the Court, through its Dred Scott decision, for much of his problem. Consequently, Lincoln censured the Court publicly—both by his words and by the contemptuous indifference with which he treated Chief Justice Taney's command in the Merryman case. Feeling as he did that the Court had been a destructive force that had helped bring on the Civil War, Lincoln took special care to pick new justices who he believed would support the Unionist cause.

In his 1932 presidential campaign, Franklin Roosevelt tossed his head derisively at the Court as another example of Republican inertia in the midst of national crisis. Five years later, he introduced his ill-fated court-packing plan. Momentarily defeated, Roosevelt nonetheless achieved his goal, thanks to judicial second thoughts by Chief Justice Hughes and Justice Roberts and an accellerating retirement and mortality rate among conservative justices. By his appointments, Roosevelt switched the Court on not only to his New Deal policies, but also to a constitutional trend that would dominate the Court's work for more than three decades: the concern for human rights.

By 1968 the United States faced yet another crisis, a crisis of confidence in itself. Richard Nixon sensed the tense national mood and suspected that the public was willing to have the Supreme Court shoulder part of the blame. By campaign time, Nixon was convinced that the Court was politically vulnerable and he would act shrewdly on that knowledge.

CHAPTER TWO

The Revolution

The view from Main Street in 1968 was deeply depressing. In Vietnam our soldiers could not win the war and in Paris our diplomats could not forge the peace. At home doves demanded an immediate pull-out and hawks a march on Hanoi. America's mainstream still longed for the old successes, combining military muscle with careful negotiation. That was President Johnson's way, bombing North Vietnam one day and pleading for peace the next. It did not work.

Across the country Americans had witnessed three years of the most destructive violence in the nation's history. Watts was aflame, then Detroit, Newark and so many lesser agonies that Americans lost count of the cities and the dead and remembered only the screen of chaos in their living rooms. Five years before, John F. Kennedy had been felled by an assassin's bullet; yet, all the explanations and presidential commissions and new resolves could not prevent another and another. Bang. The nation's leading civil rights leader was dead. Bang. A second Kennedy was cut down.

The universities, those time-honored incubators of the American dream, were in revolt. Students railed against Vietnam abroad and racism at home, locking in administrators and flouting regulations in the name of relevancy. The family reeled toward a state of disintegration. Youth flaunted its long hair, drugs and new life-style at a disbelieving, resentful older generation. The traditional source of moral solace, the church, was little help. The young were not joining and even their elders admitted that the church's influence was declining. Is God dead? Few seemed to care.

"We are living at a time when the central institutions of the traditional life of man are increasingly unable to command his allegiance and his obedience," wrote Walter Lippmann. "The great voices of authority—family, church, school and country —are silenced, confused or not listened to. The center cannot hold. . . . It is better that Mr. Nixon should have the full authority if repression should become necessary in order to restore peace and tranquility at home."

For middle America, Richard Nixon had become the unlikeliest of romantic symbols: the antihero. No flash, no profile, no uplifting rhetoric. Nixon honored the past and invited Americans to step ever cautiously into the future. He told the blue and white collars that they were right, that America's institutions had worked and would work again. Lubricate the old machinery.

No governmental institution was in greater need of overhaul, Nixon suggested, than the U.S. Supreme Court. Historically, the justices could be counted on to look grandly to the judicial past and peek at the future with a collective trepidation. If change must come by judicial mandate, it would enter with small, measured steps. What had happened, asked Nixon, to this premier national symbol for conservatism?

At a time when voters hungered for assurance in the American way of the past, the Warren Court was looking the other way, as it had for most of its history. The old traditions and mores and rusting political machinery, the Court had declared, were not good enough. After the Court had spoken, it heard precious few echoes from the other branches of government. And so the Warren Court had become the cutting edge for national reform in the second half of the twentieth century, attacking America's number one social problem, racism, rooting out rural bias in state legislatures and giving America's pariahs—police suspects as well as political mavericks—an opportunity to be heard.

In the early years the Warren Court's most vociferous detractors only strengthened the justices' legitimacy in the majority's mind. For few wanted to be associated with the rank segregationists and know-nothing right wingers who pitched the invective. If the Barnetts and Welches of the nation were against the Court, then surely the nine justices must be doing something right.

By 1968, however, the Court's supporters had dwindled dramatically. To be sure, the northern liberals and the blacks and the poor continued to back the reform-minded justices. But the Court's constituency was neither a silent majority nor a powerful minority. And new critics began to mass; respectable and influential public men became bold in their attacks on the Court. The Republican candidate for president divided the nation into peace forces and criminal forces and made clear he thought the Court was wearing the black hat of a criminal coddler. Congress passed Title II of the Crime Control Act which attempted to nullify some of the most controversial Warren Court decisions in the criminal law field. Members of the judiciary, like Judge Warren E. Burger of the U.S. Court of Appeals for the District of Columbia, began to say openly and for popular consumption that the Court had gone too far. It was all too much for America's majority. Within a single year, from 1967 to 1968, the Gallup poll showed a 9 per cent drop in the

popularity of the Supreme Court. The poll recorded the vicissi-
tudes of public opinion in an angry age. But it did not reflect
any dramatic shift in the Court's work, for there was none.
With only one brief detour, in fact, the Warren Court moved
steadily forward throughout its sixteen-year history.

The egalitarian drive of the Warren Court did not, of course,
appear full-blown when Earl Warren took the oath of office in
October 1953. The Supreme Court had been moving in that
direction since 1937. That year marked the decline of the
Court's conservative majority and the demise of a philosophy
that had dominated the Court since the days of President William McKinley. The Court had been the nation's indomitable
protector of private property rights. Contract, property, corporation disputes—these were the steady litigative diets of the
justices. When the Court ventured into public law transactions,
it was most often to smite the infidel, the misguided legislature
that had the temerity to attempt to regulate economic and
social conditions.

The Great Depression and Roosevelt's New Deal sensitized
Americans to other problems. Priorities shifted away from
property rights to the deep concerns of human rights. The faint
vibrations of a civil rights movement could be felt. Minorities,
generally, received better treatment by the majority shocked
into new postures by a race-obsessed enemy in World War II.

The Court's contribution to the human rights movement was
to give substance to language in the Bill of Rights and the
Fourteenth Amendment that had been ignored or distorted
during the gilded age of private wealth. In the thirties the Court
began to scrutinize state criminal trials for a breach of a new
fundamental fairness doctrine devised by Justice Cardozo that
referred to guarantees "so rooted in the traditions and conscience of our people as to be ranked as fundamental." A defendant who had been physically or psychologically beaten into a

confession qualified for protection under the Cardozo doctrine. Since the Court previously had concentrated its reviews almost exclusively on federal trials, its willingness to intervene in selected state cases (which represented more than 90 per cent of all criminal prosecutions in the United States) signaled a significant constitutional breakthrough.

In addition to its fresh concern for due process in state criminal trials, the Court took a harder look at the guarantees of the First Amendment than ever before. In the early forties it shielded tiny bands of nonconformists, like Jehovah's Witnesses, who would not bow to the ways of the majority even to the extent of saluting an American flag in a public school classroom. Finally, the Court backed the executive branch's initiative in the civil rights field, not yet ready to question the Court's separate but equal doctrine but at least willing to consider more seriously the second half of that legal equation.

By the late forties, however, Americans' interest in individual liberties was pushed aside by events that would create a national frenzy, bordering on hysteria. The year was 1949. Mainland China, where forces of Chiang Kai-shek and Mao Tse-tung had waged military and ideological battle for two decades, had finally been won by the Communists. The United States realized with wrenching suddenness that one-fourth of the world's population had come under the control of men whose political ideology was alien to democracy. That same year the Soviet Union exploded its first atom bomb. And by the next year, the United States had become locked in a land war with yet another Communist enemy when North Korean soldiers crossed the thirty-eighth parallel.

At home, the scene was no more reassuring. The perjury trial of Alger Hiss, a top echelon State Department official, raised unsettling questions about the Government's integrity and a swaggering opportunist, Senator Joseph McCarthy, fanned the flames of suspicion. Americans began to look over their shoulders and under their beds for the dreaded Communists. University president Harold Taylor of Sarah Lawrence offered a mocking definition of the patriotic American: "One who tells all his secrets without being asked, believes we should go to war with Russia, holds no political view without prior consultation with his employer, does not ask for increases in salary or wages and is in favor of peace, universal military training, brotherhood and baseball."

But nobody was laughing. Accusation and intimidation stifled the marketplace of ideas. Thought control became a hidden but very real threat, particularly for government employees. "If Communists like apple pie and I do, I see no reason why I should stop eating it," one federal employee told social psychologists Stuart W. Cook and Marie Jahoda. "But I would," he added sheepishly. In the Cook-Jahoda study of the social and psychological effects of the Communist crusade on government employees published in 1952 in the *Yale Law Journal,* respondents voiced a shocking concern for conformity. A certain way to stay out of trouble, some suggested, was to avoid all controversial discussions—like religion, equal rights for Negroes and atomic energy. When asked to name "safe" organizations that could be joined, one respondent limply narrowed the field to the "Knights of Columbus and perhaps the Masons." Others thought it best to snub persons with foreign-sounding names, union members, intellectuals and—persons who join organizations.

At the height of the hysteria, the Supreme Court was asked to pass on the constitutionality of the Smith Act, the antisubversive statute passed in 1940 that had become the principal tool for the investigations and prosecutions of a security-mad government. The case of *Dennis* v. *U.S.* involved eleven U.S. Communist leaders who had been convicted of teaching and advocating the overthrow of the government by force in violation of the federal statute. The federal prosecutor said that the defendants' teaching of the works of Marx, Engels, Lenin and Stalin amounted to subversive incitement outlawed by the Smith Act. The defense countered that teaching alone could not amount to a violation of the Smith Act but, if it did, the act would have to fall as an unconstitutional infringement of the defendants' First Amendment rights to free speech.

The Court, with only Justices Hugo L. Black and William O. Douglas dissenting, refused to ruffle the sensibilities of the Red hunters in and out of government. It upheld the convictions and the Smith Act. Chief Justice Fred M. Vinson's opinion centered on a constitutional doctrine, first enunciated by Justice Oliver Wendell Holmes, which said that the government could curb First Amendment rights of its citizens if it could prove that the speech, if not stifled, would present "a clear and present danger" to the public order. Vinson identified the clear danger to the public order—Communism—and then, in effect, committed all members of the Communist Party, including the eleven defendants, to its subversive purpose. The chief justice was not deterred by the fact that no evidence at the defendants' trial had proved that they had translated their teaching into action or even incitement to action. "Obviously," wrote Vinson, "the words [clear and present danger] cannot mean that before the Government may act, it must wait until the putsch is about to be executed, the plans have been laid and the signal is awaited."

Aside from the legal niceties involved, the Court was saying that it simply would not challenge the prevailing political passions of the day. If Americans wanted their government to track down Communists, even at the expense of Bill of Right guarantees, the Court would not stop them. "History teaches," warned Justice Frankfurter in a concurring opinion, "that the independence of the judiciary is jeopardized when courts become embroiled in the passions of the day and assume primary responsibility in choosing between competing political, economic and social pressures."

While the Court did little to discourage the frantic Communist chase of the early fifties, it was attentive—if not vigorous —in its concern for another aspect of human liberties: the civil rights movement. But again, as in its handling of subversive cases, the Court responded to a dominant public mood. Actually, the modern civil rights movement had gotten its most significant push in the political arena. With the coming of Roosevelt's New Deal, Negro Americans, for the first time since Reconstruction, occupied a conspicuous position on a winning national ticket. As Negroes moved outside the South and began clustering in the urban centers of northern industrial states, they flexed their political muscles with impressive results. The Justice Department created a civil rights office. FDR established a Fair Employment Practices Committee. His successor, Harry S. Truman, sent to Congress a message that included the heart of Negro demands in the late forties: an antilynching bill, the elimination of the poll tax and a permanent Fair Employment Practices Commission. By the early fifties, the armed forces were fully integrated, thanks to Truman's executive order.

Appropriately enough, the law school was to be a major battleground for the legal fight for desegregation. Thurgood Marshall, director of the NAACP Legal Defense Fund, later explained the phenomenon. "Those racial supremacy boys think that little kids of six or seven are going to get funny ideas about sex and marriage just from going to school together, but for some equally funny reason, youngsters in law school aren't supposed to feel that way. We didn't get it but we decided that if that was what the South believed, then the best thing for the moment was to go along."

And the Court went along, too. In 1951 it did not find a Negro mail carrier from Houston who wanted to be a lawyer out of line in claiming that law facilities for Negroes in Texas did not compare with those for whites. The faculty at the University of Texas' Negro law school numbered five, the white nineteen; the Negro library contained 16,000 volumes, the white 65,000. But the figures alone did not persuade the Court to side with the mail carrier. "The law school to which Texas is willing to admit petitioner excludes from its student body 85 per cent of the population of the state and includes most of the lawyers, witnesses, jurors, judges and other officials with whom petitioner will inevitably deal when he becomes a member of the Texas bar," the Court said. Clearly, the justices were looking beyond the abstract separate but equal doctrine—to get at the realities of segregation.

On the same day, the Court handed down another equally prophetic desegregation decision. Oklahoma had admitted a Negro doctoral candidate to the state university on a "segregated basis," in compliance with state law. School authorities maintained separate dining and library facilities and manuevered the Negro student into a special classroom section surrounded by a railing and low curtain and advertised "Reserved for Colored." After sympathetic white students ripped the sign, officials decided to put the Negro in a special row in the classroom which they contended in court amounted to "merely nominal" segregation. The Court ruled that Oklahoma's "nominal" segregation violated the Fourteenth Amendment's equal protection clause. Significantly, the justices considered not only physical segregation but the psychological impact that the policy would have on the black's educational experience.

By this time, the South and border states had responded to the foreboding judicial storm. White school boards initiated crash programs to build new public schools for Negroes. The aim, as Governor James F. Byrnes of South Carolina frankly confessed, was to remedy "a hundred years of neglect of Negro education, lest the Supreme Court take matters out of the state's hands." As a result, civil rights attorneys no longer had the easy arguments of patently unequal facilities so apparent in the Texas and Oklahoma graduate school cases. In five cases challenging segregation in public schools (titled *Brown* v. *Board of Education*) it was at least debatable that the tangible factors —number of teachers, quality of school buildings, faculty salaries—were very nearly equal between Negro and white. But the segregationists had done much more than build classrooms and balance budgets to shore up their legal position. They hired attorney John W. Davis, Democratic presidential candidate of 1924 and one of the great courtroom spellbinders of all time.

In 1952, Davis knew that the tide of history was running against the segregationists. He could not argue the morality of his position seven years after the defeat of a racist enemy and at a time when the United States was in a desperate Cold War struggle with the Soviet Union for the minds of nonwhite nations of the world. But Davis, a superb lawyer, also was aware that his jury was not made up of diplomats but of nine men trained in the law. Continuity with the past, respect for legal precedent had always weighed heavily with the cautious Vinson Court and it was here that Davis chose to make his stand.

Davis reminded the justices that the Supreme Court had reasserted the "separate but equal doctrine" seven times since 1896. He noted that twenty-three states that ratified the Fourteenth Amendment with its equal protection clause had later passed segregation laws. And Davis contended that Congress had annually endorsed segregation for nearly a century by maintaining segregation in the District of Columbia schools since 1862. "Somewhere, sometime to every principle comes a moment of repose," argued Davis, "when it has been so often announced, so confidently relied upon, so long continued, that it passes the limits of judicial discretion and disturbance."

The Court was deeply troubled by issues presented in *Brown* and asked for reargument in 1953, specifically requesting attorneys to focus on the purpose of the Fourteenth Amendment's equal protection clause. Did Congress intend to outlaw segregation when it passed the amendment? If not, was the Court justified in doing it? By the time the Court heard answers to its questions, Chief Justice Vinson had died and been replaced by former California governor Earl Warren.

On May 17, 1954, the country was introduced to a bold new national institution: the Warren Court. That was the day the bickering among the justices over the segregation issue stopped. That was the day that a fifty-eight-year-old legal doctrine was dismissed in a single sentence. That was the day on which a new chief justice, Earl Warren, served notice that the Court would not be bogged down by abstract legal principles when the spirit of the law moved the justices to opposite conclusions. "Separate educational facilities," Warren wrote in his historic school desegregation opinion, "are inherently unequal."

Within a few hours of the announcement of the *Brown* decision, the Voice of America had broadcast the news to foreign countries in thirty-five languages. But it was in this country that Uncle Sam stood tallest. The white majority, who for years knew that segregation was morally wrong, had a binding legal reason to reject it. And blacks? "It would be impossible for a white person to understand what happened within black breasts on that Monday," wrote author Louis Lomax. "An ardent segregationist has called it 'Black Monday.' He was so right, but for reasons other than the ones he advances: That was the day we won; the day we took the white man's laws and won our case before an all-white Supreme Court with a Negro lawyer, Thurgood Marshall, as our chief counsel. And we were proud . . . "

Somehow, all the ugly snarling from the rednecks and deft defiance of southern politicians in later years could not soil that supreme moment in American history. Even the swearing and spitting at Little Rock, the loneliness of the few black children in their "integrated" classrooms, the played-out comic-operas of the Wallaces at the schoolhouse door could not defeat or rewrite or make it disappear. The U.S. Supreme Court had spoken for America's best aspirations, had served for the moment not only as the nation's legal counselor, but its conscience.

No one on the Court in 1954 could have anticipated the bitter dialogue that would consume the justices and the South for the years to come. The "all deliberate speed" timetable that the Court laid down in 1955 seemed reasonable. But the justices underestimated the tenacious resistance of the segregationists. And that was only part of the problem. The two other branches of the federal government offered no immediate help in support of the Court's mandate. One of the most popular presidents in U.S. history, Dwight Eisenhower, could have assisted mightily in rallying the public. He remained silent. And Congress did not pass an effective civil rights bill until a decade after the *Brown* decision.

The challenge only hardened the Court's attitude. In 1958 it told officials in Little Rock, who had requested a stay of two and a half years on public school integration, that neither direct opposition nor "evasive schemes" could nullify the original desegregation ruling. In 1964 it declared that the time for deliberate speed had run out. And a year later it stated that "delays in desegregating school systems are no longer tolerable."

Both in frustration and hope, the Court developed a whole new chapter in race relations law. Segregation was struck down in public parks and playgrounds, at airports and bus terminals, on golf courses and in libraries. The Court threw out a Louisiana law requiring racial labels for candidates on the ballot. And it set aside the contempt conviction of Miss Mary Hamiliton, a black woman who refused to answer when addressed as "Mary" in an Alabama courtroom.

After a Boston lawyer named Joseph N. Welch exposed the recklessness of Joseph McCarthy at the 1954 Army-McCarthy hearings, the Wisconsin senator was never able to intimidate so effectively again. But though the hearings marked the decline of McCarthy's personal power, his followers remained potent. The House Un-American Activities Committee was still asking McCarthy's questions, impugning the loyalty of hundreds of Americans. Powerful legislative committees at the state level were destroying reputations with emulative abandon.

Until 1956, no public authority did much to curb the investigative madness. That year the Warren Court began to tip the precarious constitutional balance away from the government investigating and toward the individual being investigated. The justices did it by giving firm support to the First Amendment guarantees of free speech and association, resurrecting the Fifth Amendment's protection against self-incrimination and preaching that even congressmen and FBI agents were bound to honor constitutional considerations of due process.

In its most controversial decision since *Brown,* the Court declared that states could not duplicate the efforts of the federal government in the security field. The ruling, which barred states from prosecuting those suspected of endangering the nation's (not the state's) security, effectively voided antisubversion laws in forty-two states. That same term, the Warren Court condemned the dismissal of a Brooklyn College professor because he had invoked the Fifth Amendment before a congressional committee. "The privilege against self-incrimination would be reduced to a hollow mockery," wrote Justice Tom C. Clark, "if its exercise could be taken as equivalent either to a confession of guilt or a conclusive presumption of perjury." And finally, the Court told federal government officials that they could no longer summarily dismiss employees suspected of disloyalty from nonsensitive jobs.

The flurry of activity for a Court that only a few years ago had been so quiescent was too much for some members of the U.S. Senate. At a hearing of the Senate Internal Security Subcommittee, Senators Joseph McCarthy of Wisconsin and James Eastland of Mississippi expressed their worst suspicions:

> EASTLAND: The Court seems to be issuing just one pro-Communist decision after another.
> MCCARTHY: You're so right.
> EASTLAND: What explanation is there except that some Communist influence is working within the Court?
> MCCARTHY: Either incompetence or the influence you mention.

For conservatives, concern turned to consternation the following year as the Warren Court issued one libertarian decision after another. The first controversial ruling struck directly at FBI Director J. Edgar Hoover, who had long contended that FBI files were confidential and inviolate. Mr. Hoover and the Supreme Court started on their collision course in the case of Clinton E. Jencks, a New Mexico labor leader who was convicted of filing a false non-Communist oath in violation of the Taft-Hartley Act. At the Jencks trial two government undercover agents testified to the defendant's alleged Communist activities. Jencks' attorney demanded that the judge order the FBI to produce the undercover agents' confidential reports. Behind the request was the defense's intention of comparing the agents' reports with their court testimony to bring out discrepancies that would challenge the witnesses' credibility. It was an unexceptional request for procedural fairness. But the trial judge refused Jencks' request, siding with the FBI position that exposure of their confidential reports could threaten the nation's security. Reversing the lower court's decision, the Supreme Court said that Jencks had unfairly been deprived of the opportunity to challenge all the accusations used against him at his trial. The Court then gave the government a choice: either produce the FBI reports that formed the basis for testimony of the undercover agent witnesses or let the defendant go free.

A few weeks later the Court all but wrecked the Justice Department's drive to prosecute alleged subversives under the Smith Act. In *Yates* v. *United States,* the Court held that the Smith Act did not prohibit advocacy and teaching of the forcible overthrow of the government unless the advocacy was linked with concrete action. Although the Court did not overturn the 1951 *Dennis* decision, it took the masterfully technical opinion of Justice John M. Harlan to keep *Dennis* on the books. But the technical distinctions that Harlan made between advocacy as an abstract principle and advocacy aimed at concrete action were lost on the general public. All that most Americans remembered was that the U.S. Supreme Court had tossed out the convictions of five second-string American Communists and ordered new trials for nine more.

The Court also took dead aim at some of the more reckless investigative techniques of legislators. It reversed the contempt conviction of labor organizer John Watkins, who had been perfectly willing to tell the House Un-American Activities Committee about his past flirtations with Communism but balked at talking about his friends' associations. And the same week, the justices reversed the contempt conviction of a New Hampshire college professor who had refused to answer questions about his lectures and politics, although the questions had been asked by the New Hampshire attorney general, whose investigation had been authorized by the state legislature. In addition to the holdings, which were carefully confined to the facts of the two cases, the legislators got a lecture as well. "Investigations conducted solely for the personal aggrandizement of the investigators or to 'punish' those investigated," wrote Chief Justice Warren in his *Watkins* opinion, "are indefensible."

Congress had never shown a great talent for self-examination and had not encouraged anyone else to fill the void. So, the Court's sermons of 1957 met with predictable outrage from members of the national legislature. Senator Strom Thurmond suggested that all justices who had supported the "pro-Communist" rulings be impeached. Senator Eastland proposed a constitutional amendment that would require all of the justices to be reconfirmed by the Senate every four years. Senator William Jenner of Indiana tried to be more tolerant: "Reasonable men may err. If the Court had erred only once or twice in these decisions involving the greatest threat to human freedom, reasonable men could find excuses for it. But what shall we say for this parade of decisions that have come down from our highest bench on Red Monday after Red Monday?"

The I-Hate-the-Warren-Court Club was not confined to Congress's right wing. The Court's critics in the Senate had amassed formidable support for a bill that would have seriously curbed the Court's appellate jurisdiction; it failed to pass by a narrow vote. President Eisenhower voiced misgivings about the Court trend. Some members of the academic community such as Professor Edward S. Corwin of Princeton also found the Court's rulings excessive. Professor Corwin wrote the *New York Times* that the *Yates* decision was "nonsensical and represents . . . a recent tenderizing of the judicial mind toward the American Communist Party." And in a later letter, Corwin accused the Court of going on a "binge," thrusting "its nose into matters beyond its competence with the result that in my judgment, it should have had its aforesaid nose well tweaked."

Ike had hinted and the Congress had confirmed that the Court had rubbed raw political nerves. But before national politicians could mass broad public opinion against the Court, the justices had made a brief, dignified withdrawal from their frontline libertarian positions of 1956 and 1957. Laymen would say the Court retreated under fire; scholars would say the Court momentarily returned to the restrained judicial philosophy of Justice Frankfurter.

Frankfurter and Hugo Black had waged philosophical battle

almost since their first days on the Court in the late thirties. Ironically, the justices began in agreement—both denounced the actions of the anti-New Deal Court of the mid-thirties. Frankfurter, a close friend and advisor of President Roosevelt, was outraged by a conservative majority that violated every judicial canon he held dear. It substituted its judgment for the popular will of the legislature, showing an unpardonable (in Frankfurter's view) disregard for the prerogatives of Congress. It refused to weigh government's interest in regulating the economic life of the nation against the interests of individuals and corporations in unfettered economic freedom. It took a sledge-hammer approach to judicial review, striking down legislation as unconstitutional when narrower grounds for decision could legitimately have been found. It challenged not only Congress but the president on political issues and very nearly brought down the Court in the process.

Hugo Black, like Frankfurter, was an avid admirer of Franklin Roosevelt and one of the New Deal's staunchest supporters in Congress. He too was outraged by the action of the anti-New Deal Court. But Black's criticism of the Court was narrower than Frankfurter's. For Black, judicial intervention could be justified so long as the Court had firm constitutional guidelines to review a legislature's work. No guidelines were firmer, Black believed, than those contained in the Bill of Rights. But in the anti-New Deal decisions, Black felt, the Court relied too heavily on the fuzzy constitutional language of due process and the commerce clause. According to Black, those phrases did not invite objective analysis and, therefore, did not command judicial intervention.

How, then, to raise the Court's judgment about the political convictions and personal values of the individual judges? That really was a basic question that both Frankfurter and Black grappled with for all their contentious years on the Court. Their answers inevitably led the two great jurists to another fundamental inquiry: what is the proper role for the Court in a democracy?

Frankfurter's "judicial restraint" represented a complex philosophy that answered, to Justice Frankfurter's satisfaction, both questions. In a democracy, Frankfurter believed, all political questions were best resolved by the other branches of government. Being popularly elected, Congress and the president were more sensitive to the public will than nine isolated men who held their jobs for life. The Court could legitimately abstain from those judgments, Frankfurter contended, in a variety of ways: read prohibitions in the Constitution cautiously; balance society's interest against that of the individual; defer to Congress and the states even when their actions seemed unwise if those actions have some rational foundation. Free of political entanglements, Frankfurter believed, the Court could get on with its proper constitutional business of overseeing the federal system, reviewing its laws in pursuit of principles that would endure beyond the passions of the day.

The Supreme Court was in the center of Hugo Black's constitutional universe and the justices were the guardians of democracy's most precious document, the Constitution. By insisting on a literal interpretation of the Constitution, particularly the individual rights guaranteed in the Bill of Rights and the Fourteenth Amendment, Black believed the justices could transcend their personal predilections. Those guarantees could not, Black maintained, be contaminated by any notions of balancing the individual's interest against society's. The weighing process would defeat the purpose of the Bill of Rights as James Madison's "impenetrable bulwark against every assumption of power in the legislative or executive." Justice Black's Supreme Court was to uphold individual liberty against any attack, however subtle, and from any enemy, however formidable.

Black could count on three solid votes in support of his libertarian position. Justice William Douglas had been a consistent Black ally since FDR named him to the Court in 1939 (at the age of forty-one, the youngest appointee since Justice Joseph Story in 1811). Like Black, Douglas was an implacable foe of government encroachment on individual liberties. A prolific writer, Douglas turned out a prodigous number of legal opinions as well as books. The second activist to side with Black was Justice William J. Brennan, Jr., a Democrat plucked by President Eisenhower from the New Jersey Supreme Court. Brennan's father came to the U.S. from Ireland in 1880, shoveled coal in a brewery, joined a union and later became its business agent. The son maintained the family interest in the labor movement and, after graduation from the Harvard Law School, made labor law his specialty. A gentle man in private life, Justice Brennan wrote opinions amply fortified with both passion and pedagogical fine points. Anchoring the activist wing of the Court was Chief Justice Earl Warren, who only warmed to the Black philosophy slowly. But once he had accepted the Black position, the chief justice's devotion to it was total.

To counter the activist wing of the Court, Justice Frankfurter could usually call on four colleagues, none with his towering intellect, but all sharing his more modest ambitions for the Court. Justice Tom Clark, President Truman's attorney general and Court appointee, carried a sure sense of the public's mood onto the Court. He was a crime and Communist fighter in his early days on the Warren Court but voted with the activist majority in key cases in the sixties. In the late fifties, Clark leaned toward the conservative side. Justice John Marshall Harlan, the closest to Frankfurter in intellectual strength, was a Rhodes scholar, Wall Street lawyer and judicial craftsman of the first rank. After Frankfurter's retirement in 1962, Harlan would become the dean of the Court's restrained faction. Charles Whittaker had worked his way from messenger to senior partner in a prosperous Kansas City law firm. Appointed to the Court in 1957, Whittaker found the pressures of the job overwhelming and retired only five years later. While on the Court, Whittaker's conservative instincts placed him most often with the Frankfurtarians. Rounding out the Court was Potter Stewart, a careful writer and crisp thinker who in 1958 was serving his first term. Thought to be the swing man on the Court in the late fifties, Stewart most often swung in Felix Frankfurter's direction.

In those two final years of the so-called silent fifties, the philosophical infighting on the Supreme Court was fierce, with the Frankfurtarians usually coming out on top. The Court upheld the conviction of a Vassar College psychology instructor, Lloyd Barenblatt, who had refused to answer questions on membership in the Communist Party put to him by the House Un-American Activities Committee. Speaking for the majority, Justice Harlan said HUAC's purpose was nothing less than protecting the nation's right of self-preservation and that interest must outweigh Barenblatt's interest in his First Amendment rights.

Black did not mince words in dissent. All this lofty talk about the high purpose of "self-preservation" which the majority attributed to HUAC was so much legalistic fiddle-faddle. As far as Black was concerned, the chief aim, purpose and practice of HUAC was to punish hostile witnesses because they were or had been Communists or because they refused to admit or deny Communist affiliations. And the punishment, said Black, "is generally punishment by humiliation and shame." The First Amendment shields U.S. citizens from such treatment, Black contended, and any conclusions to the contrary could not "be justified by a congressional or judicial balancing process."

The restrained majority also held that a U.S. citizen who had voted in a foreign election could be expatriated because, in Frankfurter's view, Congress's power to withdraw citizenship in that situation was "reasonably calculated" to avoid embarrassment in the legislature's conduct of foreign affairs. Justice

Douglas, in dissent, didn't see it that way. "Citizenship, like freedom of speech, press and religion, occupies a preferred position in our written Constitution, because it is granted in absolute terms," wrote Douglas. "The power of Congress to withhold it, modify it, or cancel it does not exist."

Frustrated on the Court, Justice Black took to the public forum. Speaking at the New York University Law School in one of his rare formal addresses on a legal subject, Black strongly condemned the idea that courts should allow Congress to put "reasonable" limitations on individual liberties. "The great danger" (of the judicial balancing philosophy), said Black, is that "in times of emergency and stress, it gives Government the power to do what it thinks necessary to protect itself, regardless of the rights of individuals. If the need is great, the right of Government can always be said to outweigh the rights of the individual." The idea that there were no "absolute" constitutional guarantees, Black told his audience, "is frightening to contemplate."

The Court had stumbled along the libertarian path in the late fifties, but the fall was not fatal. Indeed, there would be no visible scar in later years. The injury, moreover, tended to blind the activists to their altogether impressive accomplishments during the early years of the Warren Court. The Court was already light years ahead of its conservative predecessors. In the 1935–36 Court term, for example, only 2 of the 160 written decisions dealt with constitutional freedoms. By the 1960–61 term the Court's 120 written decisions included 54 in which civil liberties issues had been raised. The Court, of course, did not always favor the individual against the claims of government in those cases. But it did so enough times to establish some telling constitutional trends. The Fourteenth Amendment's equal protection clause had become the blacks' constitutional wedge for equality. The First and Fifth Amendments had not

given suspected subversives comparable support from government intimidation but the Court's libertarian rulings did impose a degree of rationality to the investigative process that had
been lacking in the past. In the criminal field, the Court was still
wedded to the old fundamental fairness doctrine. (The Court
would intervene in state cases selectively and only when the
Court's vague notion of "fundamental fairness" had been
abused.) But not for long.

The case that brought the full force of the Warren Court's
supervision of the state criminal process began in the second-
floor apartment of a Cleveland woman, Miss Dolree Mapp. On
May 23, 1957, three Cleveland policemen knocked at the residence and without a search warrant, demanded entrance to
look for "policy paraphernalia" which they believed to be
stashed somewhere in the apartment. Miss Mapp, neither en-
ticed nor intimidated by the officers, called her attorney, who
advised her to lock them out. The police waited outside for
three hours and then knocked again. What followed, according
to the later Supreme Court opinion, was an incredible series of
unconstitutional actions by the police. When Miss Mapp did
not come to the door immediately, the police forced their way
into the apartment (violation one). Miss Mapp's attorney arrived on the scene and was denied entrance to the apartment
and conference with his client (violation two). A fleeing Miss
Mapp was intercepted by the police in a hallway. She demanded
to see their search warrant; an officer held up a piece of paper
which Miss Mapp promptly snatched and stuffed in her bosom.
A policeman "grabbed" her, "twisted [her] hand," and she
"yelled [and] pleaded with him" because "it was hurting" (violation three). Finally, the officers searched the entire apartment,
including trunks, dressers, photo albums and the bedroom of
Miss Mapp's daughter by a previous marriage (violation four).
They did not find bookmaking materials but did manage to
discover some off-color literature, which they seized. Miss

Mapp was later charged and convicted in a state court for possession of obscene materials. Although no search warrant was ever produced at the trial, the state court was not persuaded that Miss Mapp's constitutional rights had been violated.

The Warren Court was outraged by the police behavior in the *Mapp* case and incredulous that a state court judge would stand for it. To reverse the Mapp conviction on the basis of the fundamental fairness doctrine was not enough. The Court decision in 1961 declared that evidence illegally seized could not be used at state criminal trials. Thus, the first step had been taken by the Court to impose detailed, pervasive constitutional restrictions on state law enforcement officials.

A year later, in 1962, the Court's bravado would drive the counselors of judicial restraint to despair. In dramatic fashion, the Court entered the political thicket and promised to stay there awhile. In *Baker* v. *Carr,* the Court ruled that it had the right to review the unequal voter representation caused by malapportioned state and congressional districting plans. For the Court majority, Justice Frankfurter's long-standing advice that political problems must be solved by politicians invited a compelling rejoinder: some problems left to the politicians, like malapportionment, don't get solved.

The United States had changed from a nation of farmers in the nineteenth century to one of city dwellers in the twentieth. In 1885 only one-third of America's population lived in cities; by 1960 it was two-thirds. Traffic cops acknowledged the change; so did social workers and big city bankers. But the makeup of almost every state legislature promoted the illusion that the United States was still a frontier country with predominantly rural voters and rural values. Since the legislatures refused to redistrict according to population shifts, the country folks' votes counted for two, five, even ten times those of city dwellers.

The Tennessee legislature (challenged in *Baker*) could hardly have reflected the state's population since lawmakers had last gotten around to reapportionment in 1901. Figuring that reapportionment on the average of once a century might not solve the problem, the Court asked whether the judiciary might act. The Court majority turned to the language of the Fourteenth Amendment's equal protection clause, nodded its head and gave the green light to judicial review of the problem that legislatures had ignored for a century.

If ever he sighted a collision between the judiciary and the legislative branch of government, Justice Frankfurter spotted it here. In what turned out to be his valedictory address on the subject of judicial restraint, he warned: "The Court's authority —possessed neither of the purse nor the sword—ultimately rests on sustained public confidence in its moral sanction. Such feelings must be nourished by the Court's complete detachment, in fact and in appearance, from political entanglements and by abstention from injecting itself into the clash of political forces in political settlements."

It was not to be, and Frankfurter's replacement on the Court, Arthur Goldberg, contributed mightily to the Court's accelerating activism. President Kennedy's former secretary of labor represented the fifth solid member of the activist wing of the Court (with the chief justice, Black, Douglas and Brennan). Just as important, Felix Frankfurter was no longer present in conference to argue brilliantly for the cause of restraint. Justice Harlan would try but, in the early post-Frankfurter years, he would not be effective. Byron White, the Rhodes scholar and New Frontiersman who had taken Justice Charles Whittaker's seat, also contributed to the Court's dynamic image. White was no doctrinaire judicial liberal, particularly in the criminal law field, but he was considerably more flexible in his judicial views than either Frankfurter or Whittaker.

The nation was still waiting to hear the Court's other shoe drop in the reapportionment controversy. Although in *Baker v. Carr* the Court had asserted its right to intervene, it had left for later decisions the sticky questions of when it would step in and what standards it would use once there. The answers came soon enough. In 1963 the Court struck down Georgia's ancient county unit system, which had four times previously survived legal assault. Justice Douglas, speaking for everyone but Justice Harlan, found "inherently invidious" the extra weight the system gave country voters in state-wide elections.

A year later the Court tackled both the state and federal legislatures and, for the first time, imposed the definitive reapportionment standard: one man, one vote. The reaction to the decisions was surprisingly mild among many of the politicians who stood to lose most. After the Court ruled that Texas congressional districts, which ranged in population from 216,371 to 951,527, would have to reapportion according to the Court's egalitarian standard, the Texas delegation did not quarrel with the principle of the ruling. The most searing criticism of the rulings came from the Court itself, through the dissents of Justice John M. Harlan.

When the congressional redistricting decision was announced in the courtroom, Justice Harlan trembled with emotion as he delivered an extemporaneous historical note. "I consider the occasion certainly the most solemn since I have been on the Court and I think one would have to search the pages of history to find a case whose importance equals what we have decided today." In his written dissent, Harlan warned that "the Constitution does not confer on the Court blanket authority to step into every situation where the political branch may be thought to have fallen short."

But the activist majority was not to be denied on its reapportionment position or, indeed, on any of the positions that the Black-Douglas wing had been taking for more than two decades. The preferred position of citizenship and First Amendment rights that Justice Douglas had spoken of in his dissents of the late fifties became the law. In the sixties, the Warren Court declared that Congress lacked the authority to pass laws that deprived Americans of their citizenship without their consent. It also dealt harshly with the antisubversive laws and their sponsors. The justices reversed the conviction of a man who refused to testify about Communist associations before the House Un-American Activities Committee, and held a section of the Internal Security Act of 1950 unconstitutional. In 1964 the Warren Court gave the press its broadest protection against libel in history. The case was *New York Times* v. *Sullivan* and the Court held that the First Amendment barred recovery of damages for libel by a public official unless he could prove that the press had knowingly printed a false statement or had shown a reckless disregard for the truth.

The justices outlawed the New York regents prayer in the public schools and set off one of the spectacular controversies of the Warren Court years. Despite the opinion of a Baptist Sunday school teacher, Hugo Black, that religion was "too personal, too sacred, too holy to permit its unhallowed perversion by a civil magistrate," the preachers and politicians hopped all over the "anti-Christian" Court. Billy Graham called it "another step toward the secularization of the United States," Cardinal Francis Spellman was "shocked and frightened" and Senator Robert C. Byrd was convinced that "somebody is tampering with America's soul." Unimpressed, the Court turned to Bible reading next and declared that it too was prohibited in the public school classroom for inspirational purposes.

The prayer and Bible reading decisions were not among the Warren Court's most popular and, indeed, have been ignored by large segments of the nation's teachers and schoolchildren. But the Court never said it was running a popularity contest and its constant flogging of local censorship boards proved it.

Amid accusations that they were no more than highly paid purveyors of pornography, the Justices struggled for more than a decade to find a workable definition of obscenity that could be reconciled with the First Amendment's free speech provision. Their final creation could hardly be called the work of nine dirty old men. An obscene book, the Court decided, fit the following description: "to the average person, applying contemporary community standards, the dominant theme of the material taken as a whole appeals to prurient interests and is utterly without redeeming social value."

After arriving at that doctrinal monstrosity, the Court continued to have trouble in the obscenity field. It ruled that publisher Ralph Ginzburg's magazine *Eros* taken by itself was not obscene, but that his advertising (mailing from Intercourse, Pennsylvania, for example) made it so. By the Court's reasoning, the *Canterbury Tales,* if not outlawed in its own right, might be taken out of bookshops if the publisher mailed copies from say, Middlesex County, Virginia. Justice Potter Stewart best summed up the Court's frustration over the obscenity issue when he said he couldn't define hard core obscenity but "I know it when I see it."

The serious point to be made about the Court's efforts in the obscenity field is that the efforts were made at all. The justices could easily have ignored that legal briarpatch and let the censors and sellers fight it out at the local level. The Warren Court majority, however, felt that the free speech issue was too important to be shoved aside. As a result, the power of local censors to ban movies and books was significantly weakened. The justices' involvement pointed up a conspicuous characteristic of the Warren Court: the almost compulsive determination to keep itself and the Constitution up-to-date. If someone had to pass on the proliferating pornographic literature and film, the Warren Court seemed to think that it was best that supervision come from an institution with the highest regard for the guarantees of the First Amendment.

The Warren Court's concern for relevancy led the justices to match civil rights leaders almost step for step in the drive for racial equality. When the movement concentrated on court-room victories, the Warren Court was there to strike down segregation in the schools and buses and restaurants. And when the movement, in the early sixties, turned to sit-ins and the streets for its protests, the Court backed the demonstrators with more decisions. Given the Court's belief in the preferred position of the First Amendment, the demonstrators' free speech and association rights loomed very large indeed, even in the face of restrictive state laws and local ordinances.

Where race was an issue, the Warren Court became increasingly demanding of the states' good intentions. In the process, the Court stretched the constitutional meaning of "state action"* to new interpretive lengths. The activist majority found, for example, that the refusal of a private storeowner to serve blacks fit into its "state action" doctrine. The Court reasoned that the storeowner's segregation was influenced by the public policy of the state. Conclusion: the discrimination in the store was really the state's doing and, therefore, unconstitutional. And in 1967, the Court declared unconstitutional a voter-approved amendment to the California constitution that gave property owners "absolute discretion" in the resale and rental of housing. Justice White, for the Court majority, said that the amendment, in effect, gave homeowners and landlords the constitutional right to discriminate on racial grounds. Convinced that the amendment's intent was to discriminate, the Court ruled that it was a violation of the equal protection clause.

The Warren Court was not just supporting the blacks alone, but the underprivileged as a class. And it was not simply de-

*The Fourteenth Amendment provides that no *state* can deprive a person of due process or equal protection of the laws.

fending the individual against the excesses of state authority. It was speaking for both the individual *and* the state, encouraging the individual, on the one hand, and urging more humane policies upon the state, on the other. In fact, the Warren Court had a particular talent for the double entendre, the decision that told the defendant what his rights were and, at the same time, delivered a sermon to the state on what its duty should be. When the Court began to write a new code of criminal procedure for the nation, for example, it was not just protecting the lowly criminal suspect but lecturing law enforcement officials on what they had not done and had better do in the future.

Clarence Earl Gideon was a penniless, petty criminal who had spent most of his fifty-one years drifting, picking up the cheap buck wherever he found it. He hung out in dives and flophouses and pool halls like the Bay Harbor Poolroom in Panama City, Florida. In 1960, Gideon was arrested and convicted of breaking and entering the Bay Harbor Poolroom and marched off to the state prison to do his time. But Gideon was one of those jailhouse lawyers who delight the press and exasperate many judges with endless legal petitions for their release. Gideon was graced by a keen intellect, indefatigable energy and luck, a combination that eventually took his case to the U.S. Supreme Court. His calling card: the constitutional question of whether he, as an indigent defendant, could be convicted of a serious crime in a state court without the assistance of legal counsel.

The superbly honed legal talents of Abe Fortas, Washington lawyer and future justice of the Supreme Court, were enlisted to argue the fine points of the Gideon cause. Gideon had already put his basic problem in the proper perspective. In a letter to Florida's attorney general, Gideon had written: "It makes no difference how old I am or what color I am or what church I belong too if any. The question is I did not get a fair trial. The question is very simple. I requested the court to appoint me attorney and the court refused."

Gideon presented the irresistible image of the underdog flailing away at the tyrannies of society. He also presented a compelling argument for broad constitutional change. "That government hires lawyers to prosecute and defendants who have the money hire lawyers to defend are the strongest indications of the widespread belief that lawyers in criminal courts are necessities, not luxuries," wrote Justice Black. "The right of one charged with crime to counsel may not be deemed fundamental and essential to fair trials in some countries, but it is in ours."

Later came *Miranda* v. *Arizona,* when the Warren Court walked out of the courtroom and into the police station to do what it saw as its constitutional duty. It was not delivering guidelines for judges who had customarily looked to the Court for leadership. It was not lecturing on the law to prosecution and defense attorneys, who had studied Court decisions in law school and used them routinely in their courtroom arguments. The Warren Court was talking to cops, pure and simple. Most policemen had never read a Court opinion and in their pushing and shoving world of shakedowns and lineups, they didn't often find the need.

Suddenly, the nation's frontline crime fighters were taking orders from a new superintendent, the Supreme Court. And the new super was not mushing around with weasely terms like "unreasonable searches"; it laid down primer-like rules that every cop in the country had to abide by before interrogating a criminal suspect. In the future, the Court told the police, you will warn every suspect of his right to silence, that any statement he makes may be used as evidence against him, that he has a right to an attorney and that you will get him one if he doesn't know or can't afford one.

No one likes ultimatums and when the ultimatums promise more work and possibly less reward, then criticism turns to bitterness. "You might as well burn up the books on the science of police interrogation," said a Houston police officer. *Miranda* was another "shackle that the Supreme Court gives us from time to time in the handling of criminal cases," complained a Nevada police chief. And he added, "Some day they may give us an equal chance with the criminals."

The *Miranda* decision predated Chief Justice Earl Warren's departure by three years but, to many Americans, it provided an unfortunate last and lasting impression of the Warren Court. For many, the decision reflected the do-good philosophy of the Warren Court in which the justices saved all their good works for the criminals and cranks, almost guaranteeing a societal hell for everybody else. The impression was not borne out by the facts. Although *Miranda* became a synonym for criminal coddler in some quarters, studies of police operations in New Haven and Pittsburgh showed that the decision had virtually no destructive effects. While the *Miranda* warnings offered the suspect protection against roughhouse police tactics, they did not cut substantially into conviction rates in Pittsburgh or even, the New Haven studies showed, into the number of suspects who ultimately confessed to a crime. What *Miranda* did was to force police officers to do more legwork to get their incriminating evidence, to rely more on their professional skills and less on tricks-of-the-trade shortcuts.

What, finally, ought to be said about the revolutionary Warren Court? Its desegregation decisions, to be sure, did not change the hearts and minds of all Americans. But the Court gave the people reason to reflect and ultimately spurred them, through Congress, to follow its example. The Warren Court came on the national scene at a time of government thought control and left with the Yippies and Panthers and porno-peddlers giving their hardsells to anyone who would listen. In 1953, state legislators who voted for old towns and empty pastures counted for more than those representing suburbs and slickers. When the Court closed shop, every one of the fifty states had reapportioned according to population. The Court wielded the Fourteenth Amendment's equal protection clause with such authority that not only the blacks, but the poor as a class and the underrepresented urban voters ran successfully for its cover as well. The Warren Court entered when the criminal law was the stepchild of the legal profession; it exited at a time when the criminal lawyer and client enjoyed a high and respected position in law school and courtroom.

In moving toward that incredible record, the Warren Court breezed past many individuals and institutions not used to such cursory treatment. The Court was continually in trouble with powerful congressmen over one sweeping decision or another. In the fifties, the complaints centered on the Court's desegregation and subversive decisions. The sixties brought more tirades attacking the Court's prayer decisions and those that expanded the rights of criminal suspects. The complaints were no longer confined to politicians. High church authorities, law enforcement officers and even members of the judiciary joined the chorus. Stop trying to run this country, they were saying. By 1968 a majority of Americans seemed to be listening, if a little nervously, to the complainers.

Why did the Court fall out of favor in its last years? The answers come from reading history as much as law. By the end of the sixties, Americans had come full circle since the early days of the Warren Court. Chief Justice Warren began his duties with a nation that had lost confidence in itself and he left with an electorate in much the same state of mind. But in between, the Warren Court and the American people did important work together.

CHAPTER THREE

Paterfamilias

The chief justice holds only the most tenuous reins of Court leadership. He presides at decision conferences, states the facts of the case and assigns the opinions when he is in the majority. For the extraordinary chief justice, even those meager duties afford him the subtle instruments for leadership. But more often than not in American constitutional history, chief justices have found the tools inadequate to lead their eight fiercely independent colleagues. The frustrated chief may discover that, aside from casting his vote, he is little more than the nation's judicial custodian, keeping tabs on the Court's calendar, supervising the printing of decisions and serving as figurehead for the federal judicial system.

Not surprisingly, then, scholars have placed the mantle of greatness on precious few chief justices in the nation's history. Significantly, those chosen have come to the Court from positions of national leadership. Chief Justice John Marshall was a former secretary of state; Roger Taney, former secretary of the treasury; and Charles Evans Hughes, the Republican nominee for the presidency in 1916. All three possessed that special quality of leadership that comes with a sure political instinct, an ability to deal successfully with men of all backgrounds, intellects and temperaments.

The first great chief justice, John Marshall, enjoyed an extraordinary advantage over his successors. In Marshall's day, the justices resided in the same boardinghouse, wined and dined together, and trundled en masse to and from their courtroom in the Capitol basement. Often case discussions were laced with political commentary and gossip. Quite naturally, Marshall's dominant personality was able to work its persuasive charms on his brethren. It was not a coincidence, for example, that Marshall wrote 519 of his Court's 1,106 opinions and that he felt compelled to dissent only nine times in his thirty-four years as chief justice. But associate justices have not kowtowed indefinitely to any chief justice, even to the great Marshall. In his last years on the Court, Marshall became increasingly depressed as he failed to win a consensus to his point of view.

Divisions on a Court can sometimes be covered by an astute chief justice like Charles Evans Hughes. When the Court began its devastation of FDR's New Deal legislation, Hughes was said to have cast his vote with the conservative majority to avoid 5–4 split decisions and the impression that the Court was bitterly divided (which it was). Nothing was more important to Hughes than the maintenance of a strong and respected Court. Thus, in 1937 Hughes openly opposed Roosevelt's court-packing plan, pointing out that the Justices were not overburdened by a case backlog as the President had contended.

Hughes did not fare as well with his more recalcitrant brethren as with the president of the United States. The Court's crusty septuagenarian, Justice James C. McReynolds, was particularly immune to Hughes' persuasive powers. Once, when all the justices—save McReynolds—stood ready to convene for a Court session, the chief justice sent an attendant to inform

McReynolds of the hour. A few minutes later the attendant returned to Hughes with a message: "Mr. Chief Justice," the attendant said, "Mr. Justice McReynolds says he doesn't work for you." On another occasion, a Saturday conference session of the Court, McReynolds announced his departure for a personal engagement. The chief justice politely suggested that if all justices would only stay another twenty minutes, Court business could be finished and all could pursue their leisure activities. To which McReynolds tartly replied: "I didn't say anyone else had to leave now; I only said that I have to leave."

When Earl Warren became chief justice in 1953, the justices' disagreements were not confined to McReynolds-type cantankerousness. Philosophically, the Court was deeply divided with the Frankfurter wing in command but the activists, Black and Douglas, producing increasingly bitter dissents. With Frankfurter was Justice Robert H. Jackson, one of the most gifted writers ever to sit on the Court. Once Roosevelt's attorney general, Jackson had moved almost immediately to the Frankfurter position of judicial restraint on the Court. Justice Stanley F. Reed, another Roosevelt appointee, did not have Jackson's powerful intellect or pen. But he, like Jackson, had argued for Roosevelt's New Deal policies in the Supreme Court (Reed was solicitor general) and had taken a more cautious position on the Court than many liberals had hoped.

President Truman's three appointees were solidly in the Frankfurter fold. In addition to former attorney general Tom Clark, Truman had named two former U.S. senators from the Midwest to the Court, Sherman Minton of Indiana and Harold H. Burton of Ohio. Minton was a militant New Dealer in the thirties—and one of the most conservative members of the Court in the fifties. Burton, Truman's only Republican nominee to the Court, was former mayor of Cleveland and the junior senator from Ohio (Robert A. Taft was senior). Like Minton, Burton usually could be counted on to uphold government power when it conflicted with individual liberty.

Disagreements on the Court were more than philosophical. Justice Jackson's antipathy for Justice Black had made newspaper headlines in 1945, when Jackson was on leave as chief prosecutor at the Nuremberg war crime trials. After Chief Justice Harlan Stone's death that year, rumors spread that Jackson was in line for the chief justiceship. Truman named Vinson instead and Jackson publicly accused Black of blocking his appointment. With professional and personal animosity running high and an inept Chief Justice Vinson at the helm, the Court had moved groggily along. In 1950, for example, the justices had decided fewer cases than had any Court for a century.

The man called upon to heal the Court's wounds had never been a judge in his thirty-four years of public service. Nor had he ever exhibited the extraordinary intellect that might impress the likes of a Felix Frankfurter. And yet, when the great chief justices of the United States are listed, Earl Warren is likely to be included among them.

Like Marshall, Taney and Hughes, Chief Justice Earl Warren came to office with the impressive battle ribbons of a successful political life. He had been the most popular governor in California's history, elected an unprecedented three times, once with the backing of both major parties. In 1948 he would have been vice president, had the *Chicago Tribune*'s announcement of a Dewey-Warren sweep of the Presidential elections been more than wishful thinking. At Chicago in 1952, Warren came to the Republican convention as a strong dark horse candidate who might well have been nominated in the event of an Eisenhower-Taft deadlock.

The Warren titles, however, were not nearly so important as the qualities they represented. For Earl Warren was the model politician, sensitive enough to know the biases of others and

foresighted enough to read their aspirations. He probed tire-
lessly for a common ground among disagreeing men. His demands were deceptively difficult: honesty, good will, fairness.
But to evade, in view of Warren's own pure example, was
almost impossible. In his new role as chief justice, Warren
would call upon all of his energy and political talent.

The Warren treatment began almost immediately. A colleague would receive a telephone call from the chief justice
politely saying, "I've got a point to check with you. May I come
over?" That was the first step of the long, laborious trip that
Warren had traveled so often to find that common ground
among strong-willed men. Though Warren mainly concentrated on the professional tasks of his office, he never forgot that
nonlegal considerations were important too. So, at the injudi-
cious hour of 6:45 A.M. on an October day in 1958, the newly
appointed Justice Potter Stewart, weary and bedraggled from
an overnight train trip, walked into Washington's Union Station and the greeting of the chief justice. Other small kindnesses
abounded during the Warren years. The chief justice, for example, would have his wife bake a cake and enclose a note on the
occasion of a justice's birthday. "Our new chief may be a little
rusty on legal fine points," commented one colleague. "What
he has is far more important. It is, in the best sense, a keen
political judgment."

The Warren style produced results less than six months after
he had taken office. Speaking for a unanimous Court, Warren
ruled that segregation in public schools was unconstitutional.
After the original arguments on *Brown* in 1952 it was reported
that at least three justices were far apart from the ultimate
Court holding. But Warren brought them together, Black and
Jackson, Frankfurter and Douglas, in all, nine of the proudest,
stubbornest, most contentious men in the nation.

Colleagues and law clerks have often contributed, without
credit, to a justice's opinion. Warren boasted, however, that he

had written "every blessed word" of *Brown*. The claim was unnecessary. The opinion was pure Warrenese: simple, honest, direct talk of right and wrong. It was written in the style of a judge who had always been impatient with courts that confined themselves to precedent, courts that did not share Warren's view of the law as a living, viable instrument for reform. We can't decide this case, Warren said in *Brown*, on the basis of what men thought when the Fourteenth Amendment was passed (1867) or when the Court decided that separate but equal facilities were constitutional (1896). For Warren, abstract legal doctrine must be held up to the light of the real, contemporary world. Could the separate but equal doctrine stand it? Not by Warren. And no amount of legal precedent or stiff-lipped assurances by southern states that the buildings and courses and teachers were equal would change the chief justice's mind. There was something intangibly wrong, subtly out-of-balance, Warren declared, in bisecting a society according to race.

A year later, the chief justice again showed that he would not be bamboozled by smooth lawyer talk. It happened during oral argument in follow-up desegregation cases in which the Court was attempting to decide when and how the desegregation decree should be implemented. Addressing the attorney for a South Carolina school district, the chief justice lowered his gaze for some no-nonsense questioning:

"You are not willing to say here that there would be an honest attempt to conform to this decree, if we left it to the district court?" Warren asked.

"No, I am not," replied the attorney. "Let us get the word 'honest' out of there."

"No, leave it in," insisted the chief justice.

"No, because I would have to tell you right now we would not conform," the attorney told the Court. "We would not send our white children to the Negro schools."

A lawyer could not talk around the chief justice—nor could

a nation. Warren possessed a vision of America's future that no politician or attorney or judge was going to blur with fancified arguments. In that respect, Justice William Douglas has written, Warren must rank with Marshall and Hughes in greatness. "That rating goes to men who, seeing or sensing the strong tides of events, strive to keep the Constitution modern by making it responsive to current needs." Douglas concluded that Warren, like Marshall and Hughes, "had those subtle qualities of the spirit as well as of the mind that enabled him usually to reach an agreement with his brethren by which the constitutional compass could be reset, if necessary, to avoid dangerous shoals that were appearing."

Earl Warren, it has been said, "never had an abstract thought in his life." The comment was offered derisively but could better be taken as a generous compliment. For almost everything that Warren stood for and inspired as man and judge was learned by direct experience. Lesson one, compassion for the common man, was studied by Warren as a boy, growing up in the "railroad" section of Bakersfield, California. The family was poor, scraping by on the salary of Earl's father, Methias, a master car repairman for a division of the Southern Pacific Railroad. As a railroad call boy, Warren never forgot the tragic accidents in which railroad workers were crippled or killed, leaving their families without means or hope.

At school, Warren's impatience with classroom theories soon led to indifference. "No book or professor had a profound influence on me," Warren has said, "not even in the law school. Companionship was the greatest thing I found at the university and it still stands out in my mind today as more important than anything I learned in classes." At the University of California Law School Warren found law studies oppressively narrow for his practical mind. He did not approve of a discipline confined to the written conclusions of judges when so much that they decided depended on social, economic, political and historical factors that could not be found in court opinions.

After law school graduation, Warren spent three of the most unrewarding years of his professional life as an attorney in private practice. He then turned to the public sector and never looked back. As deputy district attorney for Alameda County, Warren was not exactly the picture of prosecutorial authority. "I'd get on a streetcar," Warren has recalled, "and I would be so tense I would hope the car would be wrecked on the way to the courthouse." But he endured and later thrived as one of the most successful prosecutors in Alameda County history. During his thirteen years as the county's district attorney, Warren convicted more than a dozen murderers a year, jailed the county sheriff for gambling graft and convicted Alameda's mayor of bribery and theft of public funds. Still, Warren "never heard a jury bring in a verdict of guilty but that I felt sick at the pit of my stomach."

Through it all, Warren built a formidable reputation for honesty and fair dealing. Typically, Warren's lectures to his staff were sprinkled with simple aphorisms. "We don't break the law to enforce it," he used to say. But his assistants soon learned that the DA's words were more than verbal posturing. "We used to get away with all sorts of things before Warren took over," a former investigator remembered. "Hell, I'd have a pocketful of search warrants and just fill in the name and date as I went along. He sure put a stop to that."

On his first day as California's attorney general in 1938, Earl Warren found two telephone messages on his desk. The first informed him that the governor's personal secretary had been selling pardons to San Quentin and Folsom prisoners on a cash basis. The second message said that the very same secretary had been appointed by the Governor to the California Superior Court the night before. Within fifteen minutes Warren was dictating charges to his secretary that would not only block the judicial appointment but ultimately send the judge-designate to jail.

Dedication to duty meant more to Warren than unassailable integrity. In the first frightening days of World War II there was no greater patriot than Attorney General Warren. Sometimes his devotion to patriotism crowded his genuine beliefs in civil liberties. When the clash came, as it did in the debate over forced evacuation of Japanese-Americans from the West Coast, Warren the patriot overruled Warren the civil libertarian.*

Attorney General Warren gave his full endorsement and cooperation to the Army's massive move of the Japanese-American population away from the coast to relocation camps at Tule Lake in northern California. In supporting the policy, Warren told a congressional committee: "We believe that when we are dealing with the Caucasian race, we have methods that will test the loyalty of them, and we believe that we can, in dealing with the Germans and the Italians, arrive at some fairly sound conclusions." Warren could not say the same for the Japanese. "When we deal with the Japanese," he said, "we are in an entirely different field and we cannot form any opinion that we believe to be sound."

Campaigning for governor in 1942, Warren's words became shriller. He urged voters to keep the Japanese from the West Coast "so long as the flag of Nippon is flying over the Philippines." And a year later, Warren told a governors' conference: "If the Japs are released, no one will be able to tell a saboteur from any other Jap."

Once the war hysteria subsided, however, Governor Warren led his state back to civility. And when V-J Day arrived, Warren was ready to welcome 25,000 Japanese-American evacuees returning to their homes. With less than twenty-four hours'

*Warren was not alone. Justice Black wrote the majority Court opinion in 1944 which found a "substantial basis" for the military policy of exclusion of Japanese-Americans from certain sections of the country.

notice of the return of the evacuees, Warren stayed up all night, calling every mayor, sheriff and police chief he knew to ask that they do everything possible to resettle the new arrivals without violence. It worked. Despite the suspicion and hostility still strongly felt by many Californians toward the Japanese-Americans, they disembarked without serious incident.

Warren's welcome of the Japanese-American evacuees was more characteristic of his civil liberties record than his earlier farewell. As governor, he proposed the state's first civil rights commission and named the first black to the California Superior Court. His reaction to mindless discrimination was immediate and heartfelt. After reading that a Chinese family had been barred from an all-Caucasian private subdivision in San Francisco, Warren wrote them: "I am not at all proud of the action of the people in your neighborhood. I am sure this is a disappointment to you and I agree with you it is just such things that the Communists make much of in their effort to discredit our system."

In his three terms as California's chief executive, Warren set a blistering progressive pace. He built more highways, schools and hospitals than any other governor in the nation. He reformed the prison system, widened unemployment insurance coverage and tried vainly three times to establish a compulsory state health insurance program. "Governor Warren faced the problems of growth and social responsibility and met them head on," former California governor Edmund G. Brown has said. "He felt the people of the state were in his care, and he cared for them."

His concern for all of the people did Warren, the Republican vice presidential candidate in 1948, very little good. He insisted on the statesmanlike stance, refusing to be drawn into partisan debate or rancorous attack on his Democratic opponents. While Harry Truman gave 'em hell, Earl Warren gave 'em the eternal verities. Nobody listened then. But four years later a man who shared Warren's love of homilies and country would. His name was Dwight Eisenhower.

At the time of Chief Justice Fred Vinson's death, President Eisenhower was engrossed in Albert J. Beveridge's four-volume work, *The Life of John Marshall.* Reportedly, Ike was struck by the similarities between Marshall and one of his chief prospects to succeed Vinson, Earl Warren. Both had a wealth of political experience and both had proved themselves as leaders in government.

Eisenhower had talked with Warren earlier about his basic philosophy and was pleased with the result of the discussion. Warren's views, according to Ike, reflected high ideals and "a quality hard to define but well understood by most"—common sense. Eisenhower also believed that Warren shared his middle-of-the-road views (Warren's middle road later proved considerably wider than Ike's). Although Eisenhower denied that politics played a significant role in Warren's selection, cynics suggested that Warren's crucial support for Eisenhower during the 1952 Republican convention's credentials fight between Ike and Taft forces did the California governor's cause no harm. Finally, Eisenhower thought Warren to be a man of national stature "who could be expected to provide a leadership that would be favorably received by all the courts of the land." Thus, on September 27, 1953, Attorney General Herbert Brownell met Governor Warren at McClellan Air Force Base near Sacramento and told him that the President planned to name him to the Court. Warren did not discover until the following week that Eisenhower not only wanted him on the Court, he wanted him to lead it.

Prognosticators were genuinely bewildered by the Warren appointment. Activists took heart in Governor Warren's progressive record, particularly in the civil rights field. But conservatives maintained cautious optimism as well, pointing to Warren's support for the states' position in the offshore tidelands dispute and his public criticism of President Truman's action in seizing the steel mills without congressional approval. In fact, in that autumn of 1953, no one was quite sure where Chief Justice Earl Warren would take the Court.

In his earliest years on the Court, Warren did not really tip his judicial hand, except on the desegregation question. It was not because of any shrewd planning on Warren's part; he simply was getting acquainted with his new job and did not want to make radical moves in either direction. During his first term, Chief Justice Warren sided frequently with the conservative majority on the Court. In civil liberties cases, for example, he agreed with conservative Justice Tom Clark in most of the cases (94 percent) and Justice William Douglas least (65 percent).

In his first year on the Court, Warren voted with the conservative majority that upheld a state gambling conviction based on incriminating conversations recorded by police in the defendant's bedroom without his knowledge or a warrant. The whole police procedure had the stench of illegality, from the moment the police entered the defendant's home without a warrant to the playing of the tapes in court. Warren later explained his action. First, the Court had only four years before refused to impose federal constitutional standards on the states in a similarly offensive eavesdropping case. "That [*Wolf* v. *Colorado*] having been such a very recent case and a majority of the Court having agreed not to overrule it at that particular moment, and I being a new justice on the Court still groping around in the field of due process, I went along with that opinion, shocked as I was at the conduct of the police."

But the gambling case was not the only example of the chief justice's restraint that first term. Warren found no constitutional bar to the deportation of an alien, a resident of the United States most of his life, who had belonged to the Communist Party in the years before it was a crime to do so. He also rejected the constitutional claim of Dr. Edward K. Barsky, whose New York medical license had been suspended after his run-in with the House Un-American Activities Committee. The state medical board had taken action against Dr. Barsky after he had been convicted of contempt for failing to supply HUAC with records of the Joint Anti-Fascist Refugee Committee. The Court majority, including Chief Justice Warren, rejected Dr. Barsky's claim that the medical board had weighed matters totally unrelated to his fitness to practice medicine, thus depriving him of his constitutional rights to due process of law.

The chief justice's identity crisis was short-lived. A man of action his entire professional life, Warren was not fit—temperamentally or philosophically—for the Frankfurtarian school of judicial restraint. He became an early dropout and soon joined the Court's activists led by Justice Black. In disagreement twenty-two times with Black in 1954, Warren quarreled with Black's judicial position twelve times the following term and, by 1956, the two opposed each other only twice.

The old Warren reappeared, comfortable in his job and firm in his convictions. No theoretician, Warren borrowed generously from Black's libertarian philosophy. "Our system faces no theoretical dilemma," Warren wrote in 1955, "but a single continuous problem: how to apply to ever-changing conditions the never-changing principles of freedom." And like Black, Warren gave the Bill of Rights and the Fourteenth Amendment top priority in facing the problem. By the end of Warren's sixteen years on the Court, it was Black who was running to keep up with the chief justice's activism. "I have heard a great many people say to me," Warren said, " 'Well, I agree with your opinions on these civil rights, all right, but don't you think you are going too fast?' Of course, the answer to that is 'We haven't anything to say about how fast we go.' We go with the cases that come to us, and when they come to us with a question of human liberties involved in them, we either hear them and decide them, or we let them go and sweep them under the rug, only to leave them for future generations."

More confident in public, Warren also became more authoritative with his colleagues, even with the feisty Justice Frankfurter. In 1962, for example, when Frankfurter added a few bitter flourishes from the bench to a written dissent, the color drained from Warren's face. He turned to Frankfurter and huffed: "I must say that although I did not file an opinion in this case, that was not the dissenting opinion that was filed. That was a lecture. It was a closing argument by the prosecutor to the jury. It is properly made perhaps in the conference room. As I understand it, the purpose of reporting an opinion in the Court is to inform the public and not for the purpose of degrading this Court."

With the nagging doubts of the early years eliminated, Warren again became the chief executive who faced the problems of social responsibility and met them head on. And like the governor of another day, Chief Justice Warren felt the people —this time those of the entire nation—were in his care. And he was determined to care for them.

When Warren's appointment as chief justice was announced in 1953, one San Francisco lawyer was heard to grumble, "I can guarantee that every one of Earl Warren's decisions will sound as if he's running for president or assistant God." In hindsight, the observation holds more than a thimble of truth. In fact, the chief justice's opinions often sounded more like civics lectures or Sunday sermons than learned expostulations on the law. There were few precious quarries of legal insight to be mined by meticulous scholars. But the chief justice's primary interest —and talent—was not in legal craftsmanship. His major concern was in results, and in two 1957 decisions curbing the legislative power to investigate alleged subversives, Warren made the point well.

In the first decision, *Watkins* v. *U.S.,* the question was whether a labor leader was justifiably cited for contempt by the House Un-American Activities Committee for refusing to tell the congressman whether acquaintances of his had ever been members of the Communist Party. The chief justice wrote a voluminous dissertation on the history of congressional investigating committees, where they had performed a public service and where they had gone astray. In his condemnation of witch-hunts, Warren could be general: "There is no congressional power to expose for the sake of exposure." And he could be specific: "An excessively broad charter, like that of the House Un-American Activities Committee, places the courts in an untenable position if they are to strike a balance between the public need for a particular interrogation and the right of citizens to carry on their affairs free from unnecessary governmental interference." But after all the fuming, the chief justice rested his decision on the narrowest of grounds: the labor official's constitutional rights of due process had been violated because he had no way of knowing whether the questions that the committee asked were pertinent to the congressional inquiry.

Warren used the same technique in the second case, *Sweezy* v. *New Hampshire,* involving the extent of the authority the New Hampshire legislature had given the state's attorney general to investigate subversive activities in the state. One of the attorney general's targets was a university professor named Paul Sweezy who refused on constitutional grounds to answer questions on his connection with the Progressive Party and a lecture he had delivered at the University of New Hampshire. When the attorney general turned the matter over to a state court, which repeated the questions, the professor again refused to answer and was cited for contempt. In his decision overturning the contempt conviction, Warren began with broad, threatening statements aimed generally at subversive investigations:

"We do not now conceive of any circumstance wherein a state interest would justify infringement of rights in these fields." He then followed the tirade with an extremely cautious decision. The actual holding in the case: the New Hampshire legislature had not authorized the attorney general to ask the kinds of questions he did, so the professor's constitutional rights to due process of law had been violated.

Warren, in a sense, had borrowed a chapter from Chief Justice John Marshall's how-to-succeed-with-legislatures book. In *Marbury* v. *Madison* (1803), Marshall had written a long, general exposition demonstrating that the Court could review acts of Congress. But in the decision, Marshall did not risk outright confrontation with the legislative branch. Since the result of the decision was that desired by Jefferson's Republicans in Congress, Marshall established the right of judicial review of acts of Congress without a showdown. In the same way, Warren scrutinized the power and scope of legislative investigations without making his actual holdings overly painful to the legislatures. In both instances, the chief justices won their battles without a shot being fired: the decisions were warnings to legislatures to be careful because there was one institution that had the right and will to supervise their actions.

In 1948, both Los Angeles County, with its six million people, and a mountain district with less than 100,000 were represented in the state senate by a single representative. That year, California voters were given the opportunity to vote down malapportionment in favor of a system of representation based on population alone. Governor Warren, along with a majority of voters, rejected the proposal. "Our state has made almost unbelievable progress under our present system of legislative representation," Warren said then. "I believe we should keep it."

In 1964 the same man, now chief justice of the United States, wrote: "The basic principle of representative government remains, and must remain, unchanged—the weight of a citizen's vote cannot be made to depend on where he lives. Population is, of necessity, the starting point for consideration and the controlling criterion for judgment in legislative apportionment controversies. A citizen, a qualified voter, is no more nor less so because he lives in the city or on the farm."

How could Warren perform such a mental somersault? The key to the change, Warren said later, lay in the nature of the two jobs. As Governor, Warren thought and acted as a politician. His constituency was limited and so was his flexibility. He practiced the delicate art of compromise, finding that highest intersection between principle and the politically possible. Warren was not deceived by the malapportionment situation in 1948. "That was not equal representation by any manner or means, but our system was getting along and the people were having an opportunity to vote on it." He added, "I went along with the thought that we were doing pretty well and we would leave well enough alone."

Why couldn't Warren, as chief justice, "leave well enough alone"? Once he became acclimated to his new position, Warren explained, he decided that he would not, indeed could not, be satisfied with the inexact science of politics. The politician's language is compromise, Warren believed; the judge's is principle—unadulterated principle. "When we come to the Court and we face a similar problem [to that of the politician] where the question of constitutionality is raised, we then test it by constitutional principles; if it violates the constitutional principles, we no longer can compromise."

Warren's reapportionment decision in 1964 not only illustrated the chief justice's break with his political past, but with his judicial past as well. If the case had come before the Court in 1954 or 1955, a time when Justice Frankfurter had Warren's ear, the result almost surely would have been different. Yet, malapportionment was as pervasive—and inequitable—in 1954 as in 1964, and arguments against judicial intervention were as potent in 1954 as a decade later. First, it was argued, reapportionment was not a matter to be pursued by courts at all, but the prerogative of the legislative branch. Second, states need freedom to work out solutions to their problems. Third, there were other considerations besides population that states with diverse economic and geographic interests had a right to consider. Why couldn't the majority of voters in Colorado, for example, give the sparsely populated mountain regions more weight in the state legislature if they chose? Finally, by jumping into the reapportionment controversy, courts would be stung by a beehive of practical problems. How, for instance, would courts solve the problem of gerrymandering? Conceivably, judges might find themselves redrawing districts themselves; when that nonjudicial function ended, another would surely begin.

In 1954 Warren might well have counseled restraint. And in 1964 he dutifully enunciated arguments against the Court's taking action. But his impatience with the arguments was apparent, even in recitation. There was no evidence of intellectual struggle with the problems, no awkward sense of uncertainty. He galloped past the problems to his conclusion: "Our answer [to the arguments] is this: a denial of constitutionally protected rights demands judicial protection; our oath and our office require no less." In other words, the chief justice found no argument to counter the Fourteenth Amendment's guarantee to urban voters of equal protection of the laws. His remedy: a representational standard based on one man, one vote.

Two years after his famous reapportionment decision, Warren wrote his most outspoken opinion of all. In the case of *Miranda* v. *Arizona,* Warren blasted away almost immediately at abusive police interrogation methods and did not stop until he had written a precise code of conduct for every state highway patrolman, county sheriff and city cop in the country. He recounted in lugubrious detail the third-degree techniques police were taught in training manuals. "To obtain a confession," Warren read from a manual, "the interrogator must patiently maneuver himself or his quarry into a position from which the described object may be obtained." Then, the chief justice offered some helpful commentary: "When normal procedures fail to produce the needed result, the police may resort to deceptive strategems such as giving false legal advice." By this time, Warren's conclusion was inevitable. "The very fact of custodial interrogation exacts a heavy toll on individual liberty," Warren intoned, "and trades on the weakness of individuals." To correct the situation, Warren wrote the famous *Miranda* rules for police interrogations.

Miranda provides a fitting climax to Chief Justice Warren's judicial development. Back in 1954, the new chief justice had stated the principle that separate facilities could never be equal. But a year later, his implementation decree, the nuts and bolts of court-enforced desegregation, had the vague quality of compromise. And the "with all deliberate speed" formula proved to be an unsuccessful compromise at that. By the late fifties, Warren was ready to deliver powerfully worded opinions, like those in the subversive cases, that had an "or else" quality to them. And by the middle sixties, the chief justice's judicial bite, reflected in the rigid rules of his reapportionment and *Miranda* decisions, was the absolute equal of his bark.

Webster's *Dictionary* defines "symbol" as "a visible sign of something invisible, as an idea, a quality." Chief Justice Earl Warren qualified. As a judge, he represented vastly more than the sum of his opinions. As a man, he suggested to the nation considerably more than even his hulking figure. The Warren symbol varied, of course, depending on the vantage point of the beholder.

Warren spoke for nine men in the first desegregation decision and most later Court desegregation opinions were written by the chief justice's colleagues. Yet, Justices Clark and Harlan and Frankfurter never suffered the indignities of racist-inspired pamphleteering. But the chief justice did, rarely venturing below the Mason-Dixon line without being greeted by segregation-forever fanatics.

During the Warren years, the Court delivered more than thirty opinions involving the First Amendment rights of those suspected—at some level of government—to be subversive. Warren wrote only a handful. But nobody bothered to print "Impeach William Brennan" bumper stickers. It was the chief justice who became the convenient target of the right wing's bitter invective. They called him a "sneaky Red" and printed a "documented record of his pro-Communist rulings." When he made public appearances, Warren could count on a welcoming committee placarding their hatred, suggesting that the chief justice "go back to Moscow." The John Birch Society was slightly more subtle; for one dollar a member or fellow traveler could purchase an "Impeach Earl Warren" kit.

But the symbolic power of Warren did not just affect the know-nothing right. "Chief Justice Warren became the image," Justice Thurgood Marshall has said, "that allowed the poor Negro sharecropper to say 'Kick me around, Mr. Sheriff, kick me around, Mr. County Judge, kick me around, Supreme Court of my state, but there's one person I can rely on.' " The Warren magic worked in foreign countries as well, Marshall recalled. Everybody knew about the chief justice, but his image was particularly vivid in the developing countries. In all his travels, said Marshall, he never failed to leave a country without someone shouting, "Give my best to your chief justice."

For the civil rights attorney of the early sixties, bruised and taunted by hostile southern communities and courts, that towering figure in the center chair of the courtroom was especially luminous. "Suddenly, you would see this paterfamilias, insisting on the justice of the black man's cause," recalls Columbia Professor Michael Meltsner, formerly a counsel for the NAACP Legal Defense Fund. For Meltsner, the chief justice was almost Old Testament in character. "Right was right and wrong was wrong. He not only said things were illegal; he said they were morally wrong."

Warren built on the Biblical image, not just with civil rights attorneys, but with other members of the bar who appeared before the Court as well. After listening to the sophisticated legal arguments of counsel, Warren might flash a troubled look at the attorney and ask: "But is it fair?" When the chief justice sniffed injustice to a suspect in a criminal case, he personalized his challenge to the government attorney: "Why did you treat him this way?"

Many in the legal community belittled as irrelevant the chief justice's questioning. But sophisticated advocates like the NAACP Legal Defense Fund's director-counsel, Jack Greenberg, contended that the Warren interrogation was fundamental to the issues of constitutional due process or equal protection of the law. Harvard's Archibald Cox has suggested that criticism of the Warren Court's deep concern for fairness shielded a profound uneasiness among the sophisticated bar and intellectual community. "No one could successfully argue that a poor man charged with a crime should not have as much chance to have a lawyer at a preliminary hearing as one who was rich, or that cows and trees should have as much voting power as people," Cox has written. "If accepted legal doctrines and institutional concepts called for a different conclusion, was not the fault in the legal and intellectual stratum and in the indifference, blindness and compromise it reflected rather than in the basic ideal?"

Warren affected thousands of attorneys—neither sophisticated nor intellectual—in a totally different way. On business or vacation in the nation's capital, they met the chief justice face to face when they stepped briskly to the center of the courtroom to the take the oath of admission to the Supreme Court bar. The ceremony was no more than a formality since any attorney with twenty-five dollars and membership in a state bar association for three years could join. But the chief justice made it infinitely more than a formality. He would address each applicant by name and extend a gracious, personal welcome.

To many observers, Warren's attentions seemed an unnecessary clot in the Court's heavily overcrowded schedule. But for others, the Warren treatment was far more valuable to the nation than a few extra hours of oral argument. "He is talking to only you," said the NAACP's Greenberg, "and he makes you feel that it is the most important thing that ever happened to you." Warren's whole attitude toward the ceremony, said Greenberg, made it appear there was a communal bond. "He's part of it; you're part of it. There's electricity in the air. It's impressive."

After talking to the attorneys who had participated in the ceremony and their wives, Archibald Cox, former U.S. solicitor general, concluded that the chief justice had accomplished a wonderous task indeed. "The warmth of the chief justice's greeting had made the Court *their court.* The bond would be enduring . . . Chief Justice Warren desired above all else, I suspect, to have both the Court and the law belong to the people —to have it serve their needs, speak to them, and voice their aspirations."

For a legal community far from the marbled courtroom, Warren's impact was equally strong. To reform-minded law students, the chief justice embodied the courage and forthrightness and principle they thought necessary to make the world better through law. And when he spoke of legal education, the chief justice warmed the hearts of those, like Warren himself, who found the case study method tedious and limiting and not always relevant. He was convinced that a law school could no longer concentrate so heavily on the so-called bread and butter courses that tell a lawyer how to make a living. "Law studies must be increasingly integrated with a study of the life of the nation," Warren told law students at the University of California. He said then the problems of a technologically advanced society were not too esoteric for legal study, and suggested that such topics as air pollution, water supply and highway construction were fit subjects for legal scrutiny. On the other hand, Warren found a legal study confined to specific community problems hopelessly empty. "In civilized life," the chief justice told an audience at New York's Jewish Theological Seminary, "law floats in a sea of ethics." Without ethical understanding, Warren said, "the law as a ship of state would be stranded on dry land. Where there is no ethical commitment to observe the law, the judicial and police systems are really helpless, and law often ceases to operate at all."

Most importantly, the chief justice exemplified to America's majority the values they most admired: honesty, fairness, patriotism and idealism. He was a man who could face the placards of hate with friendliness and dignity. And he was the judge who could make the lawyer return to his conscience, not his law books. Without Earl Warren, it is doubtful that the Court could have achieved its revolution. He became the symbolic rallying point for a nation in need of reform but fearing it, wanting a better tomorrow but clinging to the security of yesterday. Americans accepted the most important decisions of the Warren Court because, deep down, they knew those decisions were right. The chief justice told them so.

CHAPTER FOUR

Chief Justice Burger

Governments exist chiefly to foster the rights and interests of their citizens—to protect their homes and property, their persons and their lives. If a Government fails in this basic duty, it is not redeemed by providing even the most perfect system for the protection of the rights of defendants in the criminal courts.

Judge Warren E. Burger,
from an address at Ripon College, 1967

I pledge that the first civil right of every American, the right to be free from domestic violence, will again be recognized and protected in this great country of ours.

Richard Nixon,
from televised address in Presidential campaign, 1968

A month after his inauguration, President Nixon invited Judge Warren Burger of the U.S. Court of Appeals for the District of Columbia to the White House to swear in a number of administration officials. It was a routine request performed from time to time by Burger and his colleagues on the court of appeals. But the invitation ceased to be routine moments after the formal ceremony when the president asked Judge Burger to his office. There Nixon told Burger that he had read and admired his 1967 Ripon speech; he then asked the judge's views on reforms for the District of Columbia's byzantine court system.

Burger, who was not naive in the world of politics, thought perhaps the president's interest in his views was more than casual.

Two months later, Judge Burger and his wife received an invitation from the White House to attend a dinner honoring retiring Chief Justice Warren. Assuming that a few of his judicial colleagues had also been invited, Burger called one to ask for a ride. But to Burger's momentary embarrassment, he found out that his colleague had not been invited; later he discovered that he alone among judges of his court had received the honor. Curiousity aroused, Burger and his wife dressed early for the event so that they might have an unhurried look at the guest list. As his eyes ran down the list, Burger learned that he would be the lone lower federal court judge in attendance. And the company was indeed impressive: Secretary of State William Rogers, Attorney General John Mitchell, former attorney general Herbert Brownell, Thomas E. Dewey. All four served as advisors to the president; all had been mentioned as the president's possible choice to succeed Chief Justice Warren. "I turned to my wife," Burger later recalled, "and told her to be natural if she got the feeling people were looking us over."

Burger later confided to close friends that he might be under consideration for a Supreme Court vacancy, but had no idea how seriously. Unknown to Burger, the president had requested his trusted friends, Rogers and Brownell, to provide critiques of Burger as assistant attorney general during the Eisenhower administration. Both former attorneys general remembered Burger as a highly competent administrator and prosecutor. The first returns in, Nixon then asked Attorney General Mitchell to review Burger's personal and judicial record. Again, high marks. At his Camp David retreat the weekend before his announcement, the president mulled over the appointment and made his decision. It would be Burger. Nixon placed a call to Mitchell in Washington, instructing his attorney general to begin the necessary security clearances. On Wednesday, May 21, 1969, Mitchell asked Judge Burger to his office to tell him of the President's intention to nominate him to the chief justiceship. Before accepting, Burger requested permission for a physical checkup. Mitchell shrugged. That would be impossible, Mitchell said, since the president planned to have Burger at his side at seven o'clock that night to announce his appointment to a national television audience.

When the president walked with Burger into the East Room of the White House, Nixon could not disguise his satisfaction in arranging his little surprise for the nation. Although Burger's name had been bandied about the Washington cocktail circuit, few of the cabinet members or reporters present—and almost none of the millions of television viewers—recognized him. Still, Burger measured up to his starring role perfectly. Flowing white hair topped a handsomely etched face and heroic shoulders and chest. In his six-minute introduction, the President assured his audience that Burger was supremely qualified, in substance as well as appearance, for "the most important nomination that a president of the United States makes during his term of office." Nixon said, "I would evaluate him as being qualified intellectually, qualified from the standpoint of judicial temperament, qualified from the standpoint of his legal philosophy and, above all, qualified because of his unquestioned integrity throughout his public and private life."*

Although Richard Nixon and Warren Burger were only casual Washington acquaintances, the two might well have been close friends. Like the president, Burger grew up without luxuries, scrambling with others in his family to balance their meager budget. Both Burger and Nixon survived by hard work, not brilliance, by tenacity of purpose, not flashes of inspiration.

*The last qualification was a not-too-subtle reference to the failed nomination of Abe Fortas.

Each was a pragmatist in his own way, setting goals neatly within the framework of the possible. High goals to be sure, but not visionary. Step by laborious step, Nixon and Burger climbed the ladder to the American establishment, rewarded along the way for their belief in the American dream and willingness to force its reality.

Burger's father, Charles, supported his wife and seven children by inspecting railway cargo in St. Paul when he was not on the road peddling medicines or confections. Warren's early childhood was spent on the family's small truck farm, picking apples and beans and tomatoes during the week, attending Methodist Sunday school on his day of rest. When Warren was eight, the family moved to St. Paul's modest east side, the Burger boys sleeping four in a bedroom. Money was scarce and Warren helped out by selling newspapers on a street corner, then graduating to a residential route that he kept through high school. During the summers, he picked up spending money as he could, driving a truck, counseling at a YMCA camp, lifeguarding at a local pool.

Neither a top student nor athlete at John A. Johnson High School, Burger became a class leader by force of personality and iron determination. He was a 130-pound tackle on the football team, ran a leg on the half-mile relay, played coronet and sculpted. He complained about crowded halls as editor of the school newspaper and, as student court judge, tried to bring charges against one teacher suspected of peeking into the girls' locker room. Burger's good grades and nonstop extracurricular activities were impressive enough to earn a scholarship to Princeton, which he declined because it did not pay enough.

Burger stayed in Minnesota instead, working as a forty-dollar-a-month insurance clerk by day and studying for a college degree in University of Minnesota extension classes at night. Moving on, Burger enrolled at the St. Paul College of Law and graduated magna cum laude—all the while holding down his clerk's job at the insurance company and even finding time to sell insurance policies on the side. In 1931 Burger was asked to join the well-established St. Paul law firm of Boyesen, Otis and Faricy—no mean achievement, even for an honors student, in those Depression days. Drafting wills and processing corporate papers by day, teaching contracts at St. Paul College of Law at night, Burger began making an impressive name for himself in the St. Paul legal community.

"I hate to use the word stubborn, but Warren adheres to his convictions with great tenacity, and he's bored stiff if he's not advocating a cause," Burger's former law partner, James C. Otis, has recalled. Foremost among the Burger allegiances at that time were the causes of his clients, whose cases he argued with unreserved vigor. But in his off-hours, Burger found a few others. He became acquainted with another young St. Paul attorney named Harold E. Stassen and when Stassen announced for the governorship in 1938, Burger helped manage his campaign.

When Stassen went to war (Burger stayed home because of a spinal ailment), Burger left state politics to concentrate on local affairs. As the first president of the St. Paul Council on Human Relations, Burger led the crusade against abusive treatment by city police of minority groups. With a burgeoning population of blacks (porters and dining attendants on railroads) and Mexican-Americans (in town after the sugar beet harvest), the problem had become acute. Burger confronted the police chief, who casually answered that "We treat niggers the same way we treat everyone else." That said it all. Burger's group sponsored police-community relations seminars, flying in specialists to teach cops how to understand and handle the problems of the underprivileged.

Stassen came roaring back from the war, full of energy and ambition. Burger helped in Stassen's failed challenge to Thomas Dewey in 1948 and lined up as an official state delegate, pledged to Stassen, at the 1952 Republican convention. But Burger made his reputation in Los Angeles fighting for Ike, not Stassen. It happened after Stassen named Burger Minnesota's representative to the convention's credentials committee, scene of a crucial fight between Eisenhower and Taft factions over the seating of rival delegations from Texas and Louisiana. Burger seized his opportunity, coolly defended the Eisenhower position and was rewarded after Ike's election when Attorney General Herbert Brownell appointed the Minnesotan his assistant in charge of the Justice Department's civil division.

In private practice, Burger had always shown an exemplary loyalty to his client. It was no different at Justice. After U.S. Solicitor General Simon E. Sobeloff refused to defend the government's action in dismissing, on loyalty grounds, Yale professor John P. Peters as a consultant to the Public Health Service, Burger took his place. Peters claimed that he had been prevented from confronting his accusers, in violation of his constitutional rights. Burger earned the wrath of civil libertarians by taking the other side of the argument, unsucessfully as it turned out. Burger was more successful—and popular—in doggedly prosecuting Greek shipping magnate Stavros Niarchos, among others, for illegally buying U.S. war surplus vessels. Burger seized more than forty ships and ultimately worked out a settlement with the shipowners worth millions to the U.S. government.

Hard-driving as an advocate, Burger was no less aggressive after President Eisenhower appointed him to the U.S. Court of Appeals for the District of Columbia in 1956. From the outset, Burger carried on a spirited, and often bitter, debate with judicial liberals on the court, led by Judge (later Chief Judge) David L. Bazelon. The more the liberal majority expanded the rights of criminal suspects, outdistancing even the Warren Court, the more resolute Burger became in defending a tough law and order position. His fury and frustration were well illustrated when Burger dissented from the majority's reversal of the conviction of a man who had confessed to robbing a food store. The conviction could not stand, said the majority, because the defendant had not been specifically warned that oral as well as written statements could be used against him. Burger wrote: "The seeming anxiety of judges to protect every accused person from every consequence of his voluntary utterances is giving rise to myriad rules, subrules, variations and exceptions which even the most alert and sophisticated lawyers and judges are taxed to follow. Each time judges add nuances to these 'rules' we make it less likely that any police officer will be able to follow the guidelines we lay down. We are approaching the predicament of the centipede on the flypaper—each time one leg is placed to give support to a leg already 'stuck,' another becomes captive and soon all are securely immobilized. Like the hapless centipede on the flypaper, our efforts to extricate ourselves from this self-imposed dilemma will, if we keep it up, soon have all of us immobilized. We are well on our way to forbidding any utterance of an accused to be used against him unless it is made in open court. Guilt or innocence becomes irrelevant in the criminal trial as we flounder in a morass of artificial rules poorly conceived and often impossible of application."

Sometimes, Burger's outspoken opinions on the court of appeals came back to haunt him. In 1965 a three-judge federal panel, including Burger, heard a defendant argue that his Sixth Amendment rights had been violated since he had been placed in a police line-up without his lawyer present. The panel dismissed the appeal in an unsigned two-paragraph opinion. Burger, however, felt more explanation was needed and he supplied it in a concurring opinion. "Such 'Disneyland' contentions as that absence of counsel at the police line-up voids a conviction are becoming commonplace," wrote Burger. "Having found that the indigent client's sense of gratification is readily dulled by incarceration, some court-appointed counsels find it expedient to protect themselves by raising every point, however absurd, which indigent appellants suggest." Two years later, that "Disneyland contention" was made the law of the land when the Supreme Court ruled that criminal suspects had the constitutional right to counsel at police line-ups.

Known as a prosecution-minded judge in criminal matters, Burger did not always carry that reputation as a government's friend into civil law fields. "Judicial conservative" Burger could brush aside precedent when he found that a government agency, like the Federal Communications Commission, had ignored the spirit of the law.

That happened in 1966 after church leaders in Jackson, Mississippi, charged television station WLBT with deliberate racial discrimination in its broadcasting policy. As an example, they claimed that WLBT had purposely cut off a network program on race relations problems by flashing a "Sorry, Cable Trouble" message on the screen when an attorney for the NAACP was speaking. The trouble, the leaders suggested, was not with the cable but with the bias of the TV station executives. After the FCC granted WLBT a temporary license renewal in 1964, the church leaders asked the FCC for a hearing to challenge the station's qualifications. The agency denied the request, contending that it was required by law to grant hearings only to challenging parties who claimed economic injury or electrical interference. There was no legal obligation, the FCC maintained, to grant a hearing to a group of mere listeners. That was wise policy, the FCC suggested, since a more liberal hearing policy might open the floodgates of litigation to listeners with even the most frivolous gripe against a station's programming. The church leaders appealed the FCC decision to the U.S. Court of Appeals for the District of Columbia.

Judge Burger, speaking for the court majority, rejected the

government's arguments. He said that the underlying reason for an FCC hearing was to entertain complaints of those directly affected by a licensed station. The listener qualified, said Burger, even if the courts had not seen it that way in the past. Once he had determined that the listener's interest was direct and important, Burger was undeterred by the FCC's pragmatic argument that his decision might cause the agency to be swamped with new petitions. Burger matched the FCC's pragmatic arguments with his own. "Experience demonstrates," he wrote, "consumers are generally among the best vindicators of the public interest." Besides, Burger added, the expense of litigation would discourage many potential petitioners. And if that was not enough, the FCC could draft its own rules to limit hearings to responsible members of a community.

The Jackson church leaders were back in Burger's court three years later. The FCC had granted the hearing, as Burger had demanded, but had renewed WLBT's license anyway. The FCC decision was unfair, the petitioners claimed, and inconsistent with the weight of evidence they had introduced showing the station's discriminatory policies. This time Burger's opinion was more biting. He accused the FCC of "a curious neutrality in favor of the licensee" at the hearings. And though he did not announce it as such, Burger proceeded to create a new standard for FCC hearings: the agency was obligated to find an affirmative public interest in a licensee's programming to justify renewal. He warned that, in the future, the FCC must give a "hospitable reception" to citizens' groups. "Broadcasters are temporary permittees—fiduciaries—of a great public resource, and they must meet the highest standards which are embraced in the public interest concept."

Despite his expansive rulings in the FCC cases, Burger's reputation as a conservative on the court of appeals persisted. For the most part, the reputation was of his own making.

Burger's most quotable phrases ("the predicament of the centipede on flypaper . . . Disneyland contentions") appeared in his criminal law opinions. And when Judge Burger lectured outside the courtroom, he frequently chose a law and order theme.

If a judge stakes out a strong position on the criminal law, even limiting his views to criminal procedure, he virtually guarantees his own notoriety. For a judge's decisions on the procedural aspects of a criminal case not only shape the direction that a trial may take, but frequently dictate a conclusion. If a criminal suspect's confession to the police is admitted into evidence, for example, it may insure conviction; if it is disallowed, that ruling may ultimately set the defendant free. Always conscious of the underdog, Earl Warren scrutinized the government's case from police station to courtroom for any evidence of wrongdoing. Warren's concern for the defendant, often at the expense of the government, branded the chief justice as a judicial liberal. On the other hand, Warren Burger's often articulated interest in society's rights, as opposed to the criminal suspect's, made him known as a judicial conservative.

In his writings and decisions, Burger pieced together a comprehensive philosophy of criminal justice. He began with the proposition that those responsible for administering the U.S. system of criminal justice had lost sight of their ultimate goal: to protect society from criminal behavior. By concentrating almost totally on the trial process alone, Burger declared in his 1967 Ripon College speech, U.S. officials hurt both the criminal and the community. In court, Burger suggested that the offender was encouraged to continue his war with society—to fight for acquittal on the basis of legal technicalities even if he knew he was guilty. The emphasis on technical procedure, according to Burger, discouraged the right values (honesty, rededication, penitence) and encouraged the wrong ones (evasiveness, never-ending argument with society). To make matters worse, Burger maintained, those same distortions con-

tinued after conviction. In America's prisons, effective rehabilitation programs were virtually nonexistent. As a result, the
convict poured most of his creative energies into his interminable fight for freedom through the courts, busily preparing a
steady stream of motions and appeals. The commitment was
not to his innocence or readiness to make a constructive contribution to society so much as to existential escape from a futile
prison existence.

Society, Burger argued, was the big loser. It lavished huge
amounts of time and money for the trial process, which clogged
the courts with backlogs and the defendants' minds with
wrongheaded notions of justice. It gave almost no attention to
the criminal in prison, virtually assuring him a round-trip ticket
on release but not before he had taken sweet, destructive re-
venge on the society that would not offer him genuine help.

For Burger, the answers to this seemingly insoluble crime-
punishment-crime syndrome existed—some four thousand
miles away. After study visits to the Scandinavian countries,
Burger became convinced that the northern Europeans operated the most effective systems in the world. The secret to their
success, Burger suggested, was a complete reversal of the priorities that existed in the United States. The governments in Swe-
den and Norway and Denmark disposed of criminal cases in
one or two weeks that would take months in the United States.
Once a defendant was convicted, however, the Scandinavians
spared neither time nor expense on the offender in a humane
effort to prepare him for reentry into society as a constructive
citizen. In time, money and concern, then, the northern Europeans emphasized the final step of the criminal process
(rehabilitation) rather than the first (the trial).

A major step toward reform of the U.S. system was to copy
the Scandinavians, who "go swiftly, efficiently and directly to
the question of whether the accused is guilty." Burger admitted
that the northern Europeans had a few advantages. For one

thing, there was no Fifth Amendment which protects a defendant from taking the witness stand if he thinks his testimony
might incriminate him. For another, the Europeans did not
require jury trials in felony cases. Instead, three-judge panels
decided the cases, eliminating the time and expense of jury
selection and deliberation, often resulting in the saving of
weeks, even months of a court's time.

Could U.S. courts emulate the Scandinavians' efficiency
without violating constitutional safeguards? In a 1968 seminar
at the Center for the Study of Democratic Institutions, Burger
speculated on the possibilities, purposely overstating his case.
He questioned, for example, the prevalent interpretation of the
Fifth Amendment's protection against self-incrimination "as
presently applied and interpreted." U.S. courts convicted defendants from their own testimony all the time—in civil litigation. And why, Burger asked, must the standards always be so
much stricter in criminal cases? Burger also hinted that the
elimination of the jury might not be such a bad idea either, since
the Europeans had proved that three-judge panels did not
necessarily deliver an inferior product of justice.

His concern that the U.S. courts had put too much emphasis
on "techniques, devices and mechanisms" in the criminal process caused Burger to criticize some of the far-reaching decisions of the Warren Court. He took issue, for example, with the
Warren Court's decision in *Mapp* v. *Ohio*, in which the Court
ruled that illegally seized evidence could not be used at state
criminal trials. The rule, Burger suggested, gave the offender an
easy out, had little effect in curbing illegal police behavior and
ultimately punished the only innocent party involved—the
offender's next victim. Errant policemen, Burger argued in a
1964 lecture at the American University Law School, frequently didn't follow the results of their case after arrest, and
most likely wouldn't be punished by paternalistic police depart-
ments even if exposed. Instead of fighting the quixotic court-

room battle, Burger suggested, the best thing to do was create civilian review boards, independent of the police department, with legal powers to subpoena witnesses, suspend or dismiss guilty cops and expunge criminal records resulting from illegal arrests.

Burger also quarreled with the Warren Court's decisions expanding a suspect's rights in the police station, not because the illegal police activity should be condoned but because the Court had not given enough thought to the proper method of censure. In a 1967 seminar with law enforcement officers, Burger said that he favored the slower method of establishing new codes for law enforcement authorities. Rather than by Court edict, Burger maintained that the new rules should be channeled through the rule-making procedures provided in congressional legislation. By relying on the legislative process rather than the courts, Burger believed that the important foundation, built on the strength of committee hearings, expert testimony and empirical studies, could give the rules more authority and, in the final analysis, greater public acceptance. The weakness to that argument, as Burger admitted, was that the Court's rules applied to the states and no federal legislation could ever go that far. Though he was not certain that states would follow a federal example, Burger thought it worth the effort to offer them more reasons to adopt the rules than could ever be contained in a single Court opinion, like *Miranda*.

In Chief Justice Earl Warren's judicial world, there was always a place for the noble gesture, the ethical imperative. In Warren Burger's legal cosmos, more than one of the Ten Commandments had better be at issue. Burger's judgment could be harsh, as he demonstrated in an appellate opinion in which he challenged the dramatic action of a colleague, Judge J. Skelly Wright, an action that almost certainly saved the life of a mother of a seven-month-old child.

On September 17, 1963, Mrs. Jesse E. Jones was rushed to the emergency room of Washington's Georgetown University Hospital, having lost two-thirds of her body's blood supply from a ruptured ulcer. Her husband told attendants that the couple, members of the Jehovah's Witness sect, had no personal physician and would rely for care on the hospital staff. But when attendants advised the Joneses that immediate blood transfusions were necessary to save the mother's life, Mr. Jones refused to give his consent. The Joneses' beliefs, the husband said, prohibited the injection of blood into the body. Believing death to be imminent, hospital authorities called their attorneys for advice. They were told to delay a blood transfusion until the attorneys could go before a district court judge to request legal permission for the hospital to administer the blood. The judge refused. Attorneys then approached Judge Wright of the U.S. Court of Appeals for the District of Columbia.

Wright first telephoned the hospital to determine the urgency of the situation. Then, accompanied by a hospital attorney, Wright hurried to the hospital for further investigation. Mr. Jones told Wright as he had told the hospital officials that his religious beliefs forbade him from giving permission for the blood transfusions. He said, however, that if the court ordered the transfusions, the responsibility would not be his. Wright conferred with doctors who said the patient would die if no transfusion was given. "I then went inside the patient's room," Wright later recalled. "Her appearance confirmed the urgency which had been represented to me. I tried to communicate with her, advising her again as to what the doctors had said. The only audible reply I could hear was 'against my will.' "

Because of Mrs. Jones' desperate condition, Wright did not press the issue. Instead, he returned to the doctors' room, where a dozen physicians, an attorney for the hospital and the president of Georgetown University were pleading with Mr. Jones to reconsider his position. He would not, telling the anxious group that the Scriptures said "that we should not drink blood," which to Mr. Jones meant no blood transfusions. Moments later, Judge Wright signed the legal order to allow the transfusion.

Sure enough, Mrs. Jones later went to court to challenge the hospital's right to have obtained such a legal order. Her attorney argued, among other things, that the hospital had violated the patient's right to the free exercise of religion. In his opinion rejecting Mrs. Jones' arguments, Wright pointed to the urgency of the situation and the fact that, if the court had not acted immediately, Mrs. Jones would have died. "To refuse to act, only to find later that the law required action, was a risk I was unwilling to accept," said Wright. "I determined to act on the side of life."

Burger dissented on the technical ground that Mrs. Jones' suit should have been dismissed, because there was not then, nor at the time Wright acted, a justiciable controversy. Technicalities aside, Burger was saying that Judge Wright should never have signed the order in the first place since the hospital's problem, at least in the sight of the law, simply did not call for a court's solution. Burger then reminded the court of Justice Benjamin Cardozo's words: "He [the judge] is not a knight-errant, roaming at will in pursuit of his own ideal of beauty or goodness. He is to draw his inspiration from consecrated principles. He is not to yield to spasmodic sentiment, to vague and unregulated benevolence." Before embracing the noble cause too quickly, Burger said, judges had better understand that there were myriads of problems that they were professionally powerless to solve. And this, he concluded, was as it should be.

Political problems stood high on Burger's judicial verboten list. Although he once said he was not sure how he would have voted in the Supreme Court's reapportionment decisions, he voiced admiration for Frankfurter's dissent in *Baker* v. *Carr*. "There is no reason, "he contended," why we as judges should regard ourselves as some kind of Guardian Elders ordained to revise the political judgments of elected representatives of the people." When Harlem Representative Adam Clayton Powell, Jr., asked the Court of Appeals for the District of Columbia to reverse the U.S. House of Representatives' decision to exclude him, Burger's thesis was dramatically tested.

Actually, Powell's troubles began long before the House of Representatives voted on March 1, 1967 to take away his membership card. In his 22 years as Harlem's representative in Washington, Powell's freewheeling ways had antagonized formidable powers in Congress and outside. He had been a black militant long before members of his race had the pride to call themselves "black" or the courage to act militantly in a white man's world. Powell was the original "uppity nigger," playing whitey's political game superbly with guile and charm and the overwhelming endorsement of his constituents. Returned to Congress year after predictable year, Powell climbed the greasy pole to congressional power, like everyone else, through the seniority system. When he became chairman of the House Labor and Education Committee, Powell—like almost every other chairman—began to throw his weight around, holding up bills that did not please him, expediting those that did. And he began to spend the taxpayers' money a little more freely, writing himself and his congressional fellows junket tickets, putting his wife on the congressional payroll, entertaining splendidly in his oversized office. Congressmen who knew the worst of Powell's excesses could not really complain because they—or their friends—had been living the good life for years.

Then, Powell made a critical miscalculation. He publicly called Mrs. Esther James, a 63-year-old Harlem widow, "a bag woman" which, roughly translated, meant collector of graft for the police. She sued Powell for slander and eventually was awarded $55,780 in damages. But the courts of New York could never corner Powell to collect the judgment. He avoided

arrest by restricting his New York appearances to the weekends. Powell's flouting of the law coupled with his well-publicized congressional escapades slowly turned the House against
him. It voted 307–116 to exclude him for misusing public funds
and being contemptuous of New York courts and committees
of Congress.

Powell took Congress to court, claiming that he could be
excluded from the House only if he failed to meet the constitutional requirements of age, residency and citizenship. Powell
maintained he was old enough, officially resided in New York
State and had been a U.S. citizen for seven years—all that was
needed to challenge successfully the constitutionality of the
House's action. The challenge put the judiciary between Scylla
and Charybdis. If the courts let the House's action stand, the
judges would appear to be ignoring the clearest language of the
Constitution. But if they sided with Powell, the courts for the
first time in constitutional history would be asserting the
judiciary's right to supervise the internal operations of a coequal branch of government.

Fully aware of the stakes involved, Judge Burger, in one of
his last majority opinions on the court of appeals, approached
his subject with the greatest of judicial trepidation. Burger first
asked whether the Powell case presented issues which could be
decided by the courts. He concluded that it did. Then, he
approached the critical decision, the one that has always made
judges who counsel judicial restraint queasy: should the courts
settle an issue with obvious political implications even if the
Constitution allows it? Burger's answer: no. The case lacked
adequate "manageable standards" for resolving the dispute, he
contended, since the court had no realistic way to compel the
House to honor its judgment. "What would happen," Burger
later asked, "if the House ignored the Court's judgment? Could
we then send troops to the Capitol?" Aside from that frightening eventuality, Burger worried that any positive court action

would show a disrespect for a coordinate branch of government that could do neither institution any good. He deplored "the blow to representative government were judges either so rash or so sure of their infallibility as to think they should command an elected coequal branch in these circumstances." And he added: "That each branch may occasionally make errors for which there may be no effective remedy is one of the prices we pay for this independence of each coequal branch."

The Supreme Court was unwilling to pay the price. By a vote of 7–1, the Court reversed Burger and supported Powell's claim that the House of Representatives could not refuse to seat him so long as he met the explicit requirements of the Constitution. The majority opinion written by Chief Justice Warren, stated the constitutional principle with bold, uncompromising assurance, though carefully drawing back from dictating specific terms of surrender by Congress. "Our system of government requires that federal courts on occasion interpret the Constitution in a manner at variance with the construction given the document by another branch," wrote Warren. "The alleged conflict that such an adjudication may cause cannot justify the courts avoiding their constitutional responsibility."

The retiring chief justice's unflinching call to principle in the judicial process appealed mightily to the idealistic generation of law students in the sixties. Warren told the Nader Raiders and the young poverty attorneys that there need be no chasm between law and morality, between common sense and the commonweal. "They were inspired," wrote Judge J. Skelly Wright, "by the dignity and moral courage of a man and an institution that was prepared to act on the ideals to which America is theoretically and rhetorically dedicated."

On the other hand, Burger's careful balancing of competing legal interests struck a dissonant chord with the idealists. The young lawyers who wanted to change the world through the lawsuit did not easily warm to the new chief justice nor he to them. "Young people who decide to go into the law primarily on the theory that they can change the world by litigation in the courts," said Burger, "I think may be in for some disappointments. It is not the right way to make the decision to go into the law, and that is not the route by which basic changes in a country like ours should be made. That is a legislative and policy process. And there is a very limited role for courts in this respect."

Politics has always carried considerable weight in a president's selection of a chief justice. And, in turn, the appointment has always stirred political responses. When President Andrew Jackson appointed his secretary of the treasury, Roger Taney, for example, a Whig newspaper was outraged: "The pure ermine of the Supreme Court is sullied by the appointment of that political hack, Roger B. Taney." On the other hand, a pro-Jackson paper read Taney's confirmation as "the verdict of high approval which has been awarded to [Taney's] sterling worth by the American people." The Burger appointment was treated no differently. The conservative *U.S. News and World Report* proudly bannered: JUDGE BURGER: CHAMPION OF LAW AND ORDER. But the liberal *Nation* shook its head in dismay: "We pray he will not be as inadequate as his judicial record seems to predict."

Often lost in the debate over the chief justice's political soul is a function of his job that has nothing to do with his political philosophy. As head of the entire federal court system, the chief justice, if he chooses, may lobby for more money for the courts (and, therefore, more judges and court personnel) and administrative reforms that may have more to do with the quality of justice than any single opinion he writes on the Court. Some experts rate Chief Justice William Howard Taft as one of the Court greats, not because of his opinions, but because of his devoted efforts to reform an antiquated court system.

"I love judges, and I love courts," Taft once wrote. "They are my ideals that typify on earth what we shall meet hereafter in heaven under a just God." Taft was convinced that his angelic guardians on earth should have proper temples to work their miracles. In his first year as chief justice, Taft crisscrossed the country in a whistle stop campaign for reform of the courts. He spoke to bar associations, argued his case in legal periodicals and testified at length before the House and Senate judiciary committees. His efforts were handsomely rewarded the next year when Congress passed a judicial reform act that streamlined the federal judicial system by coordinating the activities of the far-flung federal districts and bringing them under surer executive control of the chief justice. That accomplished, Taft turned his attention to the problem of court congestion in the Supreme Court docket. "We made our preparations with care," Taft later said, "and it proved to be easier than we supposed." (Taft's reward was the Judges Bill of 1925 which gave the Court greater control to decide which cases it would hear.) Before he was through, Chief Justice Taft's arm-twisting (he thought nothing of calling the chairman of the judiciary committee or even talking to the president about his reforms) had succeeded in winning the Court its first permanent home—the present Supreme Court building.

Unlike Taft, Chief Justice Earl Warren did not show an overriding interest in the administration of the federal judiciary. To be sure, he was aware of the crowded court conditions and on many occasions publicly pleaded for reforms. But somehow, the man who had earned the reputation as the most effective chief executive in California history did not translate his pleas into effective programs. Two potential allies in any court reform program, Congress and the professional bar, did not rally to Warren's support, partly as a protest against the Warren Court's liberal rulings. Warren did not help matters by bitterly criticizing Congress's stinginess or by resigning from the American Bar Association in 1958 after the Conference of State Chief Justices had criticized Warren Court decisions in the chief justice's presence.

By contrast, Warren Burger showed a Taftian zeal for his administrative duties before he had ever heard an oral argument as chief justice. On June 24, 1969, exactly twenty-four hours after he had taken the oath of office, Chief Justice Burger called his first meeting to discuss the problems of court administration, a subject on which he had been lecturing bar associations for more than a decade. In 1961, for example, Judge Burger had practically committed judicial heresy by suggesting that no more than half the sixty-three new federal judgeships created that year would be needed if the sitting judges worked more efficiently.

One of Burger's first acts as chief justice was to huddle with Representative John J. Rooney, to persuade the czar of the judiciary's appropriations to grant the justices additional law clerks. A simple task? When Earl Warren made a similar request a few years before, he recalled, "you would think we were just dipping our hands in the Treasury." But Burger succeeded where his predecessor had failed.

Two months later, the new chief justice stormed into the American Bar Association's convention in Dallas with the vigor and enthusiasm of a man who did not seem to know that the ABA and the Supreme Court had hardly been on speaking terms for more than a decade. Burger had toiled long hours for the ABA, particularly as chairman of its committee on minimum standards of criminal justice. He had long believed the ABA an invaluable instrument for judicial reform and, for three days in Dallas, Chief Justice Burger vigorously embarked on a lobbying effort among the three thousand delegates to prove his appraisal correct.

Burger's activity was so frenetic in Dallas that he could have been mistaken for a political candidate wooing an important state delegation. The chief justice lingered in the meeting halls, greeting lawyers from Tucson and Indianapolis, judges and their ladies, the ABA staff. None had been so flattered in years. The chief laughed at bad golf jokes, signed autographs and accepted the heartfelt congratulations of all. "Hello, counselor, Hi Ed, Glad to meet you, Mr. Jones." That was not just a fellow lawyer, that was the chief justice of the United States telling them it was great to be with the American Bar Association.

At Sunday's prayer breakfast, the youth choir of the First Baptist Church of Dallas stirred the delegates with softly inspirational renditions of "Deep River," "My Eternal King" and "Gloria in Excelsis." The chief justice was scheduled to speak afterward on the starkly more prosaic subject of legal education. But Burger had been moved, visibly moved, by the singing as had his audience. When he stepped to the podium, he paused. "How could anyone really worry about the young people of America," the chief justice asked, "after witnessing what we have this morning?"

Burger delivered five speeches to the ABA in three days and in every speech the new chief justice dispensed with "that reminds me of a story" introductions and lofty, philosophical conclusions. His messages were serious and specific and all focused on a single objective—improvement of the administration of justice in the United States.* Burger urged the state chief justices to lobby for legislative adoption of the ABA's minimum standards for criminal justice. He told law professors that their law schools had become too abstract, too far removed from the people and problem-oriented stuff of law practice. Long an advocate of penal reform, the chief justice next asked the ABA to sponsor a sweeping reevaluation of the nation's penal system with an eye to the elimination of the "crime-punishment-crime"

---

*It would be a theme that Burger would dwell on continually. As chief justice, Burger became so immersed in his administrative duties—and opportunities—that he devoted a full one-third of his professional time, even when the Court was in session, to administration.

syndrome that had encouraged rather than eliminated the nation's crime problem. And finally, Burger called for an immediate ABA-sponsored study that would ultimately lead to a network of court administrators to streamline the clogged court calendars.

To the outside observer, the Burger proposals seemed rather modest prodding, certainly not the stuff of revolutionary change. To those who had watched the ABA move, glacier-like, for decades, even those modest proposals seemed doomed to the graveyards of committee reports. But both views missed the spirit of the proposals and underestimated the leadership of the proposer. "In my twenty-two years of attending this convention," said former justice Tom Clark, "I have never seen anyone who has so quickly and so effectively built a fire under this group as Chief Justice Burger."

The chief justice, the American Bar Association's chief justice, had come home. Burger and the ABA stood together because they shared so much. They believed implicitly in the traditional values that had built America; they believed that the legal profession was a vital instrument to preserve those values and that the development of the law, slowly and deliberately, would make the nation sturdier in the future.

CHAPTER FIVE

The Southern Strategy

During Chief Justice Warren Burger's first term on the Supreme Court, the most controversial constitutional question of the day was not argued in his courtroom. The controversy revolved around Article II, Section 2 of the U.S. Constitution, which provides that the president shall appoint principal officers of the federal government, including the judiciary, with the advice and consent of the Senate. After President Nixon nominated Chief Judge Clement F. Haynsworth, Jr., of the U.S. Court of Appeals for the Fourth Circuit, and Judge G. Harrold Carswell of the U.S. Court of Appeals for the Fifth Circuit to the Supreme Court and the Senate rejected both men, there was much discussion in legal circles and the White House of the interpretation of the Senate's duty of "advice and consent." Did the framers of the Constitution intend for the Senate to exercise the same kind of political and philosophical judgments in passing on a president's nominees that the president had done in appointing his men? If so, then the Senate's power would virtually be the equal of the president's. On the other hand, perhaps the framers wanted the Senate to play a more passive role in the appointive process, to give advice and consent, to be sure, but to place the greater emphasis on the latter part of that constitutional duty.

Finding no constitutional bar to the Senate's serious review of presidential appointments, Professor Charles L. Black, Jr., of the Yale Law School suggested a common-sense approach to the executive-legislative tug of war. Black had no quarrel with the president's right to appoint just about anyone he wanted for the executive branch, including the cabinet. "These [executive appointments] are his people; they are to work with him. Wisdom and fairness would give him great latitude, if strict constitutional obligation would not." But Black came to just the opposite conclusion on judicial appointments. "The judges are not the president's people. God forbid! They are not to work with him or for him. They are to be as independent of him as they are of the Senate, neither more nor less." For that reason, said Black, the Senate had just as legitimate a stake in passing on a nominee's potential for the national good or harm as the president. "In a world that knows that a man's social philosophy shapes his judicial behavior," Black concluded, "that philosophy is a factor in his fitness. If it is a philosophy the senator thinks will make a judge whose service on the bench will hurt the country, then the senator can do right only by treating this judgment of his, unencumbered by deference to the president's, as a satisfactory basis in itself for a negative vote."

President Richard Nixon read much more into the president's power of appointment than Professor Black. That power, Nixon believed, was not meant to be shared with the Senate. By implication, Nixon relegated the Senate's "advice and consent" to a passive constitutional function. When his nomination of Judge Carswell floundered, the President spelled out his views. "What is centrally at issue in this nomination," Nixon wrote U.S. Senator William B. Saxbe of Ohio, "is the constitutional responsibility of the president to appoint members of the Court —and whether this responsibility can be frustrated by those who wish to substitute their own philosophy or their own subjective judgment for that of the one person entrusted by the Constitution with the power of appointment. The question arises, whether I as president of the United States, shall be accorded the same right of choice in naming Supreme Court justices which has been freely accorded to my predecessors of both parties."

The president's right of choice, which Nixon said had "been freely accorded his predecessors," had been countermanded twenty-four times by the Senate before it rejected Judge Carswell. That meant that the legislators had successfully defeated nearly one-fifth of all nominees that U.S. presidents had sent to the Senate for their advice and consent. Had the senators repeatedly misinterpreted the intentions of the framers of the Constitution? Not if Alexander Hamilton was to be believed. Anticipating the Senate's advice and consent function, Hamilton wrote in *The Federalist* that, "If by influencing the president be meant restraining him, this is precisely what must have been intended." Unrestrained in his appointments, the president would be tempted, Hamilton believed, to use his power for personal favor or political advantage—to the detriment of the nation. The threat—or realization—of a Senate veto, would keep the president honest. "The possibility of rejection," wrote Hamilton, "would be a strong motive to care in proposing."

Ideally, the Senate would practice the art of high politics in reviewing the president's nominees, rejecting them only if they failed to meet Hamilton's requirements of men "who unite the requisite integrity with the requisite knowledge." Presidents from Washington to Nixon have never held their nominees to those high standards, often indulging in common politics to find their man. Throughout constitutional history, the Senate has followed suit. Almost all Senate rejections have been for reasons of political advantage, dating back to the first man who failed to be confirmed for the chief justiceship, John Rutledge.

Rutledge had been an associate justice of the Supreme Court from 1789 to 1791, but had resigned to take what was then considered a more prestigious position: chief justice of the South Carolina Supreme Court. When Chief Justice John Jay resigned from the Court to become Governor of New York, Rutledge wrote President Washington to apply for Jay's old job. The president sent word to Rutledge that the job was his. But before the appointment was officially bound by Senate confirmation, Rutledge made a critical misstep. In Charleston, South Carolina Rutledge delivered a speech vigorously criticizing the Jay Treaty with Great Britain, which the Federalist-dominated Senate had already ratified.

When news of the Rutledge speech gained circulation in the North, the Federalist press opposed the Rutledge nomination. Rumors had it that Rutledge, fifty-six years old, had reached an advanced stage of senility; otherwise, how could he have made such a preposterous speech? After the Senate rejected Rutledge, 14–10, the defeat was explained in many quarters as the result of Rutledge's supposedly decaying mental condition. But others, like Thomas Jefferson, thought otherwise. "The rejection of Mr. Rutledge by the Senate," Jefferson wrote, "is a bold thing because they [the Federalists] cannot pretend any objection to him but his disapprobation of the Treaty."

The Rutledge rejection was only the beginning. In all, twenty of eighty-one Court nominees were rejected between 1789 and 1894. Significantly, the failure rate was greatest between 1828 and 1877, a time of intense, often open, political warfare between the president and the Senate.

The first Court appointee turned down by the Senate in the twentieth century was Judge John J. Parker of North Carolina, nominated to the Court in 1930 by President Hoover. Although Parker had served for years on the U.S. Court of Appeals for the Fourth Circuit without a trace of notoriety, his elevation to the U.S. Supreme Court created a hornet's nest of controversy. First of all, the nominee was a southerner, a fact that prompted the president's adversaries to label the nomination a political offering to the South. Civil rights organizations opposed the nomination because of their belief that the judicial candidate was a racist. Organized labor attacked the nominee for his purported "antilabor" decisions, mounting a campaign against the nominee's confirmation that included public condemnation by the nation's most powerful labor leader, AFL President William Green. With such formidable opposition plus that of Progressive Republicans in the Senate like George W. Norris, Judge Parker was voted down 41 to 39.

In the fall of 1969, commentators had good reason to recall the Parker affair, for his defeat and that of another southerner, Chief Judge Clement Haynsworth, Jr., of the U.S. Court of Appeals for the Fourth Circuit, provided striking parallels. Except for conflict of interest charges leveled against Judge Haynsworth, his failed nomination contained all of the ingredients of Parker's: opposition from partisan senators, big labor and civil rights advocates. Judge Parker returned to the appellate bench to prove his critics wrong in their accusations that he was anti-Negro and antilabor. Parker proved his detractors short-sighted as well; Justice Owen Roberts, the man who took Parker's place on the Court, rendered considerably less liberal judicial opinions than Parker. That Haynsworth might well complete the analogy upon his return to the U.S. court of appeals was of little comfort to his supporters. Their man, like Parker, had been caught in a political crossfire that he could neither avoid nor effectively counter.

Haynsworth's downfall began more than a year before his nomination to the Supreme Court, at a time when his sponsor, Richard Nixon, was no more than the leading contender for the

Republican nomination for the presidency. That was the summer of 1968, when President Johnson named Associate Justice Abe Fortas to succeed Chief Justice Warren. At first, anti-Fortas forces, led by Republican Senator Robert P. Griffin of Michigan, opposed the nomination primarily because it had been made by a "lame duck" president. At the Senate's confirmation hearings, Fortas ran into deeper trouble. The chief justice-designate, it was learned, had counseled the president on national policy and had even done some behind-the-scenes lobbying on the president's behalf while sitting on the Supreme Court. Later, when Fortas admitted that he had received $15,-000 for conducting a series of seminars at American University, his ethics as well as his politics were brought into question. As a result, his nomination as chief justice languished and was finally withdrawn by President Johnson. After Fortas resumed his place on the Court as an associate justice, *Life* broke the story that charged Justice Fortas with acceptance of a $20,000 fee from the family foundation of financier Louis E. Wolfson at a time when Wolfson was under investigation by the Securities and Exchange Commission. As the days passed, it became clear that Fortas could not survive the wave of indignation that spread across the nation. Still, there was no word of a Fortas resignation.

Reports circulated that John Mitchell had met secretly with Chief Justice Warren to tell him that the Justice Department had far more serious information on Fortas' extrajudicial activities than had been made public. A legal contract, Mitchell had learned, required Wolfson's foundation to pay $20,000 a year for as long as Fortas or his wife lived. Mitchell confirmed the report that he met with the chief justice "to inform him of certain information known by me which might be of aid to him," but would not divulge the specific information he had. For Fortas sympathizers in the Senate, the Mitchell action smacked of an ugly squeeze play by the administration to force

Fortas off the bench. They did not like it but they could do nothing about it. Shortly after the Mitchell-Warren meeting, Associate Justice Fortas resigned from the Court.

The Fortas affair had profound repercussions. For the nation's judiciary, it served as a painful, conscience-searing experience. Afterward, the Judicial Conference of the United States laid down stiff new rules that forbade all federal judges except members of the Supreme Court from accepting outside fees, and required the filing of annual reports of their investments and other assets. The heat from the Fortas episode affected the High Court as well. Justice Douglas announced his resignation from a $12,000-a-year post as president and director of the Albert Parvin Foundation; the foundation's namesake enjoyed the uncomfortable distinction of having been named, though not tried, as a co-conspirator in a stock fraud case involving Louis Wolfson. Justice Brennan went further. He canceled all of his speeches, sold all of his stock, and even gave up his interest in a Virginia real estate venture.

At the same time that the judiciary was vowing financial abstinence, Senators stung by the Fortas debacle were setting their own high standards. The political caveat was clear that President Nixon's Court appointees had better be as pure as the driven snow. Nixon's first choice, Warren Burger, came through unscathed. Burger's background posed neither serious ethical nor political problems. Nixon's second nominee, Clement Haynsworth, Jr., was not so lucky.

After the Burger appointment, pressure had been building on Nixon to name a southerner to the Court. Though he had never publicly promised a southern nominee, Nixon's intentions were never seriously doubted. Aware that a judge in the South enjoyed a prestige unrivaled in any other section of the country, Nixon advisors believed that he could do southerners no higher favor than to appoint one of their own to the highest court in

the land. Even before Nixon assumed office, he had successfully
identified with the southern cause. "The one battle most white
southerners feel they are fighting is with the Court and Nixon
has effectively identified himself with that cause," wrote election analyst Samuel Lubell. "Only Nixon can change the
makeup of the Court to satisfy southern aspirations."

The president and Attorney General Mitchell came across
Haynsworth's name early. The Haynsworth background
seemed ideal for the president. He was a sitting federal judge
and, at fifty-six, the youngest chief judge on any federal circuit.
Many of his opinions mirrored Nixon's thinking. He was a
lawyer, not a theorist. He was a traditionalist, not an innovator.
Most important, Haynsworth was a southerner, a fifth generation lawyer from a respected South Carolina family.

And so the announcement came from White House Press
Secretary Ronald L. Ziegler on August 18, 1969, that Judge
Haynsworth was the president's choice. "Judge Haynsworth
meets the qualifications which the president believes are essential for an associate justice for the Supreme Court," said Ziegler. "The president feels that during Judge Haynsworth's years
on the bench, he has demonstrated judicial temperament, balance, impartiality and fairness and he is a man who at the early
age of fifty-six is an eminently qualified jurist, scholar and
intellect." The press, public and politicians were well prepared
for the president's selection. Or so the administration thought.
John Sears, former deputy counsel to the President, later recalled the administration's confidence in the Haynsworth appointment. "Here was a highly regarded southern judge who
looked and acted the part. His decisions couldn't nail him as
an imbecile. He would have been confirmed in a minute ten
years ago. But his appointment came at a time when Christ
himself would have drawn at least one 'no' vote on principle
alone."

The "no" votes of a few disgruntled Senators was one thing;

the unmitigated fury that the Haynsworth nomination produced was quite another. "This is the worst possible time for the appointment of a hard-core segregationist to the Supreme Court," charged Joseph L. Rauh, Jr., counsel for the Leadership Conference on Civil Rights. "President Nixon's appointment of Judge Haynsworth," said Rauh, "is like throwing a log on the fires of racial tension." At the same time, civil rights forces gained the ally that had spelled defeat for Judge John Parker in 1930: organized labor. AFL-CIO President George Meany labeled Judge Haynsworth antilabor and listed seven "antilabor" decisions of Haynsworth that were reversed by the U.S. Supreme Court. As relentless as the attacks on Haynsworth by civil rights and labor spokesmen were, their opposition alone would not have prevented confirmation.

Help came soon enough when anti-Haynsworth forces began poking into the judge's financial dealings, which, it was said, had made him a millionaire in less than twenty years. The stock portfolio was impressive indeed: banking, insurance, textiles, railroads, radio and television stations, hotels and construction. When Haynsworth was appointed to the Fourth Circuit by President Eisenhower in 1953, he resigned from directorships of no less than eight corporations. But despite those resignations, word passed that Judge Haynsworth had commingled his judicial business with outside business ventures, precisely the charges that had led to the downfall of Associate Justice Abe Fortas.

The first and most damaging conflict of interest charge focused on Haynsworth's involvement with the Carolina Vend-a-Matic Company, a corporation that sold drink and food vending machines. In June 1969, Haynsworth had told a Senate subcommittee investigating judicial ethics that he separated himself from Carolina Vend-a-Matic on assuming the federal bench—a statement that he contradicted under oath only three months later when testifying at his confirmation hearings. Far from separating himself, Haynsworth had remained as vice-president and director of the company for almost seven years after becoming an appellate judge. During that time, Haynsworth participated in a case in which Darlington Mills, a North Carolina textile concern that was doing $50,000 worth of business with Vend-a-Matic, had been accused of committing an unfair labor practice. Haynsworth cast the deciding vote in favor of Darlington, which had shut down its plant rather than abide by an election that would have given the victorious textile union collective bargaining rights. On the heels of the disclosure of the Darlington Mills case, Senator Birch Bayh, leader of the Senate's anti-Haynsworth forces, announced that in another decision Judge Haynsworth had voted with the majority in favor of the Brunswick Corporation, a huge conglomerate, and then purchased one thousand shares of its stock before the decision was made public. Haynsworth critics rolled out other, very minor, conflict of interest charges as well. For example, Judge Haynsworth owned three shares of the Greenville Community Hotel Corporation (annual dividend: fifteen cents) at a time that he voted against a guest who sued the hotel for injuries from a fall.

Racist, proletarian exploiter, corporate sharpie. All that remained to polish the draconian image were a few negative journalistic flourishes. The Haynsworth background and personality were irresistibly vulnerable. The quintessential southern gentleman, Clement Haynsworth, said one old acquaintance, "is the last man in the world I would approach with a dirty joke." Dour, aloof, correct, Haynsworth had few friends who could vouch for those human qualities that warm the hearts of feature writers and their readers. He never knew poverty as a youth, never sold newspapers on the street corner, never commanded a PT boat or choked up on national television about his wife's Republican cloth coat.

Short and plumpish, Haynsworth wore metal rim glasses,

combed his hair back with immaculate precision and did not give generously of his smiles even for photographers. After his nomination, the Haynsworth pictures in newspapers and magazines always seemed posed, as most of them were. Here was Judge Haynsworth peering seriously at the camera with his "Miss Dorothy" (as he affectionately called his wife) on his arm, umbrella in hand. Or the Haynsworths preparing for an evening out, Mrs. Haynsworth in long gown and Clement in dark suit. For the personal touch, Haynsworth was snapped in his greenhouse stiffly admiring one of his prized camellias.

The judge's whole life seemed meticulously programmed. He attended Furman, the university his great-great-grandfather founded, before graduating from Harvard Law School. Upon his return to Greenville, Haynsworth joined the most prestigious and powerful law firm in South Carolina. Though a nominal Democrat, he supported Eisenhower in 1952 and was properly rewarded with his seat on the U.S. court of appeals the next year. After becoming a judge, Haynsworth worked methodically week in, week out, breaking only for a forty-five-minute lunch with his wife at their $100,000 Tudor-styled home. At dinnertime, Haynsworth usually looked forward to the sounds of Brahms and Beethoven on the stereo, a quiet meal and an evening of gin rummy with his wife.

The law, for Haynsworth, was the perfect complement to his personality: steeped in tradition, free from emotionalism, strictly regulated by rules of experience and the intellect. That did not mean, as some critics charged, that Haynsworth was some bizarre relic from the nineteenth century. To the contrary, Haynsworth possessed 20–20 contemporary vision, fully capable of grasping the realities of the legal problems presented to him. Often, that practical corner of Haynsworth's mind worked against special interest groups—like organized labor.

The Food Store Employees Union had vainly attempted to organize a meat packing plant in Huntington, West Virginia for several years. In 1962, the union had requested an election and lost. Four years later, union leaders decided on an authorization card campaign, attempting to obtain the signatures of a majority of employees on cards supporting the union's collective bargaining rights with the company. After collecting cards from forty-three of the eighty employees, the union leadership asked the company president for a bargaining conference. He ignored the request. After charges and countercharges were exchanged between union and management, the dispute was submitted to the National Labor Relations Board. Among the issues presented was whether authorization cards from forty-three of the eighty employees gave a clear indication that the union represented the majority of employees. The NLRB said that it did; Judge Haynsworth, writing for his court's majority, reversed the board's decision.

"It would be difficult to imagine a more unreliable method of ascertaining the real wishes of employees than a 'card check,' " wrote Haynsworth, "unless it were an employer's request for an open show of hands." Citing a report by the NLRB to the American Bar Association, Haynsworth contended that the signed authorization cards did not necessarily reflect the true wishes of the employees. In the NLRB report, Haynsworth noted, employees were significantly more enthusiastic about the union publicly than when protected by the secret ballot. After a union presented card signatures of 50 to 70 per cent of the employees, for example, it prevailed in only 48 per cent of the subsequent secret ballot elections.

Some employees sign, according to the AFL-CIO organizer's guidebook (cited by Haynsworth), just "to get the union off my back"; free from union prodding, they might well change their mind. Making a final point, Haynsworth said that judicial endorsement of authorization cards would leave employees open to union intimidation, prevented by secret elections. A note in the *Yale Law Journal,* written in 1966, a year before the Haynsworth opinion, reached a similar conclusion. "On balance," the *Yale* article stated, "the [authorization] cards do more harm than good. . . . Secret ballot elections are not perfect. But they are the best procedure yet devised for enabling the citizen and the working man to register his choice."

The AFL-CIO's Meany said the Haynsworth authorization card opinion was antilabor; Meany's expertise on what was good for labor was not to be challenged. But that Haynsworth was biased against labor because of such decisions simply did not follow. His authorization card opinion may have been the handiwork of a biased judge, but it did not show in that carefully documented judgment. In fact, there was no consistent ideological thread to the Haynsworth opinions in the labor field.

Organized labor quite properly could be suspicious of Haynsworth's vote in the Darlington Mills decision, which backed a company that shut its doors rather than honor a union election. And it could fault him for joining a majority opinion that justified the firing of employees who walked off the job on one of the coldest days of the year when the factory heaters failed to function. But what would be labor's explanation for Haynsworth's "antimanagement" rulings? He rejected, for example, a company's contention that two factory foremen attended a union meeting "solely out of their own curiosity." Their attendance, said Haynsworth, "was clearly calculated to have a coercive effect." And when the same company fired two employees seen at the meeting, saying there was suddenly no need for their skills. Haynsworth ordered their reinstatement. "In the context of an expanding labor force and a search for the very skills those two employees had, the Board [NLRB] not unreasonably concluded they were discharged because of their union activities."

Just as labor leaders appeared more demanding of Judge Haynsworth than he of them, so civil rights advocates were uncomfortable with the judge's nondoctrinaire positions in their field. He not only earned the criticism of the leaders but also of the foot soldiers of the movement, the civil rights attorneys, as well. "Haynsworth is not committed to achieving integration," explained one attorney. "It's as simple as that—you have to push and push for integration or you won't get anywhere and Haynsworth doesn't care."

Haynsworth certainly did not "push" for integration, moving forward only when the clearest mandate was presented by the Supreme Court. And at times, he appeared to pull back by supporting a freedom-of-choice school plan and voting against forced desegregation of a North Carolina hospital. But when the fine print of even those opinions was scrutinized, it was clear that the opinions were the work of a judge, not an ideologue, by a southern gentleman, to be sure, but not a racist.

If a freedom-of-choice plan was designed to keep the races separated, Haynsworth contended, it "is an illusion and an oppression which is constitutionally impermissible." Haynsworth added that a school board had an affirmative duty to eliminate such a discriminatory system. On the other hand, the judge maintained, if the system provided what it was supposed to, namely a choice that was truly free of racial overtones or outside coercion, the Constitution did not bar it. In the North Carolina hospital case, Haynsworth issued no broad statements of policy, no attacks on the claims of civil rights attorneys. His sole contention was that the government funds accepted by the private hospital did not transform its segregation policies into state action forbidden by the Fourteenth Amendment's equal protection clause. It was a narrow interpretation by the Warren Court standards of the day. But a narrow interpretation was not synonymous with a narrow-minded one.

Would a racist judge rule that black militant H. Rap Brown be released from jail and that Brown, without posting bail, would be responsible for appearing in court? Haynsworth did, and over vigorous dissent from a colleague. Would a man closed to the prejudices working against blacks rule that lawyers for black defendants must be given the opportunity to discover if the organizations of potential jurors suggested racial prejudices? Haynsworth did. In fact, if decisions that expanded the rights of criminal defendants were viewed as primarily protecting the poor (who compose a disproportionately large number of criminal suspects), then Clement Haynsworth, Jr., looked for all the world like—a liberal.

Haynsworth struck down a conviction of one indigent defendant who had not been given counsel three months after arrest and of another after he was brought to trial three and a half hours after indictment, leaving his lawyer insufficient time to investigate the case. In another decision, he stood by the letter and spirit of *Miranda,* holding that a police officer could not avoid giving the warnings simply by questioning a suspect before his formal arrest.

Significantly, Haynsworth was most daring in interpretations of the law created and nurtured by judges, not legislatures. In ruling that a state prisoner had properly petitioned a federal court to hear his constitutional claim, Haynsworth carefully pointed out that the writ of habeas corpus, used by the prisoner, was a device fashioned by the common law courts of England to protect and extend their own jurisdiction. Since the law was the exclusive product of the judiciary, Haynsworth reasoned, it was the judiciary's prerogative to adapt it to new situations. "Judges should not hesitate to take a further step to adapt it to meet yet another need which is present, urgent and recognized, even by the state," wrote Haynsworth. The U.S. Supreme Court later agreed, upholding Haynsworth's innovative ruling.

On the ethics issue, the worst to be said for Clement Haynsworth, Jr. (and the *New York Times* said it) was that "none of his alleged misdeeds has turned out to be more than an imperceptive man's neglect in which there was neither profit nor, it would seem, expectation of profit." The Vend-a-Matic conflict of interest charge had been investigated by Judge Simon Sobeloff of Haynsworth's Fourth Circuit and Attorney General Robert Kennedy long before Haynsworth's nomination to the Supreme Court. Neither found that Haynsworth had acted improperly. After the conflict charge emerged again in 1969, Nixon's Assistant Attorney General, William H. Rehnquist, went further in defending the judge. Haynsworth's financial interest in the Darlington case was so remote, said Rehnquist, that the improper course would have been for Haynsworth to refuse to break the judicial deadlock by disqualifying himself. The opinion by a more objective observer, attorney John P. Frank, came to the same conclusion. Frank, a former clerk to Justice Hugo Black and the nation's leading authority on disqualification of judges, told the Senate Judiciary Committee that "under the law as it has clearly existed to this minute and as it existed on a given day in the fall of 1963, I do think it is perfectly clear under the authorities that there was literally no choice whatsoever for Judge Haynsworth except to participate in that case and do his job as well as he could."

Haynsworth's role in the Brunswick case similarly created the appearance of impropriety rather than the reality. First of all, Haynsworth had not taken the initiative in buying the thousand shares of Brunswick; he acted on the advice of his broker, who had given similar advice to forty other customers. Secondly, it was unrealistic to conclude that the case in which Judge Haynsworth participated—involving a dispute over the financial proceeds from ten bowling lanes and pinsetting machines—could affect the stock of a huge conglomerate that produced everything from missile components to medical instruments and did a $400 million business annually. For the record, Brunswick shares closed at $16 on the day the court ruling was made public and the next day as well.

When it looked as if the Haynsworth nomination might be doomed, an editor of a large eastern newspaper asked Attorney General Mitchell about the prospects of the nominee. "You bastards in the press," Mitchell growled, and then proceeded to give examples of what he thought was the biased reporting on Haynsworth that jeopardized his confirmation. Mitchell was right; the press in general misrepresented Haynsworth's credentials, trusting too quickly the snap judgments of civil rights and labor leaders and overreacting to ethics charges that came so soon after the Fortas affair. The media's response reflected the general attitude of a polarized nation in 1969. Both were unprepared to give a calm, rational analysis that could have moved beyond the ready stereotypes—the southerner, the conservative, the corporate man—to get at the quality of Clement Haynsworth, Jr.'s work. And who, ultimately, was to blame for the misfortune? No one more than Richard Nixon.

Even as the Haynsworth fight moved toward the climactic roll call, the president would not focus on the specific merits of his nominee. At a news conference called to reiterate his support for Haynsworth, President Nixon was defensive and highly political. He accused Haynsworth's critics of "vicious character assassination" and then defended the judge against the ethics charges, one by one. But when he had finished with the conflicts of interests explanations, the president did not discuss Judge Haynsworth's entirely competent and nondoctrinaire judicial record. Instead, Nixon matched the critics' oversimplified judicial labels with his own familiar political terms. "If Judge Haynsworth's philosophy leans to the conservative side, in my view that recommends him to me," said Nixon. "I think the Court needs balance and I think the Court needs a man who is conservative."

The word went out to Republican senators: a vote for Haynsworth was a vote for your president. The entire Republican House of Representatives delegation from Illinois swooped down on Senator Charles H. Percy to give him the message. Ohio Senator William Saxbe was invited for a chat at the White House and even found Attorney General Mitchell sidling up to him ("I'd like to have your support on this nomination," said Mitchell. "It would give us a chance to work together.") Idaho's Senator Len Jordan summed it up best: "Support of the president is urged as if it were a personal matter rather than an issue of grave constitutional importance."

On November 21, 1969, in a hushed ten-minute roll call, thirty-eight Democrats and seventeen Republicans combined to vote down Clement Haynsworth, Jr., the first Court nominee to suffer that fate since Judge John Parker in 1930. After the vote, many a senator on the winning side took the lofty stance of a statesman. Asked why they voted against Haynsworth, most suggested that their consciences would not allow them to overlook the ethical questions raised by the judge's conduct. In some cases, the explanations could not be questioned. For Senator John J. Williams of Delaware, known as the conscience of the Senate because of his puritanical values, a judge should live on his salary and devote his life to the law, standards that Clement Haynsworth, Jr., clearly did not live up to. Other Republican senators with tough reelection fights, like Albert Gore of Tennessee, had much to lose by a vote against a powerful Republican administration. But Gore risked it. Said Gore: "If a local judge in almost any town in America should do this [sit on cases in which he conceivably could have a financial stake], the local lawyers and citizens would rise up in indignation. And they should, and I want to keep it that way. The precedent of the United States Senate's condoning such practice would be watched by the entire judiciary, and the effect would be to weaken public confidence in our courts. And this would be bad. And so I voted no."

But on the whole, the senators' consciences tended to follow their political instincts. Either that, or conscience counts for more in states with substantial numbers of labor, black and white liberal voters. Both senators from twenty-one states with significant representation of those groups (Northeast, Middle West and West) voted against confirmation. Both senators from sixteen states (the South and a smattering of conservative states from the Great Plains to Alaska) voted for confirmation.

After the vote, President Nixon stayed with his political strategy. Expressing bitter regret over the Haynsworth defeat, the president said that "the Supreme Court needs men of his [Haynsworth's] legal philosophy to restore the proper balance to that great institution." No one who had read Judge Haynsworth's opinions carefully could be too sure what his "legal philosophy" was, but no one, at the same time, was puzzled about the president's meaning. "When the Congress returns for its second session in January, I will nominate another associate justice," said Nixon. "The criteria I shall apply for this selection, as was the case with my nomination of Judge Haynsworth, will be consistent with my commitments to the American people before my election as president a year ago." Three months later, President Nixon nominated Judge G. Harrold Carswell of Tallahassee, Florida.

If President Nixon's nomination of Judge Carswell failed, whispered one Washington columnist, another son of the old South was waiting in the wings. He was Judge Caleb Robert E. Lee of the Fifth Circuit Juvenile and Bankruptcy Court of Juniper County, Alabama. Judge Lee had no investments in stocks and bonds. It was reliably reported, in fact, that Lee's holdings were limited exclusively to slaves, which the judge contended should not give rise to any conflict of interest questions. "Ah don't know how owning a few darkies could affect the way ah decide the constitutional issues," drawled Judge Lee. "Besides, you have to have some balance on the Court, and right now it's heavily weighted in favor of the antislave forces."

The man to leak word of the impending Lee candidacy was pundit Art Buchwald. Typically, the savage Buchwald satire contained a deadly serious message: despite all the talk of presidential prerogatives in appointing Supreme Court nominees, the public was profoundly disturbed that their chief executive would use his Court appointments for nothing more grandiose than a political strategy. But once the official layers of Judge Carswell's résumé were peeled away, little of substance remained to recommend his candidacy. He had not won notable distinction as a law student, a private attorney, a public prosecutor or a federal judge. He was, however, a southerner with a well-documented conservative voting record as a judge.

Administration officials privately defended Carswell primarily on political grounds. Why shouldn't the attitudes of white southerners be reflected on the Court, asked one high-ranking Administration official? After all, they're part of the nation. Besides, he pointed out, Nixon was doing no more than Kennedy or Johnson did with the nominations of Arthur Goldberg (selected to represent labor and the Jews) and Thurgood Marshall (for the blacks). So why couldn't Mr. Nixon make his political points as well?

At first, Nixon's critics grudgingly conceded that the administration made an acceptable, if not inspiring case. The Court might well benefit from the views of a man whose background and ideological learnings did not fit into the majoritarian mode of the day. G. Harrold Carswell did represent the traditional philosophy of a region with one quarter of the nation's population. If Carswell's judicial views created tensions on the Court, well, that might not be so bad either, for it would provide the kinds of pressures on the justices in judicial conference that gripped the nation outside.

"Here's a southern judge," said one administration official, "that they'll know is a real southern judge." Carswell could not claim the southern pedigree of Clement Haynsworth, but no one could doubt his southern heritage. His father was George Henry Carswell, a descendant of a pioneer Irwinton, Georgia family, whose statue stood in the Irwinton town square. After his mother died of tuberculosis when Harrold was five, his father, who served in the state legislature for thirty years, cared for and captivated the young boy and his two sisters. Naturally enough, Harrold determined to follow in his father's lawyer-politician footsteps. The first stop on the journey was the Georgia Law School, a must for the state's future politicians. World War II interrupted Carswell's legal studies; when he returned from duty in the Pacific, he entered the Mercer Law School, only a thirty-minute drive from his Irwinton home. It was generally assumed that young Carswell would live in Irwinton to establish his political career and that if he did not succeed in politics, he would move away. It was no surprise, then, that after Carswell lost his first political race, for the Georgia legislature in 1948, he moved across the state line to Tallahassee, Florida.

Once in Tallahassee, Carswell made all of the right decisions. First, he joined a prominent law firm whose membership included the future Florida governor, LeRoy Collins. Secondly, he married well in a city where such decisions counted heavily in a man's financial and social future. Carswell's bride was Virginia Simmons, daughter of one of the city's leading industrialists and a member of Tallahassee's "plantation crowd." Virginia served as president of the city's Junior League and Harrold took his turn as head of Tallahassee's segregated social club, the Cotillion. In another key decision, Carswell supported Eisenhower for president in 1952. That led to a series of appointments by Republican Presidents Eisenhower and Nixon, first as U.S. attorney, then U.S. district judge for the Northern District of Florida, U.S. court of appeals judge for the Fifth Circuit, and finally the U.S. Supreme Court.

Opposition to the Carswell appointment surfaced quickly. New York University Law Professor Leroy Clark, a black who had been an NAACP Legal Defense Fund attorney in Carswell's district for eight years, called the appointment a "disaster." "Judge Carswell," said Clark, "was probably the most hostile judge I've ever appeared before. He was insulting to black lawyers. He would rarely let me finish a sentence. He was abrupt and authoritarian. He treated our arguments as if they were preposterous." Civil rights leaders quoted the findings of a Yale doctoral candidate, Mrs. Mary Curzan, who ranked Carswell eighth out of thirty-one federal district judges in the South in rulings against blacks. Mrs. Curzan also found that Judge Carswell was reversed by a higher court in 60 per cent of his civil rights decisions.

Despite the civil rights opposition, Carswell's confirmation appeared all but certain. For one thing, the Senate, particularly members of Mr. Nixon's own party, did not seem anxious to buck a president a second time. Seventeen Republican senators had crossed Nixon on the Haynsworth nomination, most of them on the "ethics" issue. Well, Carswell would not give them that out; he owned no stocks or bonds. He was a southerner, but hadn't all the statesmen in the Senate said that geography had nothing to do with their "no" votes against Haynsworth?

Within twenty-four hours, the relative calm surrounding the Carswell nomination was shattered. When Carswell's appointment was announced, a part-time newsman for a Jacksonville, Fla., television station named Ed Roeder began to dig into the local library morgue for fragments of the Carswell past. What he found sent shock waves across the nation. As a candidate for the state legislature in 1948, Carswell had told the American Legion in Gordon, Georgia, that "Segregation of the races is proper and the only practical and correct way of life in our states. I have always so believed and I shall always so act."

Hugo Black was able to ride out a similar storm in 1937 after it was revealed that as a young man he had joined the Ku Klux Klan. But Black had two advantages over Carswell. First, his Senate colleagues had already confirmed Black's nomination to the Court at the time his Klan membership was disclosed. Secondly, Black had compiled an impressive civil rights voting record in the U.S. Senate. As a consequence, when Black denounced his youthful Klan association on a national radio broadcast, the American public had powerful reasons to accept his word.

Carswell, like Black, used the national media to renounce his earlier action. On CBS-TV, Carswell said that "specifically and categoricially I renounce and reject the words themselves [in the 1948 speech] and the thought they represent; they are abhorrent to me." But the renunciation of his segregationist speech was not enough. A restive nation demanded that Carswell's disclaimer, like Black's, be backed by strong evidence that his later actions spoke as loud as his words. Unfortunately for Carswell, the record was not reassuring.

In 1953 Carswell drafted a charter for the Florida State University boosters club that opened membership to "any white person interested in the purposes." In 1956, while he was U.S. attorney, Carswell participated in a scheme to lease a Tallahassee municipal golf course, built with $35,000 of federal funds, to a private segregated club for one dollar a year. Carswell signed the incorporation certificate as a director of the private club. Although local newspapers as well as the general public knew the plan's primary purpose was to avoid desegregation of the public course, Carswell told the Senate Judiciary Committee that he was unaware of any such intention. In 1966, Judge Carswell and his wife sold land using a deed that specified "ownership, occupancy and use shall be restricted to members of the Caucasian race," a racially restrictive covenant that was outlawed by the Supreme Court in 1948.

Carswell supporters pointed to his court orders that desegregated Tallahassee's airport counters, restrooms, and waiting facilities and one of the city's barber shops. Critics, like NYU's Clark, retorted that Carswell acted only when the Supreme Court gave him no choice. When he could delay desegregation, said Clark, Judge Carswell invariably did. More damning still were some of Judge Carswell's decisions that rejected civil rights claims. Sometimes, as in a case challenging segregated public school faculties, Carswell's reasoning was as offensive to civil rights groups as the result itself. It happened in a suit brought by black students in Escambia County, Florida, asking for desegregation of public school teaching staffs. Judge Carswell did not even give them a hearing on the constitutional issue. Citing the *Brown* decision as his authority, Carswell emphasized the fact that the Supreme Court had spoken only of the desegregation of public school children, not teachers. The Carswell opinion was restrictive and gloatingly so. Carswell suggested that the students had no more business in his court challenging segregated faculties than they did complaining about teachers who were too strict or too lenient. The Fifth Circuit Court of Appeals did not think faculty discrimination based on race was quite so frivolous. It reversed the Carswell decision.

Another Carswell civil rights decision was overturned by the Fifth Circuit with a thoroughness that bordered on reprimand. The case involved four black youths who had participated in a series of sit-in demonstrations at a segregated restaurant in St. Augustine. They were arrested and convicted of criminal trespass and, after the juvenile court judge decided they were delinquent, sent to a state reformatory. The reform school was segregated and, while there, the four brought suit to challenge the apartheid policy. Before their suit reached Judge Carswell's court, the juveniles had been released on probation on the condition that they would not join any more sit-in demonstrations.

When the case was put on Judge Carswell's docket, the state moved to dismiss on the grounds that, since the boys were no longer in the reformatory, they had no legal interest in the suit. Judge Carswell agreed, ruling that the case was moot and dismissing the blacks' complaint. Judge John Minor Wisdom of the Fifth Circuit corrected Carswell's reading of the law as well as the facts of the case. To begin with, said Wisdom, Judge Carswell confused the legal issues involved. It was not a case of mootness, as Carswell had contended. The issue of mootness would be raised, said Wisdom, only if the state had desegregated the reformatory, thus giving the youths no cause of legal complaint. But segregation still existed, so the primary question of law for Carswell should have been whether the juveniles bringing the suit could be affected by that policy in the future. At that point, Judge Wisdom strongly hinted that Carswell had been disingenuous in his findings of fact. According to the evidence presented, Wisdom maintained, it should have been clear that the juveniles were still under state supervision as probationers. Since the boys might well return to the reformatory if they violated their probationary conditions, said Wisdom, they had solid reason to be in court challenging the state's segregated policy.

After reviewing Judge Carswell's decisions, Professor Louis H. Pollak, then dean of the Yale Law School, told the Senate Judiciary Committee that he "presents the most slender credentials [for the Court] of any man put forward in this century." Pollak's glum assessment, which was not confined to Judge Carswell's civil rights decisions, was echoed by legal scholars across the country. A tax expert from the University of San Diego said that Carswell's tax opinions showed an "inability to relate the facts of the case to the governing law in an adequate and persuasive manner." A law professor from the National Law Institute in the District of Columbia criticized a series of Carswell contract decisions, one of which "reveals the judge as what can best be called an absurd constructionist." The decision, said Professor Monroe H. Freedman, "violated well-established principles of contracts law as well as common sense." In one property law opinion, wrote Professor Charles Nesson of Harvard, Carswell "fails to state facts in a comprehensible fashion, fails to indicate the basis for federal jurisdiction and dismisses what appears to be the defendant's major contention in conclusionary fashion with no indication of the facts supporting the conclusion."

"Even if he [Carswell] were mediocre," said Senator Roman Hruska, "there are a lot of mediocre judges and people and lawyers and they are entitled to a little representation, aren't they?" The press had a fine time lampooning the Hruska statement. Members of the judiciary, however, were not amused. Said one high-ranking federal judge: "Although it is not necessarily good, the president has always chosen justices who he thought reflected his view of American affairs. That is his prerogative. What he should not do is appoint mediocrities. It is, among other considerations, short-sighted to do it because they simply will be swallowed up by intellectually superior colleagues."

President Nixon went down the line with Judge Carswell, declaring that his nominee's record was "impeccable and without a taint of racism." As with the Haynsworth nomination, Nixon employed a "your President right or wrong" approach. And as with Haynsworth, it backfired. Judge Carswell was turned down by the Senate, 51 to 45.

The first public reaction from the White House was mild; the president was "disappointed" in the vote. Five hours later, Nixon invited White House aide H.R. Haldeman and Attorney General Mitchell to board the presidential yacht *Sequoia* for a two-hour cruise down the Potomac for some scenery and straight talk about the Carswell defeat. Before the president let the nation in on the results of the discussion, another member of the administration family provided a preview of things to come. In the first of her famous nocturnal telephone calls, Mrs. John Mitchell, the wife of the attorney general, told an editor of the *Arkansas Gazette,* "It [the Carswell defeat] makes me so damn mad I can't stand it. "I want you to crucify Fulbright [Senator J. William Fulbright, who voted against the Carswell confirmation] and that's it."

The president's response the next day was hardly more temperate. "They [Judges Haynsworth and Carswell] have been falsely charged with being racist, but when all the hypocrisy is stripped away, the real issue was their philosophy and strict construction of the Constitution . . . and the fact that they had the misfortune of being born in the South. . . . As long as the Senate is constituted the way it is today, I will not nominate another southerner and let him be subjected to the kind of malicious character assassination accorded both Judges Haynsworth and Carswell."

Obviously, the president and Attorney General Mitchell, long a believer in the southern strategy, thought they could have their political cake and eat it, too. They intended to receive full benefit from their two southern nominees. Both were presented as southerners, tried and true. There was little attempt to smooth the ruffled feelings of those suspicious of the nominations by calling attention to the professional competence of the men. In Haynsworth's case, that approach may well have saved his confirmation; it certainly was merited by his judicial record. Carswell was another story; it is doubtful that any amount of administration explanation could have hidden the raw insensitivity of the man or the glaring weaknesses in his professional qualifications.*

The Senate rejections didn't really upset the president's political plans. He had kept his promise to the South and the failure of that southern strategy, Nixon made perfectly clear, rested with the Senate. In the middle of the political struggle between the president and the Senate was the institution that Mr. Nixon kept saying he revered so much, the Supreme Court. But between those announcements of reverence for the Court, Mr. Nixon and Mr. Mitchell gave every indication that it would be no more than a tool to realize their political ambitions.

*In his abortive campaign for the Senate after his Court defeat, Carswell seemed intent on proving that his detractors were right. He spoke of "dark evil winds" of liberalism that swept away his chances to sit on the Court and specifically blamed the "ultraliberal coalition" of the northern press and "its knee-jerking followers" for his rejection. Counseling against the liberal judicial trend, Carswell said: "I do not believe that anytime anyone comes in with a case that's got a racial angle on it, that the courts of this country should faint over and fall down and be intimidated the way they're given to now."

CHAPTER SIX

Freshman Year of the Burger Court

In his talks with southern delegates to the Republican National Convention in 1968, candidate Richard Nixon said that he believed the federal courts had taken over the legitimate responsibilities of local school boards in desegregating public schools. If elected president, Nixon suggested, there would be a greater effort on the part of the new Republican administration to distribute the responsibilities for desegregation more evenly between federal courts and local school boards, between Washington bureaucrats and the southern communities who were more aware of the problems that desegregation posed.

Less than six months after Nixon took office in 1969, his administration was already busy at work making good on Nixon's preconvention promise to the South. At the Department of Health, Education and Welfare, Nixon men had found a loophole for southern school districts that could not make the fall desegregation deadline; in an official HEW statement, officials said "there may be sound reasons for some limited delay." That same year Clifford L. Alexander, Jr., resigned as chairman of the Equal Employment Opportunity Commission because of the "crippling lack of Administration support" and the U.S. Civil Rights Commission suggested that the administration's unwillingness to enforce provisions on job bias in the 1964 Civil Rights Act amounted to subsidizing racial discrimination.

The slowdown was most conspicuous, however, in the U.S. Department of Justice. Next to the aggressive NAACP Legal Defense Fund attorneys, Justice's civil rights division lawyers enjoyed the reputation in the sixties as the most tenacious and effective courtroom warriors for desegregation in the nation. In those days, Justice attorneys like John Doar were known for their courage as well as their legal talent. Though high Justice Department officials willingly compromised with the South on many occasions, Attorney General Robert Kennedy still managed to project an idealistic public image of his men: that of a band of bright and brash government lawyers determined to enforce the Supreme Court's desegregation mandates. The image persisted through the reign of Attorneys General Nicholas Katzenbach, best remembered for his staring match with Governor George Wallace at the schoolhouse door, and Ramsey Clark, whom President Nixon and J. Edgar Hoover immortalized as a liberal softie. Under Kennedy, Katzenbach and Clark, the Justice Department became the administration's premier symbol for action, for the nitty-gritty confrontation between government and one of the worst problems that beset American society.

By July of 1969, the Justice Department under Attorney General John Mitchell was projecting an entirely different image. The law and order that Nixon had promised the American people was primarily concentrated, so far as the Justice Department was concerned, on organized and street crime and radical political movements that Mr. Mitchell felt threatened the national security. Down the list of well-advertised prosecutorial priorities was the government's obligation to enforce the desegregation that had been ordered by the Supreme Court and the Civil Rights Acts of 1964 and 1965.

It was no surprise, then, that at the end of July 1969 Justice Department attorneys asked the U.S. Court of Appeals for the Fifth Circuit for a three-month delay in the previous court order to desegregate thirty Mississippi school districts. The government's request, if granted, would effectively have postponed desegregation plans for a whole year. But without the delay, Justice Department attorneys contended, the Mississippi schools would be thrown into virtual chaos. It was emphasized that the Justice Department was not against desegregation; it was simply putting the educational interests of the children, black and white, ahead of bureaucratic demands that schools meet an arbitrary desegregation deadline. The appeals court favored the government's argument and the NAACP Legal Defense Fund, now opposing the Justice Department for the first time ever in a school desegregation case, appealed.

Given the conspicuous slippage of the Justice Department's resolve in the desegregation area, it was fitting, if a little embarrassing, that when the argument reached the U.S. Supreme Court on the Mississippi desegregation plan, Justice's civil rights chief, Jerris Leonard, was paired with Mississippi's John Satterfield, a longtime arch-segregationist. For his part, Leonard tried to keep to the straight and narrow of pragmatic argument. He told the Court that if "instant integration" was ordered, there would not be enough "bodies" to enforce the order.

In the old Warren Court days, Leonard's chances for a favorable ruling from the Court would have been considered remote, if not nonexistent. But Chief Justice Warren had retired and his successor, Warren Burger, was known for his more conservative judicial outlook—and his pragmatic weighing of competing constitutional values. Would the Nixon-appointed chief justice sympathize with the administration's arguments and, if so, would he be able to persuade his colleagues to do the same? The answer to both questions, a resounding "no," was delivered in a two-page unanimous decision by the new Burger Court. The unsigned Court order stated that the "continued operation of segregated schools under a standard of allowing 'all deliberate speed' for desegregation is no longer constitutionally permissible. Under explicit holdings of this Court the obligation of every school district is to terminate dual school systems at once and to operate new and hereafter only unitary schools."

The Court's action was a major setback for the Nixon administration's "go slow" policy on desegregation. It was also a personal embarrassment for the president, who had made much of his desire to appoint men to the Supreme Court who would be "strict constructionists," meaning conservatives. In his first major decision, Chief Justice Burger appeared to be performing well below conservative expectations. At a news conference after the decision had been announced, the president expressed disappointment in the Court's action. Still, the decision, even with the participation of Nixon appointee Burger, had not sullied the President's image in the South. "The Nixon administration stood with the South in this case," said Senator Strom Thurmond, "but the Court has chosen to override both the State of Mississippi and the Department of Justice."

The president's disappointment in the Court's performance may not have ended after the Mississippi desegregation order. The first post-Warren Court gave no indication that it was ready to be molded in the new president's image or that of his first Court appointee, Chief Justice Burger. The Court majority not only served notice that there would be no backsliding on Warren Court initiatives but almost seemed bent on undercutting the Nixon administration's carefully laid political plans.

The Justice Department's sensitivity to the problems of southern whites not only affected its attitude toward school desegregation but caused it to take a more sympathetic look at discrimination in other areas as well. It opposed, for example, the extension of the Voting Rights Act of 1965, offering in its place a watered-down version that would have eliminated the special sanctions that the 1965 statute imposed on recalcitrant southern officials. But at the same time that the Nixon administration was wobbling, the Supreme Court was issuing decision after unequivocal decision backing the Warren Court's desegregation mandates. The Court broadened the legal protection against discrimination in public restaurants and frowned upon a suburban home-*cum*-recreation-association scheme that rejected black members. And a unanimous Court held that a prima facie case for jury discrimination had been made in one Georgia county where 178 persons were turned down for grand jury duty as "unintelligent" or "not upright"; 96 per cent were black.

While the Justice Department was keeping a suspicious eye on anti-Vietnam War protesters, the Court was giving those same protesters firm constitutional protection. It would not allow a Minneapolis draft board to accelerate the induction of a registrant who had deposited his draft registration certificate on the steps of the federal building in Minneapolis in protest against the war in Vietnam. The Court also reversed the convictions of fifteen antiwar protesters in Baltimore who had been arrested for disturbing the peace after picketing an army recruiting office, passing out antiwar leaflets and generally giving the police a hard time. Since it was never clear whether the protesters were convicted for disturbing the peace or the sensibilities of pro-Vietnam War onlookers, the Court threw the case out. In another decision, the justices were not persuaded that a performer wearing an army uniform during an antiwar skit in Houston should have been thrown in jail for showing disrespect for the armed forces. The majority was not so much concerned with the survival of "guerilla theatre" as the First Amendment. A federal law, wrote Justice Brennan, "which leaves Americans free to praise the war in Vietnam but can send persons like Schacht [the defendant] to prison for opposing it, cannot survive in a country which has the First Amendment."

As John Mitchell's Justice Department was clearing the way for its much publicized war on crime, the Court was still insisting on fundamental safeguards for criminal suspects. The Court held that a criminal suspect was entitled to a lawyer not just at his trial but at his preliminary hearing as well. It found that a robbery suspect who was arrested in 1960 but not put on trial until seven years later had been deprived of a speedy trial guaranteed by the Sixth Amendment. The Court also demanded a stricter standard of proof in the trials of juveniles.

But despite the evidence that the Court was not retreating from frontline Warren Court positions, it was also clear that the new Burger Court did not speak with the confidence and assertiveness of the Warren Court. The decisions on desegregation, free speech and criminal law telling the Nixon administration that backtracking was not for the judiciary also suggested that the days of Warren Court daring were over. These were not landmark decisions that charted new constitutional directions or introduced sweeping new judicial initiatives. Moreover, a study by the American Jewish Congress indicated that the Burger Court was pulling back in the area where the Warren Court had been most aggressive: civil liberties. According to the AJC study, the Burger Court majority favored the asserted liberty in only 55 per cent of its decisions the first term compared with an 81 per cent record by the Court in the last term of Chief Justice Warren. Every justice, the study also showed, had a more conservative voting record in the civil liberties area in the 1969–70 term than in the last under Chief Justice Warren. Chief Justice Burger, the only new Court member, was given the lowest civil liberties rating of all. A year before, the Court majority had favored the government in criminal prose-

cutions in only eight of twenty-six cases; in the Burger Court's
first term, the majority sided with the government prosecutor
eighteen of twenty-nine times.

The new caution of the justices was seen in individual cases
as well as in statistics. It was on exhibit, for example, when the
Court refused to throw out a ceiling on state welfare payments
in Maryland that was challenged by poor petitioners with large
families who claimed that the restrictions deprived them of
equal protection of the law. Justice Stewart, speaking for the
Court, returned to the "rational purpose" test of constitutionality that had served the Frankfurtarians so well in their cautious
rulings on political liberties in the fifties. Though a state law
might result in some inequities, said Stewart, it need not be
struck down as unconstitutional so long as the state classification had some reasonable basis. That the welfare cutoff hurt
large families who might receive the same payments as smaller
families was undisputed. But there were other, positive considerations: the state policy could encourage gainful employment,
provide incentives for family planning, discourage discrimination between welfare families and the families of the working
poor and insure the most prudent allocation of limited state
funds. Stewart did not endorse any one of the positive arguments but only said that the state had met the test for the
rationality of its restrictions.

A more cautious Court majority was also happy to brush
aside the controversial suit, like the one brought by a couple
from Colorado who were not allowed to vote in the 1968 presidential election because they had not lived in the state for six
months. Justice Brennan, a stalwart of the activist wing of the
Warren Court, wanted to take the case, maintaining that it
involved "the fundamental right to vote—the right preservative
of other basic civil and political rights." But the majority, noting that the Colorado legislature had reduced the residency
requirement to two months (after the Court indicated that it

might review the case), suggested that the couple's complaint
was no longer important enough to merit Court review. When
it did not reject the controversial case, the Court often simply
postponed it. So, the justices put off decisions in cases involving
the constitutionality of busing to achieve school desegregation,
capital punishment and the right of a young man to refuse
military service because he objected to the Vietnam War.

There was no dearth of explanations for the Court's shift
into low gear. The most obvious, of course, was that for the
first time since Justice Robert Jackson had gone to Nuremberg to prosecute war criminals a quarter century ago, the
Court was forced to sit for almost an entire term with only
eight members. Quite simply, a crippled and often divided
Court was not anxious to take on more constitutional trouble than it had to. Even when the eight Justices wanted to
decide close issues, they were sometimes frustrated by a 4–4
split in opinion. In addition to those reasons for judicial
caution, it was entirely conceivable that the justices had
been reading the election returns, as Mr. Dooley once suggested. Mr. Nixon had won the presidential election, all the
while talking of the overreaching Supreme Court. It could
not have been pleasant for the justices to contemplate further attacks on their reputation or independence.

And finally, there was the indisputable fact that the nation
really was governed by men, not abstract laws. As a result,
when the personnel of the Court changed, so did the Court's
performance. The absence of Chief Justice Warren and Associate Justice Fortas did make a critical difference, eliminating two
votes for that faction of the Court with a ready appetite for the
controversial case—and decision. Now the activists—Justices
Brennan, Douglas and Marshall (Black had grown more conservative in his last years)—were looking for support. The first
prospect for their proselytizing, Chief Justice Burger, was not
promising.

The associate justices did not have to wait until Chief Justice Warren Burger cast the last vote in judicial conference to know they had a new leading man. The change, literally, was all about them. The new chief justice redecorated the wood-paneled conference room by hanging paintings borrowed from the National Portrait Gallery—as well as a few of his own. He also moved his desk, previously in the smaller personal office of the chief justice, into the conference room. As the fourth-ranking member of the U.S. government, Burger felt that he should greet visiting dignitaries in the impressive conference room rather than in the cramped chief justice's office (the smallest of any member of the Court). Burger's handiwork followed the justices into their private dining room, where the chief justice removed the depressing potted ferns from each corner, hung more paintings and placed flowers in the window sills. He also lengthened the lunch break, which had traditionally lasted only a half hour, to a full hour. In the courtroom, Burger replaced the justices' old water tumblers with handsome silver goblets and began making plans for a new, half-hexagon-shaped bench for the justices and high intensity lights overhead. And somehow, the enterprising chief squeezed out an extra two hundred dollars from the limited Supreme Court budget to purchase potted geraniums for each of the four interior courtyards of the Court. The changes were reassuring. The new chief justice, like the old, would make those personal small gestures to his colleagues that would lower the tension, encourage a relaxed working atmosphere.

As the presiding officer in the courtroom, Burger was equally low key, assured and assuring. In bearing and manner, Burger was remarkably similar to Warren. With their white manes, ruddy complexions and broad shoulders, both men commanded attention physically. Burger, like Warren, gave attorneys his steady gaze and attention throughout oral argument. Neither chief justice would interrupt to ask a question without showing unfailing courtesy. Throughout Court sessions the two chief justices exuded a quiet dignity, never forced, but always present.

And yet, the deep philosophical differences between Chief Justices Warren and Burger could be readily learned by studying their professional concerns on the bench. Chief Justice Warren's questions almost invariably focused on the the fairness of the law; they were often instinctive probings into the moral position of government authorities. The technical queries Warren happily left to his colleagues. Chief Justice Burger spent almost no time on such moral questions. When he strayed from the technicalities of a case, it was usually to question the impact of the appellant's asserted right on the entire system. Concern for the underdog tended to be lost in Burger's judicial overview. There was none of the outrage, the righteous indignation that so often crept into an exchange between Chief Justice Warren and an attorney.

Chief Justice Burger declared his judicial independence from his predecessor most dramatically in his written opinions. The camaraderie with colleagues, the geraniums and the silver goblets were forgotten. The controlled, ever courteous presiding officer of the courtroom was absent. The new chief justice was continually provoked by what he considered a persistent "activist" trend of the Court in his first term. In his opinions, Burger shared his deep annoyance with the rest of the Court. Burger accused his colleagues of being unreasonable and irrational in their analysis, of making bad sense and worse law in their decisions.

The more isolated Burger became, the more intent he seemed on making his judicial points. The chief justice's unhappiness with his colleagues—and determination to tell them so—was well illustrated in a card game robbery decision. The case involved six men who were playing a friendly game of poker at Lee's Summit, Missouri, into the early morning hours when four intruders announced a stickup. Armed with a sawed-off shotgun and pistols, the robbers went around the table taking money and valuables from each poker player, then fled in the car of one of the victims. Three men were later arrested near the abandoned car and all were charged with robbery of each poker player. The state decided to try each suspect individually. At the first trial, the prosecution presented a weak case against the defendant, never clearly establishing that he was one of the robbers. Two of the poker players could not identify the suspect, a third said only that his voice sounded familiar and a fourth placed him only by size and height. The defense thought the state's case was so thin that it offered no testimony and waived a closing argument. The jury agreed, returning a verdict of "not guilty due to insufficient evidence." The district attorney was not discouraged. Six weeks later he brought the same suspect to trial, but this time tried him for the robbery of a second poker player. The prosecution was able to present stronger evidence at the second trial, the defendant was found guilty and sentenced to thirty-five years in the state penitentiary. The convicted man's attorney appealed the decision, contending that his client had been tried twice for the same crime, which violated his Fifth Amendment right to be protected from double jeopardy.

The Supreme Court, with only Chief Justice Burger dissenting, said the conviction in the second trial could not stand. The only jury issue in both prosecutions, wrote Justice Stewart for the majority, was whether the defendant had been one of the robbers. The first time around the jury said he was not, so why, asked Stewart, should the state be given a second chance to litigate the same issue? "No doubt the prosecutor felt the state had a provable case on the first charge," wrote Stewart quoting from the state's brief, "and when he lost, he did what every good attorney would do—he refined his presentation in light of the turn of events at the first trial." But

Stewart concluded that "this is precisely what the constitutional guarantee forbids."

The majority's conclusion provoked Burger into writing a highly emotional dissent which dwelled upon a familiar law and order theme. "What the Court holds today must be related to its impact on crimes more serious than ordinary housebreaking," wrote Burger. "To understand its full impact we must view the holding in the context of four men who break and enter, rob and then kill six victims . . . or alter the crime to four men breaking into a college dormitory and assaulting six girls. What the Court is holding, in effect, is that the second and third and fourth criminal acts are 'free' unless the accused is tried for the multiple crimes in a single trial. . . . No court that elevates the individual rights and human dignity of the accused to a high place—as we should—ought to be so casual as to treat the victims as a single homogenized lump of human clay."

Shrill denunciations of the Court majority by its new chief justice recurred time and again that first term. When the Court ruled that an indigent defendant was entitled to counsel at a preliminary hearing before his trial, both Burger and Stewart dissented. Stewart, in typically prudent, low-key fashion, wrote that he was troubled with the majority decision because it appeared to stand on a principle alone without regard to the facts of the case. His main point was that no evidence presented at the preliminary hearing without counsel had been used against the defendant at his trial. As a result, said Stewart, the defendant's claim that he had not received a fair trial was theoretical, not real.

Burger's dissent, unlike Stewart's, told as much about the chief justice's mood as his judicial view. It was a sweeping attack on the Court majority—on its reading of history, on its philosophy of constitutional law, on its ability to analyze the simplest judicial problems correctly. "While I do not rely solely on 183 years of contrary constitutional interpretation," wrote the chief justice, "it is indeed an odd business that it has taken this Court nearly two centuries to 'discover' a constitutional mandate to have counsel at a preliminary hearing." Taking another swipe at the Court's interpretation, Burger said: "By placing a premium on 'recent cases' rather than the language of the Constitution, the Court makes it dangerously simple for future Courts, using the technique of interpretation, to operate as a 'continuing Constitutional Convention.' " Such "strict constructionist" views, commented an unimpressed Professor Philip B. Kurland of the University of Chicago Law School, are "usually identifiable by their ready resort to hyperbole in support of their literalness."

Rather than confining himself to the particular facts of each case, the new chief justice seemed intent on broadening his specific conclusions to universal truths. It was almost as if the chief justice were more interested in promoting a judicial philosophy than deciding the cases before him. In the area of criminal law and procedure, the chief justice clearly was backing the "peace forces" against the "criminal forces" or, less politically, the law enforcement authorities more often than the criminal suspects. If the criminal justice system needed renovating—and Burger freely conceded that it did—it should be done by legislatures or the judicial and legislative branches together through the laborious rule-making process. But, most decidedly, not by the courts alone.

"It is not for nothing that one of the symbols of the law is the tortoise," Burger reminded a New York audience honoring Justice Oliver Wendell Holmes. "This is why Holmes argued so vigorously all his life for the right of the political branches to experiment in the search for answers." Burger wanted to give not only the executive and legislative branches of the federal government more breathing room, but the states as well. In criminal law opinions, Burger emphasized "the importance of allowing the states to experiment and innovate." The view carried over to other areas, like censorship, where the chief justice suggested that "we should not inflexibly deny to each of the states the power to adopt and enforce its own standards as to obscenity and pornographic materials."

The Court rarely heeded the chief justice's advice that first term, but Burger remained undaunted. After the Court majority ruled that welfare recipients had a constitutional right to formal hearings with trial-like safeguards before government officials could strike them from the welfare rolls, the chief justice again castigated the Court majority. Burger first noted that the Department of Health, Education and Welfare had introduced new procedural protections for welfare recipients that were similar to those required by the Court. "Against this background," said Burger, "I am baffled as to why we should engage in 'legislating' via constitutional fiat when an apparently reasonable result has been accomplished administratively." By imposing "the heavy hand of constitutional adjudication," Burger contended that needed experimentation would be discouraged. The chief justice continued on an exasperated note: "The Court's action today seems another manifestation of the now familiar constitutionalizing syndrome: once some presumed flaw is observed, the Court eagerly accepts the invitation to find a constitutionally 'rooted' remedy."

Chief Justice Burger's freshman year performance stood in stark contrast to that of his predecessor. For Earl Warren, the first year was a time of learning, of getting acquainted with his colleagues, of settling into a new life-style. He offered his views cautiously and with great consideration and courtesy for his brethren. He rarely risked isolation from the majority view. Aware that the Court had been bitterly divided in the past, Warren determined to show the face of unity to the public, even to the point sometimes of voting with a majority position that he was not totally convinced was right.

Many observers expected Warren Burger to take the same approach to his new position. He assumed leadership of the Court at a time when internal divisions were deep, the Court's integrity was questioned and its recent judicial conclusions had been pounced upon by politicians like Richard Nixon as wrong and threatening to the national majority. It was suggested that the Court would do well to lower its national profile, to consolidate its judicial gains cautiously, and slow the pace. But after the initial "desegregate now" order to Mississippi school districts, in which the Court spoke with one voice, the justices went off in all directions and no one was doing his judicial thing more conspicuously than the chief justice himself. Why?

For one thing, there was less mystique attached to the Court for Burger than for his predecessor. Warren had never worn the black robes of a judge in his life—then suddenly he occupied the center seat on the highest court in the nation. It was an honor to humble even a man of Warren's impressive political accomplishments. The consideration that Warren showed his colleagues in his first term was not only dictated by courtesy and humility—but need as well. Warren's colleagues had been struggling with the slippery terms of "due process" and "equal protection" for years; so who was he to tell them so soon that his judicial vision was clearer? Besides, this man who had come to Washington with a giant reputation as a mediator was not about to arouse his colleagues' ire when discreet silences might pay off a later day.

Warren Burger approached the Court with radically different professional experience and expectation. He had been a federal judge for thirteen years, the first chief justice in history to be appointed directly from a lower federal court. Moreover, his court, the U.S. Court of Appeals for the District of Columbia, more nearly approximated the Supreme Court, in both composition and calendar, than any other in the nation. Members of the D.C. Court of Appeals represented all parts of the United

States, so that Judge Burger from Minnesota often crossed judicial pens with J. Skelly Wright of Louisiana. More important than geographical distribution was the D.C. Court of Appeals' mixture of cases. Because of its proximity to the seat of national government, the appeals court received a disproportionately large number of potentially landmark cases in constitutional law. As a result, when Burger took over as chief justice there was not the sense of awe that engulfed his predecessor. The cases he would hear in the Supreme Court were, in fact, pretty much of the same order as those he had been hearing down the street.

Earl Warren had made his reputation and owed his appointment as chief justice largely to his abilities as an extraordinary conciliator. Burger did not. In fact, if anything, Burger owed his appointment more to his strong-willed refusal to give in to the views of his more liberal judicial colleagues. On the appellate court, Burger was the chief dissenter from the liberal majority, often delivering uncompromising criticisms of his colleagues' positions. His inability to win a majority to his side only made Burger more determined; his dissents were often vitriolic and his public speeches and law review articles no less so. Those outspoken views were the ones that Richard Nixon noticed, respected and, ultimately, acted upon in appointing Burger to the chief justiceship.

Though vigorous dissents had been a part of Burger's professional life for years, there was a special urgency to his criticism in his first year as chief justice. At sixty-one, Burger seemed determined to get things done in a hurry. With his judicial philosophy well settled and generally known to his colleagues, the chief justice appeared unconvinced that patience and quiet persuasion would be effective. He wanted agreement with his views immediately and was willing to risk some rousing rhetoric to get it. In short, Burger seemed prepared to split the Court internally in an effort to heal what he saw as the more damaging division between the Court and the public. And though the chief justice often seemed to speak in desperation that first term, help was already on the way. In the fourth week of June, the last of the 1970 term for the Court, the Senate confirmed the nomination to the Court of Harry A. Blackmun, an old friend and philosophical ally of the chief justice.

Harry Blackmun's father opened a combination grocery and hardware store on St. Paul's east side and moved his family into a house just six blocks from the Charles Burger family. Harry Blackmun and Warren Burger first met at Methodist Sunday school to which both boys were sternly dispatched by their parents. The two boys soon discovered that they had much in common, not the least their modest economic circumstances. They chummed around together through the formative years, in school and on the tennis courts, in bull sessions and on camping trips. Though they were separated as teenagers by different high school districts, the two still remained close friends. They were often together when important decisions were made: Blackmun was best man at Burger's wedding.

Like all close friends, Blackmun and Burger had their disagreements. In 1924 Blackmun supported Calvin Coolidge for the presidency while Burger backed Robert LaFollette. And on matters more personal and immediate, the two sometimes chose different paths. At the time Burger received a tuition scholarship from Princeton and turned it down because of the family financial situation, Blackmun got word that he had won a similar scholarship to Harvard. Blackmun accepted his and, upon arriving in Cambridge, set about to supplement his tuition grant by painting the university handball courts and caulking Harvard's half-dozen shells. His pay was fifty cents an hour. Blackmun's precise and logical mind steered him to his college major (math), extra spending money (math tutoring) and academic honors (summa cum laude). Believing that his high mathematical aptitude could be put to further use, Blackmun chose to study at the Harvard Law School where precise and logical analysis was also appreciated.

Between clerking for Judge John B. Sanborn of the U.S. Court of Appeals for the Eighth Circuit and succeeding him later on the bench, Blackmun went about his professional career with methodical determination. In 1934 he began a sixteen-year career with the Minneapolis law firm of Dorsey, Colman, Barker, Scott and Barber, one of the largest and most prestigious in the state. He first specialized in tax law, then helped senior partners with general litigation and finally headed the firm's trust and probate department. The Dorsey firm had always done substantial law work for the Mayo Clinic, the giant medical treatment and research center, and had traditionally sent one of its members to be the clinic's general counsel. In 1950 Blackmun was chosen for the assignment and remained in that position until his appointment to the U.S. Court of Appeals for the Eighth Circuit in 1959. As an attorney, Blackmun was that rarest of species: a gentle advocate. Always considerate and quiet in manner, Blackmun was enormously successful in handling trust and probate matters, where tact and attention to detail were essential. He was thoroughly disciplined, indefatigably conscientious and well schooled in the intricacies of the law. He could not have been anything but a successful lawyer.

Blackmun carried his meticulous work habits and knowledge with him to the court of appeals and, again, they served him well. First, the enormous caseload perfectly suited the unusual Blackmun appetite for work. Every weekday morning at 7:15 Blackmun would leave his modern redwood and glass home overlooking Rochester, Minnesota, jump into his tiny VW and head for his office in the Rochester Towers, returning home invariably at 6:15 P.M. On weekends, he would jog the routine only slightly, Saturdays working from 8 A.M. to 3 P.M. and

Sundays attending services at the First Methodist Church of Rochester between short doses of work at his downtown office. Unlike many judges who rely on their clerks to do the brunt of their legal research, Blackmun did most of it himself. He drafted and redrafted his written opinions many times before making them public. The results of Blackmun's prodigious labor were consistently well documented, carefully written and ploddingly thoughtful judicial opinions.

Few who knew Blackmun's work were willing to categorize him beyond certain predictable generalizations. As a rule, Blackmun, like Burger, was "conservative" in his views of criminal procedure and generally shy in breaking new judicial ground. After patiently reciting a defense attorney's argument for a innovative judicial decision, Judge Blackmun would often turn to a familiar refrain: if new constitutional law is to be written, the authors should be members of the U.S. Supreme Court, not his court of appeals. On civil rights matters, Blackmun gained the reputation of a moderate, which meant that he would not stand for desegregation delays that he suspected were inspired by prejudice. To most professional acquaintances, Judge Blackmun was unpredictably open-minded. Attorneys felt that if their arguments were sound, regardless of the cause they advocated, Judge Blackmun was available for a favorable ruling.

One of Blackmun's most publicized appellate opinions—a ruling on the constitutionality of capital punishment—displayed the judge's most telling judicial traits. The defendant in the case was William Maxwell, a twenty-one-year-old black man from Arkansas, who was charged with the rape of a thirty-five-year-old white woman. An all-white jury had quickly found Maxwell guilty and sentenced him to death by electrocution, not an unusual verdict to be given a black man accused of the rape of a white woman in a southern state. What made the Maxwell case stand out, however, was that attorneys from the

NAACP Legal Defense Fund chose it to challenge the constitutionality of the death penalty. Led by Professor Anthony G.
Amsterdam, a brilliant scholar and courtroom advocate, the
LDF set about to prove that the death penalty could not be
reconciled with the U.S. Constitution.

Key testimony for Maxwell came from Professor Marvin E.
Wolfgang, a criminologist from the University of Pennsylvania,
who had undertaken an extensive study of rape convictions that
resulted in the death penalty in eleven southern states, including Arkansas. The study, which cost $35,000 and utilized the
talents of numerous scholars as well as more than a score of law
students, concluded that juries were considerably more anxious
to demand the death penalty for blacks than whites convicted
of rape. In a word, there was discrimination based on race.

Based on Wolfgang's testimony and the study, attorney Amsterdam argued that blacks historically had been singled out for
capital punishment. William Maxwell, said Amsterdam, was an
unfortunate statistic in the historic pattern. Since southern juries had insisted on rougher justice for blacks, including Maxwell, Amsterdam contended that Maxwell had been denied
equal protection of the law.

Addressing himself to that issue, Judge Blackmun credited
Professor Wolfgang's study for its "interesting and provocative" findings. The judge was so intrigued by the study that he
devoted more than a quarter of his opinion to the discussion of
its intricacies—and almost as much space to explain why he did
not find its conclusions persuasive in the Maxwell case. Although the study covered nineteen counties in Arkansas com-
prising 47 per cent of the state's population, Blackmun pointed
out that Garland County, where Maxwell was convicted, was
not included in the survey. But even if the study had included
Garland County, Blackmun suggested that more than broad
generalizations were needed. Had the Maxwell jury, in fact,
discriminated against the defendant? No statistical pattern

could be ascertained, said Blackmun, since Maxwell was the only man, black or white, to be sentenced to death for rape in the county's history. Having satisfied himself that neither the broad Wolfgang study nor the specific facts in the case before him proved racial discrimination by the Maxwell jury, Blackmun concluded: "We are not yet ready to condemn and upset the result reached in every case of a Negro rape defendant in the state of Arkansas on the basis of broad theories of social and statistical injustice."

Like all good lawyers, Amsterdam had not relied on a single argument for his constitutional challenge. Broadening his attack on the death penalty to all persons, not just blacks, Amsterdam argued that no jury possessed rational standards to decide whether a man should be put to death or given life in prison. And finally, Amsterdam asserted that Maxwell had been denied due process of law because the jury had convicted and sentenced the defendant in one sitting, though proof of a man's innocence often worked at cross purposes with that presented to show that a defendant should not be put to death. A defendant who claims his innocence at trial, for example, is unlikely to project the proper picture of repentance that might gain the sympathy of the jury at sentencing time.

Blackmun was unpersuaded by either argument. On the first point, Blackmun said that the jury's choice was no more arbitrary than that facing many judges who are authorized by statute to decide whether a convicted defendant should receive five years or twenty-five years in prison. The judge contended that legislators rightly credited jurors as well as judges with the necessary judgmental qualities. "The jury system," wrote Blackmun, "appropriately assumes that jurors in their factual determinations bring into play their common sense and the experience of life." In dispensing with Amsterdam's single verdict argument, Blackmun relied less on common sense and more on the rules of his profession. As he did in many cases in which one side was asking the court to write new law, Blackmun backed off, supporting his judicial shyness with arguments that precedent counseled caution and that if new law was to be made, another court—the U.S. Supreme Court—should make it.

The Maxwell opinion was unmistakably Blackmunesque. It revealed an almost interminable exposition of the facts and arguments of the case, unpretentious analysis of the issues, reverential concern for judicial precedent and the prerogatives of the Supreme Court. A final Blackmun touch was saved for the last paragraph. The Maxwell case, wrote Blackmun, was "particularly excruciating for the author of this opinion who is not personally convinced of the rightness of capital punishment and who questions it as an effective deterrent." Blackmun, the citizen, was questioning the death penalty as Blackman, the judge, would not. Always mindful of what he believed to be the limitations on courts, Blackmun did not want to do what he conceived as the legislature's work. The abolition of capital punishment, he believed, was a policy issue more properly decided by legislators.

After President Grant had named two men to replace Chief Justice Salmon Chase and both had to be withdrawn because of opposition to the nominations, the president's next choice, Morrison Waite of Ohio, was greeted with a collective sigh of relief by the nation. "On the whole," one newspaper editorialist wrote, "considering what the president might have done and tried to do, we ought to be very thankful and give Mr. Waite a cordial welcome." Americans were equally thankful for the nomination of Judge Harry Blackmun, who, from all appearances, seemed certain to succeed where Judges Haynsworth and Carswell had failed. Still, the nation held its breath as politicians and scholars anxiously scrutinized the Blackmun record.

At first there was a sinking déjà vu feeling: Blackmun on

three occasions participated in cases involving corporations in which he owned stock. While owning $2,500 worth of Ford Company stock, the judge had participated in two appeals involving minor damage suits against Ford. He also ruled in a case involving a regional telephone company while owning $1,350 worth of American Telephone and Telegraph stock. An attorney for the losing plaintiff in the telephone company dispute shook his head ominously: "I certainly don't think it was a very good idea [for Blackmun to participate with his $1,350 stake in a multimillion-dollar corporation]. The appearance is bad—it looks bad." But the absurdity of an ethics charge against prim, proper and ministockholder Blackmun caught up with the doubters.

On other items of the judicial checklist, Blackmun gave the public cause for more than resigned support. His civil rights record, the first snag in the Carswell candidacy, was correct—neither too liberal for the South nor too desultory for blacks. The mediocrity issue—introduced unfairly in the Haynsworth candidacy but with considerably more reason in the Carswell case—simply had no application to Blackmun. Clearly, Blackmun deserved the highest judicial rating, which the American Bar Association gave him. His nomination was even lauded by scholars like Professor Yale Kamisar of the Michigan Law School who did not agree with Blackmun's basic judicial caution. It was heartily approved by lawyers who had appeared before him, judges who had sat next to him and clerks who had researched under him.

As the testimonials piled up, each one more favorable than the last, the Blackmun confirmation became a foregone conclusion. The Senate Judiciary Committee questioned the nominee for only three hours before unanimously supporting his candidacy. The full Senate followed the example. The debate lasted less than an hour before the nomination of Judge Harry Blackmun for the U.S. Supreme Court was confirmed by the Senate, 94–0.

The most intriguing question surrounding the Blackmun nomination was not whether he was qualified to serve on the Court. Plainly, he was. Rather, it was how the judge would conduct himself as a member of the Court to which he had passed the buck in so many opinions. Would he now show more enthusiasm to make constitutional law rather than follow it? And would Blackmun, so long a friend and confidant of Warren Burger, discover the chief justice's presence seriously compromising his judicial independence?

"We do not always see eye to eye," said Blackmun when asked of his relationship with the chief justice before confirmation. "If by chance this thing should go through, he would be the first to expect that we would disagree." But that might prove more difficult once a member of the Court than nominee Blackmun suggested. Personal relationships, as chief justices from Marshall to Warren proved, could count for a great deal on the Supreme Court. It would not, then, be surprising if the newest justice felt a subtle pull toward the man he had known since kindergarten, the judge whose philosophy was so close to his own and the chief justice who, reportedly, had recommended him for the highest court in the nation.

CHAPTER SEVEN

No More Fire and Brimstone

In 1962, eight years after the school desegregation decision, human arrangements in Jackson, Mississippi, were not altogether different from those in Johannesburg, South Africa. Racial boundaries were neatly outlined by state law, city ordinance or southern tradition. Jackson's blacks drank from different water fountains than did whites, relieved themselves in special restrooms and waited for buses in isolated areas of the public terminal. It was part of what the U.S. Court of Appeals for the Fifth Circuit called the state's "steel-hard, inflexible, undeviating official policy of segregation."

That year, Jackson's ruling white elite received the unwelcome news that Mississippi's segregation policies were unconstitutional. Without telling officials precisely what to do, a U.S. district court judge strongly hinted that if the segregation policies were not abandoned voluntarily, the courts would force the change. It was advice well taken. Within the year, Jackson's public parks, libraries and zoo had been desegregated. Jackson officials insisted on only one exception to their new desegregation policy: the city's public swimming pools would remain separated by color, with whites admitted to four of the five municipal pools and blacks to the remaining one.

That interracial bathing stood only slightly below marriage in the segregationists' pantheon of fears was evident by both the words and actions of Jackson's mayor, Allen C. Thompson. Nine days after the federal court's decision, Mayor Thompson announced: "We will do all right this year at the swimming pools . . . but if these agitators keep up the pressure, we would have five colored swimming pools because we are not going to have any intermingling." And a year later, Thompson reiterated his determination to keep the races segregated, announcing that "neither agitators nor President Kennedy will change the determination of Jackson to retain segregation." When a committee of blacks formally requested that the mayor act on their demands for desegregated swimming facilities, Thompson chose to tell them of the new plans Jackson had for building more and better segregated facilities for the city's Negroes. As the desegregation pressure built up, Thompson became less open in his resistance but just as determined. By May 1963, the mayor reported that there would be a delay in opening the city's pools "due to some minor water difficulty."

Jackson did not reopen its swimming pools to the public. Instead, it sold one, surrendered a lease on another and shut down the remaining three indefinitely. In court in 1965, the city admitted that the pool closings were precipitated by the district court's 1962 desegregation ruling. But attorneys for Jackson claimed that the underlying reasons for the decision were pragmatic, not personal. Had the city opened its swimming pools on an integrated basis, the city argued, race riots would likely have ensued. Besides, the whites' displeasure with the pools' new customers would have been so intense that business—at least among the traditional white clientele—would have dropped off dramatically. Given the already hefty deficit of the public pool operation, the city maintained that it would find itself locked into an economically suicidal venture.

The black petitioners countered that the Fourteenth Amendment's equal protection clause made no concessions to red ink economics or speculative social unrest. A long line of Warren Court decisions supported their position. The Warren Court did not hesitate to side with blacks, for example, in a dispute with officials of Prince Edward County, Virginia, over the right to close the public schools rather than desegregate them. In the Virginia case, the Court heard testimony that the official good intentions covered a determination to prevent mixture of the races; county funds were later diverted to "private" schools that operated on a segregationist basis. The Warren Court brusquely rejected Virginia's claim. "Whatever nonracial grounds might support a state's allowing a county to abandon public schools, the object must be a constitutional one and grounds of race and opposition to desegregation do not qualify as constitutional."

Fortunately for Jackson officials, the personnel of the Supreme Court had changed just enough since the Prince Edward case to tip the balance in their favor. The five-man majority opinion written in 1971 by Justice Black made precious distinctions between the Jackson and Prince Edward County cases to justify the different results. Unlike the previous case, wrote Black, where there was concrete evidence that the Virginia county and state governments were perpetuating a segregationist policy (through financing), no one could claim that the city of Jackson was financing private segregationist swimming pools. Any vague notions that Jackson officeholders were motivated in closing the pools by segregationist sentiment could not, said Black, be the basis for a court decision. Once the Court had eliminated the "motivation" argument (which the Warren Court refused to do), the city of Jackson was home free. Nowhere in the Fourteenth Amendment or any act of Congress, Black pointed out, was there a positive obligation on states to

operate public swimming pools. And when public swimming
pools are closed to all, reasoned Black, blacks and whites are
treated equally.

Though Black's was the majority opinion, concurrences by
Chief Justice Burger and Associate Justice Blackmun were at
least as significant, since the two newest justices represented the
decisive votes in the case and their opinions reflected a penchant
for judicial caution that would find its way into majority opinions with increasing frequency. The chief justice was particularly reluctant to get the courts into the slippery business of
figuring out the motives of every governmental official. It could
produce only inexact results, he contended, some of them not
beneficial to the public good. Specifically, Burger feared that
second-guessing by the Court could well "lock in" municipal
policy to perpetuate services, once opened, that were neither
efficient nor economically viable simply because the charge of
racism might be raised upon closing.

In characteristic one-two-three-four order, Justice Blackmun
listed his reasons for going along. One: the city had shown its
good intentions by desegregating all other municipal services.
Two: swimming pools represented a "nice-to-have-but-not-
essential variety" of public service. Three: it was undeniable
that the Jackson pools had operated at a deficit. Four: it was
unfair to read the pool closings as an official expression of black
inferiority, as had Justice White in dissent.

Taking the Black, Burger and Blackmun opinions together,
the overriding impression was that the Court chose not to risk
its prestige on what it considered the tangential desegregation
problem of public swimming pools. It was not an irrational
decision but neither was it totally rational. For it had been
shown through the long and painful years since 1954 that
desegregation does not just happen and that, given half a breath
of flexibility, southern officials could present half a dozen reasons to back their segregationist policies. That was why the

Warren Court became almost doctrinaire on the desegregation-ist issue; to do otherwise promised certain impotency. As Judge John Minor Wisdom of the U.S. Court of Appeals for the Fifth Circuit ruefully noted in dissent when the Jackson case was before his court, a judicial wavering did much more than keep the swimming pools closed. It taught that "the price of protest is high," said Wisdom. "Negroes . . . now know that they risk losing even segregated facilities if they dare to protest."

The Jackson case underscored the new judicial spirit of the Supreme Court, suggesting the desire to quiet things down both in the courts and outside. That the Court could do this in the area of desegregation, where the Warren Court had spoken with such force and where new Court members Burger and Blackmun had solid civil rights records, gave powerful testi-mony to the Court's new resolve. Even when the Court favored a civil rights cause, its decision was usually punctured with so many judicial caveats and qualifications that it was drained of the moral drive of a Warren Court opinion.

Busing had become America's first scare word of the seven-ties. The issue brought every racist and demagogue to the public platform to describe the dreaded vision of little children being moved away from familiar surroundings to antiquated schools, strange teachers and new classmates. The issue touched the raw nerves of so many voters that even the moderate and liberal politicians were reluctant to back forced busing. For increas-ingly insecure Americans, a sweeping revision of the educa-tional system meant that another piece of their world was no longer safe and secure.

In that charged emotional atmosphere it was not surprising that a complex opinion of Chief Justice Burger in four desegre-gation cases was bannered by the popular media as "the busing decision." At the outset, the chief justice's tone was reassuring. The Court, he suggested, was saying no more than the Warren

Court had been saying for seventeen years. Since *Brown,* the
Court had ruled that state-sponsored segregated schools were
unconstitutional, and what had followed was only the hows and
whens of the dismantling process. The Burger Court would do
neither more nor less than the Warren Court had promised.
That meant that, yes, busing could be employed, as well as
other measures, to break down dual school systems, but that the
choices would largely be up to the lower courts to do all or
nothing—as was necessary to satisfy the constitutional mandate. It was a gentle proposal compared to the fire and brim-
stone language that characterized Warren Court decisions.

The Burger opinion intended no more than to maintain the
status quo. It spoke only of breaking down the dual system, a
purpose that had been long enunciated by the Warren Court.
It carefully excluded the more ambitious goal of eliminating de
facto segregation in the suburbs. But the chief justice's care to
emphasize the pure ordinariness of this desegregation order was
to no avail. For the Court had said that school districts in the
South were required to eliminate segregation if at all possible,
and, with busing as a tool, it was usually possible. Because of
the Court decision, busing debates sprang up in communities all
over the country. The issue revivified the presidential aspirations of George Wallace and, ultimately, pressed President
Richard Nixon into the dubious constitutional posture of
proposing a statute to take the courts out of the busing business
altogether.

The chief justice was chagrined by the political storm the
Court's opinion had caused but, at the time, was helpless to do
anything about it. When lower courts seemed to overreact to
the Court opinion, handing one busing order after another as
if on direct orders from the High Court, the chief justice reen-
tered the picture. Five months after the original decision,
Burger wrote a ten-page opinion (refusing, as it turned out, to
stay the enforcement of a lower court's busing order) to clarify

the Court's position. The chief justice stated that judges in lower courts were misreading the Supreme Court if they were ordering busing in the belief that the Court required racial balance in every school. The Court, Burger cautioned, had no formula in mind. No rigid black-white ratios were required, but rather a down-to-earth determination by judges to see that school systems were desegregated as much as practicable.

While the Burger Court quietly held to the Warren Court line on desegregation, it was not so loyal to its predecessor in other areas. The promises to the underprivileged, implicit in Warren Court rulings, were not being honored by the Burger Court. That message was delivered piecemeal and with judicially honed sophistication, but it was delivered nonetheless. It came, for example, in a challenge to a Louisiana statute which forbade a bastard to inherit from a father who neglected to make a will. The Burger Court denied the child's claim only a few years after the Warren Court had struck down another illegitimacy statute by the legislature of the same state. This time, however, the Court chose to emphasize that the value judgment—whether illegitimate children could be discriminated against—was for the state legislature, not the Court, to make. The majority opinion brought a swift rebuttal and reminder of things past by Justice William Brennan, Jr. With the high moral fervor so familiar in the Warren Court era, Brennan said that the decision upheld "the untenable and discredited moral prejudice of bygone centuries which vindictively punished not only the illegitimates' parents, but also the hapless, and innocent, children."

That the Court majority was no longer giving special attention to the nation's poor could also be seen in a case involving a New York City mother on welfare who refused to let a caseworker inspect her home. The refusal was grounds under New York's welfare law for cutting off welfare payments. When the payments stopped, the welfare mother sued, charging that the state had violated her Fourth Amendment right to be protected from unreasonable searches.

In his first important majority opinion, Justice Blackmun rejected the mother's claim with methodical ease. First, Blackmun pointed out that there was no forced entry—which could have been a constitutional violation. If the mother refused entrance to the social worker, Blackmun reasoned, no search took place. That deprivation of the funds for food and rent might be a form of coercion, in its own way just as devastating as a forced police search, was not discussed. Even if the welfare recipient had been forced to open her home, Blackmun suggested that the forced entry was not unreasonable. Since the focus of the welfare program was on the child, said Blackmun, inspection of the home surroundings was a reasonable request. According to Blackmun, welfare recipients were in a position no different from those receiving private charity. "One who dispenses purely private charity naturally has an interest in and expects to know how his charitable funds are utilized and put to work," wrote Blackmun. "The public, when it is the provider, rightly expects the same."

Depending on the point of view, the Warren Court either reached its high—or low—point with its *Miranda* decision demanding that police give specific warnings to criminal suspects. Arguments of both supporters and detractors had merit. The *Miranda* opinion was the logical extension of a line of Warren Court decisions that insisted on fair treatment for all criminal suspects. It was also the most extreme example of the Warren Court's imposition of standards on the states and came very close, in its explicitness, to language more familiar in criminal codes drawn by lawmakers. The *Miranda* decision provoked spirited dissents from three members of the Warren Court who remained after the appointments of Chief Justice Burger, an outspoken critic of *Miranda,* and Justice Blackmun, well known for his deference to legislative policy-making.

With the Burger and Blackmun appointments, there was widespread speculation that the *Miranda* decision might well be overruled since the anti-Miranda minority had now become the majority. The opportunity to reverse the *Miranda* decision came in the case of *Harris* v. *New York,* which involved a twenty-three-year-old drug addict and high school dropout, who had quit school after the tenth grade, Viven Harris, who was picked up by police for questioning about an illegal drug sale that had taken place a few days before. Police interrogated the suspect without giving the *Miranda* warnings; the suspect made statements linking himself to the drug transactions.

At his trial, Harris testified in his own behalf and denied committing the crimes. On cross-examination and over the objections of Harris's lawyer, the prosecutor read Harris's statements to police in the station house and asked the witness if he remembered making them. He said he did not remember all that happened at the police station. The jury was instructed to consider the station house statements only for the purpose of weighing Harris' credibility on the witness stand, not for determining his guilt. Harris was convicted on one count of narcotics sale and the conviction was affirmed on appeal.

The Burger Court upheld Harris' conviction but refused to overrule *Miranda.* According to the chief justice's eleven-paragraph majority opinion, he did not have to. Burger acknowledged that police officers had not given the *Miranda* warnings but wrote that Harris had not claimed his statements had been coerced or were involuntary. So long as the evidence was trustworthy, said Burger, it could be used to impeach the witness's testimony. Although there was language in the *Miranda* opinion which suggested that confessions without the warnings could not be used for any purpose, Burger contended that the language was not part of the core decision and, therefore, not controlling on his Court. The chief justice decided that the "speculative possibility" that the decision might encourage police abuse was outweighed by the deterrent effect of showing that the "shield provided by *Miranda* cannot be perverted into a license to use perjury. . ."

When he announced the *Harris* decision from the bench, Chief Justice Burger went out of his way to play down its importance. It was, he said, a decision "of interest mostly to members of the bar" and not significant enough to describe in detail in the courtroom. The written opinion, only four pages in length, appeared to corroborate the chief justice's view. Within days, it was clear that Burger had been whistling in the dark. The reaction among civil libertarians was swift and bitter. The *Harris* decision, they charged, was a model in deception since it overruled *Miranda* without saying so. They agreed with Justice Brennan who, in dissent, had said that the Burger opinion manufactured distinctions from *Miranda* that were not there and tossed out as tangential language from the earlier decision that was central to both the word and spirit of the Warren Court opinion. In practical terms, it was asserted, police were given a bonus for not issuing the *Miranda* warnings, since *Miranda*-less confessions could be used profitably at trial. A second consequence, it was charged, was that defendants would be discouraged from taking the stand for fear that their statements made without the *Miranda* warnings would be introduced. Once such statements were in evidence, some jurors might not be sophisticated enough to limit judgment to whether the suspect had told the truth on the witness stand; their view of the defendant's guilt or innocence might well be colored.

In a *Yale Law Journal* article, Professors Alan M. Dershowitz of Harvard and John Hart Ely of Yale said the *Harris* opinion showed "a total absence of analysis and provides no support for its result." First of all, the two professors contended that the chief justice had incorrectly stated crucial facts in the cases. Contrary to statements in the Burger opinion, they said that the defendant had claimed at every level of his court fight that his station house statements had been involuntary.

They also charged that the chief justice had been disingenuous in saying that the language in *Miranda* was not binding on the Burger Court. "*Miranda* not only 'can' be read to require the reversal of Harris' conviction, it can be read no other way," said Dershowitz and Ely. Further, the two scholars maintained that Burger smoothed over very real and serious policy considerations that were neither adequately discussed nor properly resolved. The decision, Dershowitz and Ely suggested, would encourage police abuse at the expense of a defendant's legitimate constitutional rights.

"The Court's philosophy obviously is changing and doubtlessly will continue to change as more appointments are made," concluded Dershowitz and Ely. "Ideological ebb and flow is an inherent, though generally more gradual, part of the American judicial system. But failures of logic and candor are neither inherent nor desirable in our highest Court. In that regard, the *Harris* opinion seems to have taken an overdrawn academic caricature of the Warren Court's methodology and used it as a recipe. What is vice in a liberal, however, is not necessarily virtue in a conservative."

Could it be, as the *Yale* article suggested, that the Burger Court majority was falling to the right of center with the same heavy steps that critics had said made awkward stumbling for the Warren Court to the left? A major criticism of the Warren Court majority was, after all, that in its zest for the "good" result, the justices did not bother to explain how and why they got to that result. It was not only sloppy craftsmanship, critics charged, but intellectual dishonesty. And now, the civil libertarians were charging, the Court had come full circle with no better justification and even less justice. For Burger Court critics, the case of *Rogers* v. *Bellei* fit into the developing pattern.

Aldo Mario Bellei was born in Italy in 1939; his father was an Italian citizen and his mother a native-born American. At birth, Bellei became a citizen of Italy and, by statute, the United States. But Congress further provided that if foreign-born citizens, like Bellei, failed to live in the United States continuously for five years between the ages of fourteen and twenty-eight, they would lose their U.S. citizenship. Bellei challenged the constitutionality of the residency requirement.

In defending his legal position, Bellei relied heavily on Warren Court rulings that had expanded the rights of citizenship and, at the same time, contracted Congress's role in regulating those rights. The Warren Court, for example, had ruled that a naturalized citizen who had voted in a foreign election could not be deprived of his citizenship although the vote was grounds, under a federal statute, for expatriation. In that decision, the Warren Court said flatly that a U.S. citizen could not lose his citizenship unless he voluntarily relinquished it.

A five-man Burger Court majority sidestepped the Warren Court precedent and stripped Bellei of his U.S. citizenship. A crucial distinction made by Justice Blackmun, who wrote the majority opinion, was that the petitioner in the Warren Court decision was a citizen naturalized in the United States while Bellei was not. Therefore, said Blackmun, Bellei was not "a Fourteenth-Amendment-first-sentence citizen" (that sentence protects "all persons born or naturalized in the United States"). The Blackmun opinion left Justice Black grumbling in dissent about the earlier Warren Court decision, which guaranteed the right of every U.S. citizen "to remain a citizen in a free country unless he voluntarily relinquishes that citizenship." With his fine factual distinctions, Blackmun had cut the Court off from the spirit of the Warren Court rulings. And the decision did much more.

After the Court decision, there was widespread panic among many naturalized American citizens living abroad. Ad hoc committees formed in European cities to urge repeal of the residency statute; hundreds of distressed Americans began signing protest petitions and writing congressmen. The Court decision threatened to divide families, even famous ones like violinist Yehudi Menuhin's. Gerard Menuhin, son of the famous violinist, had been born in Edinburgh while his father was there for a music festival. Though he had lived much of his life in the United States, Gerard Menuhin was in jeopardy of losing his U.S. citizenship because he had not fulfilled the residency requirement that had snared Bellei. At the same time, his brother, Jeremy, had spent less time in the United States but had had the good fortune to have his mother and father conveniently located in the United States at the time of his birth. Under the Blackmun interpretation, Jeremy was a "Fourteenth-Amendment-first-sentence citizen," but Gerard Menuhin was not.

In the judgment of the University of Chicago's Philip Kurland, Chief Justice Burger's second year on the Court would be marked in American history as the most important in seventeen years, since the year of *Brown* v. *Board of Education*. If the 1954 term was the judiciary's atomic explosion at Hiroshima, Kurland suggested, the decisions of the 1971 term could be compared to the actions of the American strategic bombing command over Europe in World War II. "We are witnessing in the Court's work not one major explosion," said Kurland, "but a large number of smaller but by no means insignificant ones, cumulatively perhaps as devastating [as *Brown*]."

To switch the metaphor from warfare to sports (neither image inappropriate during the Nixon administration), the Burger Court had stopped the momentum of the Warren Court, which —as sportscaster Howard Cosell would be the first to admit— is of critical importance. Since the major Warren Court decisions were not overruled, it was not a whole new ball game. But the Court had surely begun a new quarter with fresh reserves,

Burger and Blackmun. And the substitutes obviously felt no obligation to follow the Warren Court's game plan.

It was clear, in fact, that Burger and Blackmun had no intention of following the example of their predecessors, Warren and Fortas. The new appointees did not see the Court as a major instrument for reform in the country; indeed, the word "reform" was virtually anathema to the Burger and Blackmun judicial vocabulary. For "reform," the two new members would substitute "restraint." Let the president, the Congress and the state legislators make policy. Burger and Blackmun were content to stick to their cases, deciding them, hopefully, without broad policy connotations.

The appointment of Chief Justice Burger alone had not dictated any drastic shifts in the direction of the Court. Despite the new chief justice's exhortations, the Court continued on its activist way, though at a noticeably slower pace. But once Burger was joined by Harry Blackmun, important things began to happen. The two new Court members, both wanting to take the Court to a more conservative position, were countered by the veterans, Douglas, Brennan and Marshall, who insisted on going the other way. Black, now eighty-five years old, never did like to be pushed in any direction and, at this last stage of his brilliant career, he became more unpredictable than ever.

On the close questions before the Court, it was extremely unlikely that the conservative faction (Burger and Blackmun) could count on the liberals (Douglas, Brennan and Marshall) to attain a majority. By the same token, the liberals could hardly expect any more cooperation from the two new members. The judicial balance of power, therefore, was held by the three Court middlemen—Harlan, Stewart and White. Less dogmatic than their brothers, the three centrists were more likely to be persuaded and, at the same time, be persuasive in the give and take of the judicial conference. They were more cautious than their brethren on either side and, because their votes were crucial, they caused their colleagues to be more conciliatory, in many cases, than they might have liked. To understand the new stance of the Supreme Court of the 1971 term is to understand the men who guided it—Harlan, White and Stewart.

Law and distinguished public service had for generations been the most outstanding characteristics of the Harlan family. Justice John Marshall Harlan was named for his grandfather, a distinguished member of the U.S. Supreme Court for thirty-four years, who had himself been named for a nonrelation, John Marshall, the great chief justice of the United States. John Marshall Harlan was born in Chicago, where his father served as the reform-minded mayor of the city. Harlan made his way in blissful comfort through one preparatory school after another until he reached Princeton and later Oxford, as a Rhodes scholar. He returned to the United States a confirmed Anglophile, which, on a personal level, meant that trans-Atlantic friendships were continued throughout his life. On a professional level, Harlan never blushed in his admiration for the British legal tradition. Harlan attended the New York Law School and joined one of Wall Street's most prominent law firms, Root, Clark, Buckner & Howland, which boasted such legal luminaries as Emory Buckner and, later, Thomas Dewey.

With only a brief stint as assistant to Buckner when he was U.S. attorney in New York, Harlan made his living and formidable reputation as a trial lawyer for private, and mostly wealthy, corporate clients. Throughout his career, however, Harlan remained supremely aloof from the cause he represented—except in the courtroom. There he left no argument untouched, no judicial precedent unstudied. As with most great trial lawyers, Harlan owed his success to two rather unspectacular traits: thorough preparation and impeccable organization of his case.

When Harlan was only thirty-two, the executors of the will of Ella Wendel came to his firm with a bizarre legal tangle. The late Miss Wendel was well known for three things: eccentric tastes, a reclusive nature and, most of all, money. Ella Wendel left an estate of between forty and fifty million dollars and designated in her will that most of the fortune be divided among five charities. Some uncharitable relatives suggested that Miss Wendel was not of sound mind when her lawyer drew up the will. Their challenge to the will brought Miss Wendel's executors to the office of Buckner, a senior partner in Harlan's firm. Buckner picked Harlan and a younger associate, Henry J. Friendly (now chief judge of the U.S. Court of Appeals for the Second Circuit) to help protect the true relatives from the phonies. Since there was a crowd of men and women claiming genealogical affinity with Miss Wendel, it was no small task. After Buckner became ill, that major responsibility was left to Harlan and his assistant, Friendly.

After making a trip to Europe to trace the Wendel family history, Harlan established twenty-three tests for genealogical authenticity. He then dispatched Friendly to investigate the claims of each challenger to the will and match the individual background against the Harlan tests. Friendly, a thorough lawyer, triumphantly reported his results on twenty-one of Harlan's tests. Quietly but with firmness, Harlan asked his colleague to check out the other two.

When he finally went to court, Harlan knew the details of each challenger's background down to the last third cousin. Though the tall, patrician Harlan was rarely attired in anything less formal than a staid three-piece suit, his manner was never imperious. On the witness stand, Harlan treated each challenger with perfect courtesy. Even when a witness offered what Harlan knew was a blatantly false explanation, the lawyer would retain his composure, his manners and his insistence that the witness describe every detail of his claim. When the witness had finished, Harlan, again quietly and with utmost courtesy, demolished his story, pointing out contradiction after embarrassing contradiction until the witness found there was very little left of his original claim. Harlan's performance was so effective that he not only knocked out fake claims but caused the trial judge to order the prosecution of one witness for perjury.

At the beginning of World War II, Harlan turned his great energy and intellect to the Allied military effort, heading the section of the Eighth Army that had active responsibility for bombing operations in Europe. Harlan time and again observed bombing operations first hand and often made recommendations for bombing method changes that were soon implemented. He returned from the war with the rank of colonel and recipient of the Legion of Merit from the U.S. government and the Croix de Guerre from the French.

After the war, Harlan devoted most of his time to the practice of law with his old firm, but took off eight months in 1951 to serve as chief counsel for Governor Dewey's New York State Crime Commission. By the time President Eisenhower reviewed the Harlan résumé for appointment to the U.S. Court of Appeals for the Second Circuit in 1954, it was irresistible. Harlan was a Republican, a Presbyterian and a first-rate lawyer. Nine months later, Ike elevated Harlan to the Supreme Court. After his appointment was announced, it was noted in the newspapers that Harlan owned a seven-room apartment in New York City with a view of the river, a nine-room house in Weston, Connecticut, and indulged in the genteel hobbies of fishing and golf. "It does sound awfully tame and correct, doesn't it," the justice-designate suggested to one interviewer. And then, with whimsical aside, Harlan offered, "If it helps any, we don't have a terribly good view of the river—sort of an on-an-angle one—and I don't play golf at all well."

After his confirmation to the Court, Harlan immediately transferred the spartan work habits of his private practice to the Court's business. He labored for prodigiously long periods and, though a naturally amiable man, tolerated no diversions from his staff. That did not mean, however, that he was inaccessible. Harlan encouraged his clerks to argue over the fine points of a case and, in fact, this give-and-take made a Harlan clerkship one of the most coveted among all the justices. Harlan's attention to all of the cases, even the "peewees," as Harlan called the less significant ones, was well known to his colleagues. At the regular Friday conferences of the Court, Harlan always entered with carefully prepared positions on each case. But though his thoughts had been carefully organized beforehand, Harlan was always open-minded to the better argument of a colleague.

To label Harlan a "conservative" or "liberal" even in the judicial sense is a risky business. His conclusions trailed too closely after the facts of a particular case for that kind of categorizing. Still, there were themes that recurred in Harlan opinions, none more important nor more frequently articulated than the justice's belief in federalism. John Harlan believed that it was sheer judicial arrogance for judges to try to correct every wrong in a tripartite federal system. Harlan simply did not trust the minds and good intentions of nine men untouched by an electorate's veto. It was this anxiety that led Harlan to castigate the Court when it rendered the one man–one vote rulings. Harlan wrote: "These decisions give support to a current mistaken view of the Constitution and the constitutional function of this Court. This view, in a nutshell, is that every major social ill in this country can find its cure in some constitutional 'principle,' and that this Court should 'take the lead' in promoting reform when other branches of government fail to act. The Constitution is not a panacea for every blot upon the public welfare, nor should this Court, ordained as a judicial body, be thought of as a general haven for reform movements."

But if that opinion would properly place Harlan in the "conservative" judicial mold, others would give pause to such labeling. Harlan wrote the opinion that established for the first time freedom of private association as a fully guaranteed constitutional right. In the early sixties, it was Harlan who first saw the sit-in demonstration as a legitimate form of free expression. In what turned out to be his last year on the Court, Harlan wrote the majority opinion that gave indigent women the right to sue for divorce with the states picking up the tab. And finally, the dignified and very proper Mr. Justice Harlan wrote that the Constitution's free speech provision was broad enough to protect a man wearing a jacket in public embroidered with the words "Fuck the Draft."

Harlan's reputation for high scholarship never diminished during his losing battle with old age and bad health. That was impressively illustrated in his majority opinion, delivered only six months before his death, in which Harlan rejected constitutional challenges to jury procedures in death penalty cases. Harlan traced the history of capital punishment from the common law of medieval England to a 1971 report on the subject by the National Commission on Reform of the Federal Criminal Laws. The history lesson was not an exercise in judicial pedantry. Harlan's opinions never were. Instead, Harlan was attempting to show, through history as well as tight judicial reasoning, that standards in capital punishment cases had troubled the makers of Anglo-American law for almost as many centuries as there had been such law. But, alas, no judicial reform had ever been able to devise satisfactory standards for the ultimate judgment of whether a man ought to live or die. To impose general standards was not the Court's function anyway, said Harlan. "The Federal Constitution, which marks the limits of our authority in these cases, does not guarantee trial procedures that are the best of all worlds, or that accord with the most enlightened ideas of students of the infant science of criminology, or even those that measure up to the individual predilections of members of this Court. The Constitution requires no more than that trials be fairly conducted and that guaranteed rights of defendants be scrupulously respected."

For all of his well-earned accolades as a scholar, John Harlan was first and last a lawyer, studiously attentive to factual detail, stubbornly resistant to dogma from any quarter. Harvard's Paul Freund wrote of Harlan that "his basic responsibility, as he conceives it, is to decide the cases before him, with that respect for its particulars, its special features, that marks alike the honest artist and the just judge." Harlan was so impartial in approach to the facts of cases, John Frank has written, that neither shrewd defense attorney nor prosecutor would, given the choice, single out Harlan to decide his case. But if defense and prosecution *together* had to choose, Frank wrote, Harlan would be their man.

> There was very little money around Wellington [Colorado] and I suppose you could say that by the normal standards of today we were quite poor, although we didn't necessarily feel poor because everyone was more or less the same. Everybody worked for a living. Everybody. You started working early. A friend of mine who lived across the street and I went to work in the beet fields when we were seven or eight . . .

Justice Byron White's memories say much about the man. He chooses his words economically; yet, no word or phrase is wanting. He speaks dispassionately about very personal and, surely, wrenching human experiences. There is no play for pity or favor. Tough, self-reliant and coolly confident of his ability to cope in any situation, Byron White found opportunity in every challenge from childhood in the farm supply center of Wellington in northern Colorado to maturity as an associate justice of the U.S. Supreme Court.

White's father, Albert, was the branch manager for a lumber supply company in Wellington. In a town of 350 during the depths of the Depression, nobody, not even the president of Wellington's one bank, enjoyed much financial security. So Byron, like the other boys in town, went to the sugar beet fields (school let out early for the harvest), thinning and harvesting by hand for a dollar or two a day. It was not pleasant work but it had to be done and White did it. Despite the hard times, White was always told by his parents, who had never finished high school, that education was the most important activity of his life. Aware that the first person in the graduating class of every high school in Colorado was automatically given a scholarship to the state university, White "made a noticeable effort to be first." And he was.

At the University of Colorado, White was a junior Phi Beta Kappa and valedictorian of his graduating class. But White was better known for his superior talents as an athlete, not as a scholar. "Whizzer" White became the nation's most exciting college football star for three years, culminating in Colorado's undefeated season in 1937. That year, White, a six-foot-two, 190-pound halfback, led the nation in scoring (sixteen touchdowns, twenty-three extra points). On the football field as in the classroom, White combined talent and hard work to make his way. The touchdowns he scored by returning punts, for example, were a testimonial to White's natural speed and agility; but the thirty to forty-five minutes he spent every day in practice, catching punts at full speed, had something to do with his phenomenal success as well.

White picked up two extraordinary honors, fittingly divided between his talents as an athlete and a scholar. He won the coveted Rhodes scholarship to Oxford, which enabled him to study English law and legal history. At the same time, White signed on with the Pittsburgh Steelers professional football team for $15,800 a year, then the highest salary ever paid a professional football player. White managed both scholarship

and football with characteristic aplomb, leading the National
Football League in rushing his first year before pursuing his
studies at Oxford.

After Oxford, White entered the Yale Law School and
earned the highest grades in his first-year class. He was invited
to join the school's prestigious law journal but declined "to play
football [for the Detroit Lions] and make some money instead."
The bombing of Pearl Harbor interrupted studies and football.
White was a Naval Intelligence officer in the South Pacific who,
early in the war, briefed PT boat squadrons based on the Solo-
mon Islands.

During the briefing sessions, White renewed his acquaintance
with a young man he had first met in England, John F.
Kennedy. One of White's assignments was to write the report
on the famous accident in which Kennedy's PT boat was sunk.
As a result of interviews on land and in Kennedy's new PT
boat, White "began to get a strong feeling about what kind of
fellow he was. He proved himself to be very intelligent in the
way he ran his boat, as well as cool and courageous under fire.
I concluded he was a pretty solid sort of person."

After the war, White finished at Yale (graduating magna cum
laude) and clerked for Chief Justice Fred Vinson.* He later
turned down offers from two of Washington's most prominent
law firms when they would not meet his demand for a partner-
ship after two years. It was not a modest proposal that White
put to the firms; but then, White did not have much reason to
be modest. Instead of settling in Washington, White chose Den-
ver for his law practice. For the next twelve years (1947–59),
White was content with a prosperous law practice, quiet participation in local civic activities and thorough enjoyment of
Colorado sports and outdoors.

"One day in the summer of 1959 while I was driving back
from an AAU track meet in Boulder, I got to thinking about

*White was the first Court clerk to become a member of the Court.

the coming presidential campaign," White later recalled. "I began to feel that Jack Kennedy would be my preference." And so, White organized the Colorado Committee for Kennedy and, after his candidate's nomination, the nationwide Citizens for Kennedy. Robert Kennedy was so impressed with White's administrative abilities that he asked his brother to appoint White deputy attorney general, the second-ranking job in the Justice Department.

The fresh legal talent that was infused into the Justice Department in the early sixties, including men like Burke Marshall, Louis Oberdorfer and Nicholas Katzenbach, was largely due to the recruiting efforts of White. As deputy attorney general, White had no time for aimless talk but all the time in the world to work out the solution to an intricate legal problem. "If you wanted to talk about a legal problem and get skeptical questioning," Burke Marshall remembered, "Byron had as fine a mind for that as anyone around." The men at Justice also knew that no political current would disturb White's cool, analytical mind. "He would never act on rumor," said Marshall, adding that "he just would not be pushed into a position that might have seemed momentarily expedient."

White was not a man to make speeches to promote his own values or impose his political ideas on others. He was no civil rights crusader, but he believed implicitly in the rule of law. So when the first freedom riders were met by raucous, rioting crowds in Alabama in May 1961, White's private convictions and public obligations to enforce the law merged to draw him personally into the tense situation. The trouble began when the first integrated buses in the "freedom ride" caravan reached Alabama. One bus was destroyed by fire and a dozen persons were injured. As the buses moved through the state, the tension built. Street fighting broke out in Birmingham; a hostile mob in Montgomery promised even more serious violence. After a Justice Department officer was injured in a Montgomery riot,

White decided to act. He borrowed a turbo jet from the Civil Aeronautics Administration, grabbed an assistant attorney general who was a native of Alabama, his personal secretary and a load of law books and headed for Alabama. In flight, White calmly drafted the legal papers necessary to impose judicial order on the Montgomery tinderbox. In Montgomery, White took charge of the Justice Department operation, held a terse conversation with Alabama governor George Wallace and, assured that peace had been restored, returned to the nation's capital.*

After President Kennedy appointed White to the Supreme Court, the new justice, like Chief Justice Warren, withdrew from the political scene entirely. Though he always enjoyed a freewheeling political discussion, Justice White no longer allowed himself that luxury. He did not move in high Washington social circles, though he could have had he wished. If his lawyer friends had cases pending before the Court, White even cut himself off from social activity with them, at least until the case had been decided.

But the robes and self-imposed isolation did not hide the essential Byron White. Like the Kennedys, White was a pragmatist with all the strengths—and contradictions—that the Kennedys gave the term. With a quick but careful mind, White attended fact, not dogma. He was a leader of high intentions but realistic goals. On the Court, White disappointed those liberals who liked their leaders' ideas and values neatly packaged for predictable delivery.

Justice White declared his independence from liberal doctrine early when he established himself as a hardliner in the criminal law field. His dissent in the *Miranda* decision, for example, contained some of the familiar trappings of law and

*White's dry humor could sometimes break the tension under which the Justice Department civil rights attorneys were then working. Informed that Alabama prison guards had been deputized to help control a threatening crowd, White drolly replied: "That's fine, but which side are they on?"

order rhetoric. White charged that the *Miranda* ruling "will return a killer, a rapist or other criminal to the streets and to the environment which produced him, to repeat his crime whenever it pleases him. As a consequence, there will not be a gain, but a loss in human dignity. The real concern is not the unfortunate consequences of this new decision on the criminal law as an abstract, disembodied series of authoritative proscriptions, but the impact on those who rely on the public authority for protection and who without it can only engage in violent self-help with guns, knives and the help of their neighbors similarly inclined. There is, of course, a saving factor: the next victims are uncertain, unnamed and unrepresented in this case."

Frequently, White fended off constitutional claims of the criminal suspect to get at the root problem of his guilt or innocence. That happened in the case of *Alford* v. *North Carolina* in which Henry C. Alford was charged with the capital crime of first-degree murder. The state of North Carolina, where the crime took place, had gathered strong evidence of Alford's guilt. The defendant was unable to counter the State's case with substantial evidence showing his innocence. Alford's appointed counsel recommended that his client plead guilty to second-degree murder, a plea that would save the state the cost of a trial and the defendant, conceivably, his life. Such "plea bargains" are struck daily in every courthouse in the country and though, on the surface, they appear to be nothing more sophisticated than a crude legal bazaar, both defense and prosecution find the process enough to their advantage to perpetuate it.

On his lawyer's advice, Alford struck the bargain, pleaded guilty to second-degree murder and was sentenced to thirty years in prison. Throughout the legal process, all the while agreeing to the plea, Alford insisted that he was innocent. From prison, Alford asked the federal courts to intervene and set aside his conviction on the grounds that the plea bargain was involuntary because the principle motivation for the defendant's plea was the fear of the death penalty.

White began his Court opinion by challenging the crucial assumption of the defense. In attacking the plea-bargaining process, Alford had argued that the choice of proclaiming his innocence (and risking the death penalty) or pleading guilty to a lesser offense was really no choice at all. For White, that conclusion could only be made if the facts of the case supported it. And for White, in the *Alford* case, they did not. Carefully reviewing the case record which showed "overwhelming evidence" of Alford's guilt, White concluded that, realistically, Alford "had nothing to gain by a trial and much to gain by pleading." A preference that the issue be settled by a judge out of court rather than in a formal trial, said White, was a free and entirely rational choice by the defendant.

But if White seemed impatient with legal technicalities that benefited the criminal suspect, he could be equally uncomfortable with official subterfuges that worked to the advantage of segregationists. It was a White opinion, for example, that threw out California's constitutional amendment that allowed voters to skirt fair-housing regulations. And it was White who wrote the persuasive dissent in the 1971 Mississippi swimming pool decision. Typical of White's opinions, this dissent consisted of a detailed recitation of the facts (showing that the city of Jackson's primary purpose was to maintain segregation through the pool closings) followed by a careful analysis of the law (showing that the Warren Court had intended for judges to scrutinize the motivations of officials in desegregation cases). Finally, White concluded: "The equal protection clause is a hollow promise if it does not forbid such official denigrations of the race the Fourteenth Amendment was designed to protect."

Cincinnati, Potter Stewart's hometown, was solid Republican territory where the Taft family served as the Republican saints-in-residence. The Stewarts, middle-class, well-established and Republican, fit in perfectly and, in fact, were both friends and admirers of the Tafts. As a small boy, Potter was called "little Jimmy" by Chief Justice William Howard Taft. The chief justice was referring to Potter's father, James Garfield Stewart, who was active in the Republican Party, serving several times as mayor of Cincinnati before his appointment to the Ohio Supreme Court.

High achievement came early and easily to Stewart. At Yale, he was one of the biggest men on campus, editing the *Yale Daily News,* serving as his class orator and graduating Phi Beta Kappa. Stewart toyed with the idea of a career in journalism after Henry R. Luce offered him a job at Time, Inc. Instead, he decided to accept the prestigious Henry Fellowship for study at Cambridge. After his study abroad, Stewart returned to the Yale Law School, where he served on the law journal and graduated with honors. He then took the road of least resistance for many a bright Yale Law graduate, joining a very proper and prosperous Wall Street law firm. But the war disrupted Stewart's plans and he left law practice to serve in the Navy as a deck officer on oil tankers in the Atlantic. It was a job that Stewart described as "floating around in a sea of 100 octane gas, bored to death 99 per cent of the time and scared to death 1 per cent of the time." Stewart returned to New York with three battle stars and a growing suspicion that New York corporate law practice was not for him. As a New York lawyer, said Stewart, "you work harder and harder to become more and more successful so that you can move further and further away from town and see less and less of your family." So Stewart packed for Cincinnati to join a law firm in his home town.

Although he dabbled in local politics, serving two terms on the Cincinnati city council, Stewart always knew that his field was law, not politics. When President Eisenhower in 1954 offered him a seat on the U.S. Court of Appeals for the Sixth Circuit, Stewart, then thirty-nine, quickly accepted. For the next four years, Stewart built a reputation for fairness and judicial craftsmanship. He could, however, speak with controlled indignation, as he did when Hillsboro, Ohio, school officials argued for a postponement of a desegregation order because it would result in overcrowded classrooms. Stewart replied that "the avoidance alone of somewhat overcrowded classrooms cannot justify segregation of schoolchildren solely because of the color of their skins." Still, Stewart did not welcome the opportunity to be outspoken and when, after his appointment to the Supreme Court, he was asked to label his judicial philosophy, Stewart responded uneasily that "I like to be thought of as a lawyer."

When Potter Stewart was elevated to the Supreme Court in 1958 at the age of forty-three, the justices were almost evenly divided between those supporting the activist philosophy of Hugo Black and those following Felix Frankfurter's counsel for judicial restraint. Stewart was immediately seen as the "swing man" in important constitutional areas. And, not surprisingly, the new justice—the second youngest to be appointed since pre-Civil War days—was wooed in much the manner of an uncommitted delegate at a political convention. Members of each faction would occasionally corner Stewart to clarify their point of view or send him informal memoranda arguing a legal point as they saw it. Stewart was told to call Justice Black "Hugo" and Justice Frankfurter "Felix," commands not without awkwardness since Stewart had studied the opinions of "Mr. Justice Black" and "Mr. Justice Frankfurter" when he was a law student.

All of the attention, of course, did not make Stewart's job any easier. He felt very young and singularly unprepared to take an ideological view urged upon him by either of the competing philosophical factions. For the time being, Stewart decided, he would write his opinions on the narrowest possible grounds. In that way, he could fulfill the responsibilities of his office without committing himself to any specific judicial doctrine. To a large degree, that original Stewart strategy still holds, no longer because of any lack of confidence on his part, but because Stewart believes that the narrowest decision is often the best one.

Always skeptical of absolutes, Stewart has never assumed that strong governmental measures were, automatically, bad; but he has not tolerated government regulations that have been abusive. He has rejected attempts to impose total prohibitions on government regulation in the area of censorship but, at the same time, has insisted that a victim of censorship be given a fair hearing to defend his controversial product. Stewart could strike down a state regulation requiring public school teachers to list all of their organizational memberships but might uphold specific questions that directly relate to a teacher's fitness. He won't shield all U.S. citizens from congressional statutes providing expatriation, but he will be sure that the statutory provisions are not arbitrary and that the individual has been guilty of the conduct Congress had in mind when it passed the statute.

If fairness is Stewart's first judicial consideration, federalism is his second. When the action of another branch of government is rational, Stewart will accept it, even if he thinks it is unwise. His judicial restraint is rooted in practical as much as philosophical considerations. Like Harlan, Stewart just doesn't trust judges to make government policy. Judges are generalists, hopefully intelligent ones, but generalists nonetheless. And unlike legislators, judges do not have access to the experts or all the information necessary to make policy decisions. Besides, Stewart draws assurance from the ready check on legislative judgments—the ballot box—whereas there is none for life-tenured judges.

In exceptional cases, Stewart has been willing to abandon his restrained approach to join his colleagues in issuing broad judicial decisions, like *Gideon v. Wainwright*. Before *Gideon*, the Court had tried to protect indigents in court by reversing convictions in blatantly unfair cases. But that cautious approach had not worked. Too often, indigents without lawyers justifiably appealed to the Court for help and the Court's piecemeal approach simply couldn't handle the legal traffic. Several states realized the futility of an indigent's courtroom battle without an attorney and passed legislation requiring counsel years before *Gideon*. Experience showed that those state laws helped the poor defendant without clogging the courts. With all of that accumulated knowledge—the Court's frustration and the states' success in guaranteeing a fair trial for the poor—Stewart believed that *Gideon*'s day had come.

But four years after the *Gideon* decision, Stewart was unwilling to join the Warren Court majority in extending the *Gideon* guarantee to juveniles. Stewart did not quarrel with the majority's conclusion that the juvenile in the case before the Court had been deprived of fundamental procedural safeguards. But the majority had gone beyond the specific case to impose a broad code of procedure in all juvenile cases without, in Stewart's view, the knowledge and experience that had been the basis for the broad judgment in *Gideon* (it was only the second major case on juvenile proceedings to reach the Court in twenty years).

Stewart's philosophy could be traced to any number of Court giants—Holmes, Brandeis, Frankfurter and Harlan. But no man stood higher in Stewart's judicial hagiology than Justice Robert Jackson. At a Jackson testimonial dinner, Stewart said as much about his own philosophy as the man he came to honor. "He [Jackson] saw that 'judicial activism' could be a deadening and stultifying force. He knew that every coercive and centralizing court decision deals a blow, if sometimes only a little blow, first to the ability and then to the will of the democratic process to operate with responsibility and vigor. He understood, as only an experienced advocate could understand, the shortcomings of the adversary process as a substitute for the give-and-take of informed self-government. He understood, as only a wise and sophisticated judge could understand, how fallible the judges of even a final court can be. He knew that the right answer to a problem of New York might not be the right answer in North Dakota. He knew also that there might be a better answer tomorrow than the best of today's. He knew, in short, that the great strength of the federal union our Constitution created lies in its capacity for self-innovation and change."

CHAPTER EIGHT

The Pentagon Papers

At midnight, June 14, 1971, the telephone rang in Mrs. Yetta Bickel's Manhattan apartment. Professor Alexander M. Bickel of the Yale Law School, an overnight visitor at his mother's residence, groggily picked up the receiver. The voice at the other end was that of Harding F. Bancroft, executive vice president of the *New York Times*. Usually perfectly controlled in speech, Bancroft this time sounded tense.

He told Bickel that the *Times* had received a telegram earlier that evening from Attorney General Mitchell demanding that the newspaper cease further publication of documents from a voluminous history of United States involvement in the Vietnam War, commissioned by former secretary of defense Robert McNamara. Bancroft read the telegram to Bickel: "I have been advised by the secretary of defense that the material published in the *New York Times* on June 13 and 14, 1971 captioned 'Key Texts From Pentagon's Vietnam Study' contains information relating to the national defense of the United States and bears a top secret classification. As such, publication of this information is directly prohibited by the provisions of the Espionage Law, Title 18, U.S. Code, Section 793. Moreover, further publication of information of this character will cause irreparable injury to the defense interests of the United States. Accordingly, I respectfully request that you publish no further information of this character and advise me that you have made arrangements for the return of these documents to the Department of Defense."

In a telephone call from Assistant Attorney General Robert C. Mardian to Bancroft that followed the Mitchell telegram, the *Times*'s executive was told that the Justice Department would immediately seek an injunction to bar further publication if the *Times* did not comply with the Government's ultimatum. Bancroft and other top executives of the *Times* pondered their dilemma. Should the *Times* continue publication and invite the inevitable showdown with the Justice Department? Or should the newspaper stop publication of the series and, in effect, submit the nation's most powerful and revered newspaper to government censorship?

When he heard of the Justice Department's telegram that Monday night, the *Times*'s general counsel and vice president, James C. Goodale, had anxiously placed a call to Bancroft to gauge the initial response of the *Times* hierarchy. Bancroft asked Goodale's advice. The attorney was quick and adamant. "That's easy. We won't stop publication. We don't do that." That had been Goodale's opinion all along; he had been one of the most insistent voices urging publication of the Pentagon Papers before the final decision was made, and his position had not changed. But Bancroft, a careful and diplomatic man, did not share Goodale's sense of urgency before publication nor did he that night. He told Goodale that no decision had yet been made and that the newspaper's executives were meeting to discuss the *Times*'s future course.

By the time Goodale's taxi pulled up in front of the *Times* offices, Managing Editor A.M. Rosenthal and Vice President Sidney Gruson were already "screaming and yelling at each other." Gruson counseled caution, mindful of the view of Louis Loeb, an attorney whose firm had represented the newspaper in major litigation for decades, that the *Times* could not take it upon itself to jeopardize the security interests of the United States. The *Times* should not continue publication of the series, Loeb advised. Rosenthal argued vigorously against the Loeb position, expressing the newsman's natural revulsion to censorship from any quarter. But as he sensed the tide of opinion in the room shifting to the Loeb position, Rosenthal demanded that the final decision be left to Publisher Arthur O. Sulzberger, who was then in London. After Sulzberger was reached in his London hotel room, Goodale took the phone and said: "We cannot afford for the future of this newspaper to stop publication now. It would be terrible." Sulzberger quietly gave the order to continue publication.

Bancroft sent the telegram to the attorney general that would assure the legal confrontation. "We have received the telegram from the attorney general asking the *Times* to cease further publication of the Pentagon's Vietnam study. The *Times* must respectfully decline the request of the attorney general, believing that it is in the interest of the people of this country to be informed of the material contained in this series of articles. We have also been informed of the attorney general's intention to seek injunction against further publication. We believe that it is properly a matter for the courts to decide. The *Times* will oppose any request for an injunction for the same reason that led us to publish the articles in the first place. We will of course abide by the final decision of the court."

After Bancroft had reviewed the extraordinary events of the evening for Professor Bickel, he told him that Lord, Day and Lord, Louis Loeb's firm, had refused to argue the *Times*'s case in court. Loeb and another senior partner of the firm, Herbert

Brownell, had previously advised the *Times* not to publish the materials. That night, Bancroft told Bickel, Brownell had flatly said that Lord, Day and Lord would not represent the newspaper in its tangle with the Nixon administration.

Rejected by Loeb's firm, the *Times* turned to Professor Bickel. Actually, Bickel had entered the picture earlier in the day after he, Goodale and Floyd Abrams, another New York attorney, had met to discuss other *Times* legal business. When the Pentagon Papers controversy was touched on briefly in conversation, Bickel said that he had found the first installments of the Pentagon Papers very interesting, that it was good that the documents had been made public and that he did not think the government would take any action against the *Times*. Coming from Bickel, a prominent constitutional scholar who did not make a practice of impetuous judgments, the remarks were both welcome and reassuring. When Bickel's name was mentioned that night, Goodale enthusiastically backed the recommendation.

Would Bickel take the case, asked Bancroft? The Yale professor thought about the proposal for a few minutes, pondering the immediate difficulties (he was due in Washington the next day to testify before a congressional committee) and the longer-range problems (he would need the help and facilities of a first-rank New York law firm). He would cancel his Washington appearance the next day. Could he get assistance from a New York firm? Floyd Abrams had promised his immediate help, Bancroft said, and would try to enlist his firm, Cahill, Gordon, Sonnett, Reindel and Ohl, in the effort the first thing the next morning. Bickel accepted. Bancroft said that Abrams would pick him up in a taxi shortly and that the two could go to work immediately at the Cahill, Gordon offices.

Cahill, Gordon is one of the large, prosperous New York firms that demands long hours from its lawyers but tries to make the work conditions as pleasant—and efficient—as possible. For nocturnal professional adventures such as Abrams and Bickel were about to embark on, the firm retained twenty-four-hour secretarial services, around-the-clock hot coffee and scrambled eggs. Abrams and Bickel loosened their ties, grabbed cups of coffee and started to work.

At the outset, the *Times*'s attorneys faced a large problem. "We didn't know what the hell was in the Pentagon Papers," Bickel later recalled. Under the circumstances, Bickel and Abrams decided there was only one effective strategy open to them. "It seemed to me," said Bickel, "the only chance of winning quickly and possibly at all was to say—the government's action is unauthorized. As a matter of law, the government has nothing to rest its case on. In order to prove that, we have to knock out the statutory authority (the Espionage Act) and the inherent powers (the president's constitutional obligation to protect national security). Then we come to the First Amendment issue—a fact issue."

Bickel was criticized by some civil libertarians for not resting his entire argument on the First Amendment's protection of the press. That absolutist approach, Bickel contended, was for what he called "the First Amendment voluptuaries." Bickel had never been comfortable in the absolutist school of constitutional law, in fact had become one of its chief antagonists. But now, Bickel had practical as well as theoretical objections to that approach. "If you represent the American Civil Liberties Union, you're only interested in the First Amendment," said Bickel. "But not if you have a client. I wasn't interested in a blow for freedom. I wanted to win."

After reading the statutory provisions cited by Attorney General Mitchell in his telegram and studying several of the most important decisions based on Espionage Act prosecutions, Bickel concluded that Congress had not intended the act to cover the *Times* situation. To invoke the inherent powers doctrine,* Bickel thought the government would have to make a prima facie case that the Pentagon Papers contained materials that would directly and seriously harm the security interests of the United States. Though he had read only that much of the Pentagon Papers as had appeared in the *Times,* Bickel intended to hold the government to the narrowest possible test of "harm to the national security." If he could knock out both the statutory and inherent powers justification for the government's action, Bickel could argue that it was a case of censorship. And that was forbidden by the First Amendment.

By 3 A.M. Bickel began dictating a memorandum that he would use in court later that day. At 6:00, the secretary went home, leaving Bickel to type the last four pages of his ten-page memo. When he had put in the last sentence, Bickel felt tired but satisfied. He had argued that the government had a heavy constitutional burden to justify the prior restraint of a newspaper's publication. According to Bickel, neither the Espionage Act nor the executive's inherent constitutional power provided the government justification to suspend the First Amendment. Bickel had not had the time to do the research that he—or any lawyer—would have liked to carry his arguments "to the last decimal point." But Bickel felt he was as prepared as he could be, under the circumstances, to argue that afternoon in U.S. District Judge Murray I. Gurfein's courtroom that the Government's request for a temporary restraining order to halt further publication of the *Times* series should be denied.

The issues in what would soon be known as "the Pentagon Papers" case monopolized the time of two U.S. district courts, two U.S. courts of appeals and, ultimately, the Supreme Court of the United States. Amid a tense and highly emotional public

*Included in the president's constitutional right to protect the national security, the Government would argue, is the "inherent" power to prevent publication of sensitive security documents.

debate of the controversy, the courts would listen to the arguments and deliver their decisions within days, sometimes hours,
after hearing the lawyers argue points that they themselves
admitted had not been thoroughly researched. The Supreme
Court would settle the issues on June 30, only seventeen days
after the *Times* presented its readers with the first installment
of the series entitled "Vietnam Archive." The entire controversy pushed forward to its dramatic conclusion with such
ineluctable suddenness that it was reminiscent of one of those
old Hollywood movies in which the omniscient, deep-voiced
narrator, aided by an ordinary desk calendar, would flip
through years of history in a matter of seconds.

And yet, the drama that ran its public course in little more
than two weeks was five years in the making. It began, roughly,
in 1966 when Daniel Ellsberg, an intense, 35-year-old middle-
echelon Defense Department official, began to have serious
doubts about the wisdom of American involvement in Vietnam.
It had not always been that way. Only a year earlier, Ellsberg,
an honors graduate with a doctorate in economics from Harvard, had supported the government's Vietnam policy at university teach-ins across the country. In the middle of 1965
Ellsberg volunteered to go to Vietnam to help assess the pacification program in the South Vietnamese provinces. After numerous field inspections, Ellsberg began to write pessimistic
reports and became increasingly skeptical of the more sanquine
accounts of progress written by others. By 1967, Ellsberg
looked back on two years of field work that "had discredited,
in my eyes, any hopes of success, in almost any terms, in Vietnam, given the course we were following and the obvious un-
likelihood of our changing it."

After he was hospitalized with hepatitis in 1967, Ellsberg
returned to the U.S. and civilian life as an economic analyst for
the Rand Corporation. That same year, Ellsberg was called to
Washington to contribute to a massive retrospective study of

U.S. decision making in Vietnam that would later be known as the Pentagon Papers. Ellsberg's serious doubts about U.S. policy turned to total disillusionment as he read classified government documents on the war. He concluded that the goals of U.S. policy makers were both politically and morally bankrupt. What had begun as a quiet recommendation by Ellsberg that the U.S. seek a negotiated exit from Vietnam became an urgent demand that the U.S. leave Vietnam, with or without a negotiated settlement. By 1969, Ellsberg had joined a tiny band of Rand radicals who voiced increasingly bitter opposition to U.S. Vietnam policy. Finally, six of them wrote a letter to the *New York Times,* urging a total withdrawal of U.S. troops from Vietnam within a year. "Past U.S. promises to the Vietnamese people are not served," Ellsberg and his colleagues wrote, "by prolonging our inconclusive and highly destructive military activity in Vietnam."

The next year, shortly after U.S. troops entered Cambodia, Ellsberg appeared before Senator J. William Fulbright's Foreign Relations Committee. "I think that what might be at stake if this involvement goes on," said Ellsberg, "is a change in our society as radical and ominous as could be brought about by our occupation by a foreign power." By 1971, Ellsberg was comparing U.S. policy makers, including himself, to those of Nazi Germany. Both, said Ellsberg, participated in a criminal war, willfully, irresponsibly and with neglect of human consequences.

But disillusionment had prodded Ellsberg into more than a war of words. Before he left the Rand Corporation to join the Massachusetts Institute of Technology faculty as senior research associate, Ellsberg spent his evenings in September 1969, xeroxing the Pentagon Papers study for what he considered the future good of the nation. Ellsberg first presented his xeroxed study to Senator J. William Fulbright, chairman of the Senate Foreign Relations Committee, but Fulbright was reluctant to make the study public without its official release by the Department of Defense. Secretary of Defense Melvin R. Laird refused to release the study. Senator George McGovern, like Fulbright, an outspoken critic of U.S. policy in Vietnam, was approached by Ellsberg. But he too was unwilling to take on the responsibility of making the study public. Growing increasingly restless, Ellsberg looked for other channels of public distribution. After he read and admired a long and probing book review discussing U.S. involvement in Vietnam by *New York Times* reporter Neil Sheehan, Ellsberg made his move.

In late March 1971, Sheehan visited Ellsberg in Cambridge and then returned to Washington with a bundle of photocopies of government documents that were the Pentagon Papers. Sheehan discussed the documents with his boss, Washington Bureau Chief Max Frankel, and Frankel briefed the *Times* New York editors on Sheehan's find. The initial response was less than euphoric. "We had to wonder: What are we going to learn from yet another Pentagon history?" recalled one high-ranking *Times*man. "What confidence can we have of its authenticity and its comprehensiveness?" But, as people like Frankel discovered as they dug into the study, the Pentagon Papers loomed as something considerably more provocative and important than just another analysis of the Vietnam War. "I remember saying to Neil very early on," said Frankel, "that if this is the quality of most of the thing, it's a gold mine."

The *Times* managing editor, A.M. Rosenthal, saw similar merit to the study and quickly organized "Project X," putting Foreign Editor James L. Greenfield in charge of preparing the Pentagon Papers for publication. Greenfield's assistant, Gerald Gold, was dispatched to Washington to plan the overall project with Sheehan. After Gold and Sheehan had holed up in a two-room suite in the Jefferson Hotel for two weeks of study, they concluded that the *Times* should run a long series on the Pentagon Papers.

Managing Editor Rosenthal and Greenfield, a former assistant secretary of state for public affairs under Kennedy, spent ten days poring over forty-two books written by former government officials about the Vietnam War. They concluded that classified information had been leaked so regularly and used so consistently by former officials, sometimes for commercial gain, that the whole question of top secret papers "had become almost academic." Most of what had once been confidential, said Greenfield, "had been very well moved over and walked over and revealed." Still, the *Times*'s editors imposed their own system of classification. The documents were rated for publishing priority with some items—such as an admiral's suggestion that the United States should introduce nuclear weapons in Vietnam—omitted as being sensational and unrepresentative of thinking by U.S. policy-makers.

"Project X" soon engaged the full-time services of *Times* correspondents Sheehan, Hedrick Smith, E.W. Kenworthy and Fox Butterfield. The four were charged with the responsibility of reading the Pentagon study, selecting the most important documents and building a telling narrative around them. The massiveness of the project had dictated a shift in locale from the *Times* offices on 43rd Street to a three-room suite at the New York Hilton, furnished with desks, chairs, typewriters, filing cabinets and safes. Even this setup proved too confining and so the work area was eventually expanded to five hotel rooms, with a *Times* security guard watching over the empty rooms at all times.

Meanwhile, the *Times* hierarchy had still not decided whether the series ought to be published. Led by attorney Loeb, the antipublishing faction of executives argued that publication would put the *Times* in the indefensible position of determining what was in the national interest. General Counsel Goodale, Rosenthal, and columnist and vice president James Reston countered that freedom of the press was being tossed aside on the speculative possibility that some document, yet undiscovered, would jeopardize the national security.

In the middle was Publisher Sulzberger. He had given the initial go-ahead for preparation of the series, but as opposition to publication mounted within the *Times* hierarchy, the publisher began to hedge. He sliced the space for the series from the originally agreed-upon twelve daily pages to six. Even as the deadline neared, Sulzberger's position was thought to be so shaky that Rosenthal and Washington Bureau Chief Frankel nervously talked out their strategy in case the boss changed his mind at the last minute. To their relief, Sulzberger did not change his mind. Still, he left the final decision on the published version to Bancroft, since Sulzberger planned to be in Europe when the series went to press.

A ninth-floor office of the *Times* was ordered stripped of all furniture. The walls were covered with masonite, and bright fluorescent lights replaced soft, indirect units. In came a huge page proof press, six automatic typesetting perforators, a galley proof press, a printer's saw, storage cabinets, makeup tables, proofreading desk and paper shredder (to destroy extra proofs). A watchman stood at the door and admitted no one who was not included on a secret list. Specially selected printers began typesetting on Thursday night, June 10, working around the clock until the first editions of Sunday's paper were ready for printing on Saturday.

> QUESTION: Mr. Secretary, can you give us the basic reasons for the Gulf of Tonkin patrol?
>
> SECRETARY McNAMARA: It is a routine patrol of the type we carry out in international waters all over the world.
>
> *News Conference, August 5, 1964*

On Sunday, June 13, 1971, readers of the *New York Times* knew that Secretary McNamara had deceived the American public that day in 1964 and that high U.S. officials, including President Lyndon Johnson, had taken part in countless deceptions before the 1964 Gulf of Tonkin attack. In fact, as documents from the Pentagon Papers published in the *Times* showed, there was nothing routine about the Gulf of Tonkin patrol. It was part of a carefully calculated plan of the United States to increase military pressure on North Vietnam.

The Pentagon Papers revealed what the most outspoken critics of U.S. involvement in Vietnam had only suspected: U.S. policy-makers had never seriously considered a negotiated peace in Vietnam so long as the South Vietnamese government was in danger of ultimate defeat. The domino theory lived—in the White House, the Pentagon, the State Department—indeed it had been the touchstone for every diplomatic and military move that the United States made in Southeast Asia since the administration of President Harry Truman. Believing that the fall of South Vietnam to Communism would lead to a massive surrender of U.S. interests throughout Southeast Asia, U.S. policy-makers routinely hoodwinked the American public about the war. They said war was peace (or pacification) and defeat was victory because, in the long run, they believed history would prove their decisions sound, their purpose honorable. President Johnson could, for example, ridicule Republican presidential candidate Barry Goldwater as a Dr. Strangelove while the President's advisors were plotting U.S. bombing missions to North Vietnam.

The gap that separated the American people from the truth about U.S. policy in Vietnam was only a part of the Pentagon Papers story. As startling was the chasm that separated U.S. policy-makers from the truth about the Vietnam War. Memorandum after crisp memorandum revealed that the Rostows and Bundys of the Johnson administration consistently miscalculated both the strength of the enemy and the effectiveness of U.S. military power. Beyond the deceptions and miscalculations was a pervasive arrogance among U.S. policy-makers. The

Pentagon Papers showed, for example, how U.S. Ambassador to South Vietnam Maxwell Taylor had played the role of exasperated schoolmaster with a group of plotting South Vietnamese generals. "Do you all understand English?" Taylor began. "I told you all clearly at General [William C.] Westmoreland's dinner we Americans were tired of coups. Apparently, I wasted my words. Maybe because something is wrong with my French because you evidently didn't understand. We cannot carry you forever if you do things like this."

The Pentagon Papers also exposed an intellectual smugness among presidential advisors. The strategy for peace in 1964 was very simple, as Walt W. Rostow presented it to the president. The United States would suggest to the North Vietnamese that it was in their best interests to leave South Vietnam alone. If Ho Chi Minh did so, according to Rostow's scenario, the following steps would follow:

a. peace;
b. accelerated economic development;
c. Asians taking a larger hand in their own destiny;
d. as much peaceful coexistence between Asian Communists and non-Communists as the Communists wished.

The Rostow memo was only a single example of the how-to-arrange-the-world-in-one-page-memos mentality that was reflected time and again in the Pentagon Papers documents. Those documents were not the whole story of U.S. strategy but they said enough.

Secretary of Defense Melvin Laird learned of the *Times* series from aides after the first installment appeared on the Pentagon teletype Saturday afternoon, June 12. Laird placed a telephone call to Attorney General John Mitchell to confer on what the proper government response ought to be. The immediate problem, for Laird, was that the secretary was scheduled to appear on CBS-TV's *Face the Nation* program Sunday morning. If he were asked about the Papers, Mitchell told Laird, the secretary of defense was to say that the disclosures endangered the national security and that the Justice Department was studying the matter for possible legal action. The contingency plan was not necessary, however, since the newsmen did not mention the Pentagon Papers on the telecast. Sunday passed without an official response to the *Times*'s series and the newspaper readied for the second installment.

By Monday afternoon, the second installment was in print and there was still no word from the Nixon administration. At that time, however, Attorney General Mitchell and his Director of Internal Security Affairs, Robert Mardian, had retreated to Mitchell's Watergate apartment to draft a formal answer to the *Times* challenge. By 7:30 P.M. Mitchell and Mardian had sent the telegram to the *Times* ordering immediate cessation of the series and followed with the Mardian telephone call warning that the Justice Department would take the *Times* to court if it did not accept the Government ultimatum. It was a tough, uncompromising stand, the kind that had become John Mitchell's trademark. There would be no middle ground, no compromise settlement with the *Times*.

Once the *Times* and the Justice Department had made their positions public and irreconcilable, supporters for each side climbed aboard. "We say the federal government does not have a constitutional leg to stand on in its effort to censor the contents of a newspaper," editorialized the *Washington Post*. But the conservative *San Diego Union* lamented that the Pentagon Papers "are documents for which our enemies would pay a king's ransom—and they are getting them for free." A citizens' group tried to join the *Times* in court in the interest of the people's right to know the truth about the Vietnam War. But White House Press Secretary Ronald Ziegler suggested that the real public interest was to keep diplomatic lines uncluttered by press leaks and that the United States could not operate a foreign policy effectively if it could not "deal with foreign powers in a confidential way." Secretary of Defense Laird issued a statement of concern by the Pentagon about "the disclosure of publication of highly classified information affecting national security," while William G. Florence, a retired Pentagon official, was contending that "at least 99½ per cent of those classified documents could not be prejudicial to the defense interests of the nation."

The Pentagon Papers controversy bottomed on two basic—and competing—constitutional claims: the press's right to publish versus the Government's right to protect the national security. Although the Supreme Court had never faced the stark confrontation before, it had previously spoken to the government censorship issue. That happened in 1931 when the justices were confronted with the prosecution of the publisher of a viciously anti-Semitic Minneapolis newspaper by the state of Minnesota on the grounds that the publication was "largely devoted to malicious, scandalous and defamatory articles." The Court divided 5–4 in that decision, *Near* v. *Minnesota,* with the majority favoring the right of the publisher to print his articles. Chief Justice Hughes wrote the majority opinion, declaring that even "Miscreant purveyors of scandal" are protected by the First Amendment's freedom of the press. The chief justice then laid down the standard for prior restraints that was to exist up to the Pentagon Papers case. There could be no question, said Hughes, that the press was not totally free to print when confronted with other, equally important, public interests. National security, for example. Hughes said that "a government might prevent actual obstruction to its recruiting service or the publication of sailing dates of transports or the number or location of troops."

The burden of sorting out the confusing facts and law surrounding the publication of the Pentagon Papers fell to a new

U.S. district judge, sixty-three-year-old Murray Gurfein. In his first official day on the bench, Tuesday, June 15, Judge Gurfein heard Assistant U.S. Attorney Michael D. Hess argue that the *New York Times* had violated section 793 of the Espionage Act, which forbade serious injuries "on our foreign relations to the benefit of other nations opposed to our form of government." Hess, a thirty-year-old Harvard Law School graduate, asked Gurfein to grant a temporary restraining order barring the *Times* from going forward with publication of the series.

The *Times*'s Bickel countered that granting the Government's motion would give the judicial stamp of approval to a "classic case of censorship." Then, moving to the point he had spent most of the previous night preparing for, Bickel said that the Espionage Act was never intended to be used against the press of the country. To rely on that statute, Bickel warned, would set a dangerous precedent for the nation. "A newspaper exists to publish," said Bickel, "not to submit its publishing schedule to the United States government."

A troubled Judge Gurfein weighed the opposing arguments and then granted the Government's request for the temporary restraining order. At the same time, Gurfein scheduled a full hearing on the issues for Friday, June 18. In a case so important to the future of Government-press relations, said Gurfein, any temporary harm to the *Times* "is far outweighed by the irreparable harm that could be done to the interests of the United States if it should ultimately prevail." Though Gurfein's ruling was temporary, it nonetheless made history. For the first time, a federal judge had forbidden a U.S. newspaper to publish a specific article.

While the *New York Times*'s lawyers worked and its readers waited, editors at the *Washington Post* were scrambling to catch up to their competitor's journalistic coup. Ever since the *Times*'s first installment had hit the newsstands, the *Post*'s editors had tried to figure out a way to wiggle out from under the *Times*'s shadow. At first, the *Post* ran stories on the Pentagon Papers by combining materials from the *Times*'s series with reporting from the *Post*'s own sources. It was not a happy solution for the *Post*'s proud news staff or its aggressive executive editor, Benjamin Bradlee. "The score was 36 to 0," Bradlee later recalled, "and we were trying to get even." By Wednesday, the day after the *Times*'s series was suspended by court order, the *Post* was very close to a score.

The *Post*'s Assistant Managing Editor, Ben H. Bagdikian, had known Daniel Ellsberg when both were working on projects at the Rand Corporation. When the Pentagon Papers were first published, Bagdikian immediately thought of Ellsberg as the possible source of the leak. Bagdikian's suspicion was confirmed in a telephone conversation on Wednesday, June 16, with Ellsberg, who was in Cambridge. The *Post* wanted to publish its own Pentagon Papers series, Bagdikian told Ellsberg. The *Post* editor was instructed to take a night air shuttle to Boston and bring a large suitcase with him. On Thursday morning Bagdikian phoned Bradlee from Boston: mission accomplished. When he returned with the documents to Washington, Bagdikian headed straight for Bradlee's Georgetown home, where the executive editor had arranged a greeting party of three of the *Post*'s top reporters, all with Pentagon or Vietnam experience, editorial page editor Philip L. Geyelin, the newspaper's lawyers and Bradlee.

Differences of opinion, both editorial and legal, arose immediately. Should the *Post* publish a series in the same manner as the *Times,* with both a narrative and the documents? For reasons of space and readability, the group decided that the *Post* would present an analysis of the documents but not the documents themselves. The *Post*'s Chalmers M. Roberts was given the assignment of writing the series' first installment for the next day's editions.

In much the pattern that developed at the *Times,* the *Post*'s newsmen and lawyers divided, roughly, into opposing camps on the proper legal course for the newspaper to follow. The newsmen contended that the *Post* had the duty to publish; the lawyers, initially joined by the *Washington Post* Company's chairman of the board, Frederick S. Beebe, argued that the newspaper could not really be sure that it was not violating the nation's security. At the very least, the lawyers pointed out, the *Post* could be found guilty of violating the provision of the Espionage Act which stated that anyone with reason to believe that publication would seriously damage the United States was in violation of the law. The *Post*'s Bradlee later recalled, "A case could be made that we had reason to believe that. The attorney general had said so publicly. So had the secretary of state. And so had a federal judge in New York."

Bradlee, the driving force behind the *Post*'s rush for the Pentagon Papers, seemed to waver, at least in the eyes of some of his reporters. But the executive editor said the reporters had misread his listening to the lawyers' objections for support for the lawyers' views. "My problem as executive editor was to reach the decision to publish as quickly and painlessly as possible." Ultimately, the *Post* went ahead with publication of the Pentagon Papers series, with Bradlee convinced "we were not endangering the national security." He came to that conclusion "because all of the information was at least seven years old, because much of it had been published, though of course not in the compelling detail, and because collectively we probably had a hundred years of expertise that afternoon in my house on what endangers and what does not endanger the national security."

Friday morning, June 18, Professor Bickel began his oral argument before Judge Gurfein in support of the *Times*'s position by pointing to the handiwork of his client's competitor.

Since the *Washington Post* had now taken up where the *Times* left off with the Pentagon Papers, Bickel argued, Judge Gurfein's temporary restraining order on the *Times* served no valid purpose.* Gurfein's order, Bickel noted, did not affect the 345 client newspapers of the *Washington Post–Los Angeles Times* news service, whose readers would be reading an analysis of the Pentagon Papers, courtesy of the *Post*, at the same time they would be reading about the court's frustration of the *Times*'s efforts to do the same thing. What Gurfein was doing, said Bickel, was penalizing the *Times* readers—and nobody else. The *Post*'s action, besides rendering Gurfein's restraining order ineffective (the nation would still read about the study), showed that the Government's claim of security breaches was exaggerated, said Bickel. Even a second exposure of the Pentagon study, Bickel noted, had not compromised the nation's defense. "The republic stands," he observed, "and it stood the first three days [of the *Times* series]."

Judge Gurfein, understandably cautious in his first week on the federal bench, was not anxious to clear his calendar of what was, perhaps, the most important case that he would hear in all of his days as a judge. No, there would be no quick verdict in favor of the *Times*. Actually, Bickel had not expected to win the point; indeed, the Yale professor did not think that his chances of winning on any point in Gurfein's court were all that good. After all, Gurfein was a former colonel in U.S. Intelligence in World War II, not a man a *Times* lawyer would assume to be naturally sympathetic to his case. The judge would listen carefully to the argument of U.S. Attorney Whitney North Seymour, Jr. "These are stolen documents," Seymour told the court. "They are classified. They compromise our current military and defense plans and intelligence operations and jeopardize our international relations."

---

*The court's restraining order would seem even more futile after portions of the Pentagon Papers later surfaced in the *Boston Globe, Chicago Sun-Times, St. Louis Post-Dispatch* and *Los Angeles Times.*

Gurfein's questions during the oral argument were searching, almost painful, attempts to get at the newspaper's motivation in printing the study. It did not come easily to the judge. "I don't understand, though, frankly why a patriotic press should not be willing to subject these papers [to government inspection], not to censorship of any kind except from a limited security point of view. I wish you would answer that because it is troubling me." And later: "I am concerned about materials sent by foreign governments which do not belong to the United States . . . or perhaps revelations of intelligence gathering all of which as patriotic citizens I think the press as well as anybody else agrees should be kept sacrosanct, not to deprive anybody of a right to express an opinion, mind you, but in order to protect what is dear to all of us, the security of the country."

Gurfein appeared to be searching for a compromise verdict, one that would spear out one or two documents that he could say jeopardized the national security while letting the *Times* print the rest. In that way, the judge could uphold the principle of the First Amendment but make it clear that the nation's security was an equally important interest. But to do that, the Government would have to go beyond the conclusionary generalizations that publication of the Papers jeopardized the national security. "Show me where the shoe pinches," Gurfein kept telling U.S. Attorney Seymour in closed sessions. Show me specific documents, Gurfein was saying, show me materials whose public exposure would so clearly endanger the national security that I would be justified in suspending the First Amendment to see that that does not happen.

"Without revealing the content of the testimony," Judge Gurfein wrote in his opinion, "Suffice it to say that no cogent reasons were advanced as to why these documents, except in the general framework of embarrassment previously mentioned, would vitally affect the security of the Nation . . . Fortunately upon the facts adduced in this case, there is no sharp clash such as might have appeared between the vital security interests of the Nation and the compelling constitutional doctrine against prior restraints. If there be some embarrassment to the Government in security aspects as remote as the general embarrassment that flows from any security breach, we must learn to live with it. The security of the Nation is not at the ramparts alone. Security also lies in the value of our free institutions. A cantankerous press, an obstinate press, a ubiquitous press must be suffered by those in authority in order to preserve the even greater values of freedom of expression and the right of the people to know . . ."

The *Times* had won the first round, and a very popular victory at that. U.S. Attorney Seymour later compared the courtroom drama to the old-fashioned celluloid kind. Whenever the good guys, the *Times* in this case, made a point, the visitors' galleries would roar with laughter and applause. When the heavies, in this case the government attorneys, argued, there was silence or disapproving muttering from the back of the room. It was "a veritable cabal of the nation's press," Seymour complained; "We are villified on all sides." But Seymour's turn came less than forty-eight hours after Judge Gurfein handed down his opinion. For when the government appealed the Gurfein opinion to the U.S. Court of Appeals for the Second Circuit, it was Professor Bickel, not Seymour, who was given the rougher time.

Bickel's important strategic mistake before the Second Circuit was in underestimating the tension-laden atmosphere in the courtroom. Bickel discovered his error quickly enough, after he began his argument by challenging the government's contention that the *Times* materials were "stolen." In arguing that the term "stolen" should not be used, Bickel wanted to eliminate that highly emotional reference so that he could get on with his legal arguments. The request should be honored, Bickel suggested, since nothing about how the *Times* had obtained the documents had been proved in the lower court.

Chief Judge Henry Friendly and his colleague, Judge J. Edward Lumbard, immediately pounced on the Bickel position. What do you mean, the documents weren't stolen? Did the government simply hand them over to the *Times* to satisfy the editors' curiosity? Were they found on the sidewalk on 43rd Street? Of course, the documents were stolen, so don't waste the court's time on such pettiness. By the time Bickel had backpedaled out of that legal traffic jam, ten minutes and the court's patience had elapsed. The Yale professor never fully recovered, never was able to put his basic arguments to the court with the coolness and precision that he had hoped.

The judges were left to ponder U.S. Attorney Seymour's point: who should have the role of declassifying government documents, the *New York Times* or the Government itself? In the unsigned opinion, Chief Judge Friendly and Judge Lumbard joined three of their colleagues in a majority ruling that ordered a further delay of the *New York Times* series. The majority said the *Times* could only resume publication of the series with those materials which the Government said did not threaten the national security. Judge Gurfein was ordered to conduct a secret hearing with Government representatives and the *Times* to carry out the appellate court's decision. The *Times* immediately announced that it would not continue the series on those conditions. To do so, said the *Times,* would be to submit to government censorship. The newspaper would appeal to the Supreme Court.

The *Washington Post* fared better. On the *Post*'s first day of publication, June 18, attorneys from the Justice Department asked U.S. District Judge Gerhard A. Gesell to grant a temporary restraining order barring further publication of the *Post*'s series. Gesell, son of famed pediatrician Dr. Arnold Gesell and a judge known for his liberal and often controversial opinions, answered the Government the very same day. "What is presented is a raw question of preserving the freedom of the press as it confronts the efforts of the Government to impose a prior restraint on publication of essentially historical data," wrote Gesell. Although he admitted that the Pentagon study could cause embarrassment to the government, Gesell said he had no basis to conclude that the publication would endanger the national security. The government's request was turned down.

Five hours later, Gesell was overruled by a three-judge appellate court, which halted further publication of the *Post* series. The two judges in the majority, Spottswood Robinson and Roger Robb, of the U.S. Court of Appeals for the District of Columbia, wrote why they had sent the case back to Judge Gesell for a full hearing on Monday. "Freedom of press, as important as it is," said the two judges, "is not boundless." Judge Gesell should have granted a full hearing to give the Government the opportunity to show why the publication would harm the national security. So the two appellate judges tossed the case back to Judge Gesell over the impassioned dissent of Judge J. Skelly Wright. ("As if the long and sordid war in Southeast Asia had not already done enough harm to our people, it now is used to cut out the heart of our free institutions and system of government.")

In his second opinion, this one commissioned by the court of appeals, Judge Gesell took a swipe at his judicial superiors. He did not welcome "the role of quasi-censor" that the appellate judges had imposed upon him, particularly, said Gesell, because they had given him no standards to apply. Nonetheless, he followed orders and came to the same conclusion he had three days before. "There is not here a showing of an immediate grave threat to the national security which in close and narrowly defined circumstances would justify prior restraint on publication," wrote Gesell. "The Government has failed to meet its burden and without that burden being met, the First Amendment remains supreme." As he finished reading the opinion, Gesell glanced at the courtroom clock. It showed twenty minutes to five, the hour the courts closed. Addressing the government attorneys who he knew would immediately appeal his decision, Gesell said, "You have twenty minutes. I am sure they are waiting for you upstairs."

At 11 A.M. on Tuesday, the day the court of appeals had scheduled the government's appeal, Attorney General John Mitchell asked the Solicitor General of the United States, Erwin N. Griswold, to come to his office. Mitchell said that he wanted Griswold to argue the government's appeal before the D.C. Court of Appeals in three hours. Griswold hesitated. After all, Griswold, the former dean of the Harvard Law School, had not worked on the case. He had not even read the briefs written by Justice Department attorneys for Judge Gesell. Well, said the attorney general, "if you want me to get someone else . . ." He would do it, Griswold quickly replied. The solicitor general hastily retreated to his office and called his wife. Since he was due in court in less than three hours, Griswold asked if Mrs. Griswold could bring some sandwiches to the Justice Department. Also would she bring a quieter tie and a pair of black shoes, more appropriate for the court appearance of the U.S. solicitor general.

While he waited for the sandwiches, Griswold jotted down notes on paper at his desk. The notes, taken without reference to a single law book, would serve as the basis for Griswold's appellate argument. "What chance is there going to be to carry on the SALT talks," asked the solicitor general in court that afternoon, "if the people on the other side think anything they might say, particularly if they put it in writing, would show up in the American press?" The Government, Griswold tried to show, need not be confined to troop movements or military codes (the *Near* case) in showing that documents could jeopardize the national security. But the next day, in rejecting Griswold's argument, the court of appeals decided that the government had still failed to meet the heavy burden of showing "irreparable harm" to the nation that would override First Amendment interests.

At the outset, most scholars had predicted that the issues raised by the Pentagon Papers publication would ultimately be decided by the Supreme Court. The case presented a classic confrontation between the government and the private sector and between competing constitutional interests (national security versus free press). When the D.C. Court of Appeals and the U.S. Court of Appeals for the Second Circuit, two of the federal system's most prestigious appellate courts, could not agree on the proper judicial solution to the conflict, the Supreme Court's entry into the controversy was inevitable.

The solicitor general learned of the Court's decision to hear the Pentagon Papers cases in a telephone call from Chief Justice Burger at 11:30 A.M., Friday, June 26. The Court, Burger told Griswold, had scheduled oral arguments for 11 A.M. the next day. Justices Black, Douglas, Brennan and Marshall had dissented from the Court's decision, declaring that they favored freeing both the *Times* and *Post* to print their series without hearing the Government's arguments. The four dissents could only discourage the Government; that meant, in all probability, that the four dissenting justices would again assert their belief in the preferred position of the First Amendment when the Court's decision on the merits of the case was finally delivered. For Solicitor General Griswold, the dissents forced him to concentrate on the five other justices, for he would need every one of their votes for his courtroom victory.

Less than twenty-four hours before he was to argue the case in the Supreme Court, Griswold still had not seen the source of the entire controversy—the Pentagon Papers. So his first decision was to arrange for all forty-seven volumes of the Pentagon Papers—seven million words—to be brought to his office in the Justice Department. The solicitor general also requested that three government representatives—one from the State Department, one from the Defense Department and one from the National Security Agency—come to his office to advise him on the documents whose publication would jeopardize the national security. He asked them to tell him which documents, if published, would endanger the nation. Griswold emphasized that he was not interested in documents that could embarrass the U.S. government, but only those that could cause it serious harm. The three representatives submitted forty-two items to the solicitor general that they felt met his criterion.

Both the mass of material he had to study (one of the forty-two items consisted of four bound volumes of the study) and the maddeningly short time left for preparation convinced Griswold that he would need help. He called in his assistant, Daniel M. Friedman, and assigned Friedman the job of writing the government's brief on the legal issues involved. Griswold concentrated on selecting those documents whose publication, he would tell the justices of the Supreme Court, were not in the national interest. He scanned all forty-two items proposed by the three government representatives. The solicitor general reduced the number of "security risk" items to eleven, still including the four volumes (on the history of secret diplomatic efforts to end the war). By the time Griswold had finished dictating the crucial portions of the secret documents to his secretary, it was 3:15 A.M. Saturday, seven hours and forty-five minutes before the solicitor general was due in court. His assistant, Daniel Friedman, had left only fifteen minutes before and Griswold's secretary stayed until 4:00 to finish the typing. All three were back at Griswold's office at 8:30 to assemble the legal papers.

At 5:45 that same morning Richard L. Baltimore, a Harvard Law student from New Rochelle, New York, waited at the doors of the Supreme Court. He would be the first person

admitted to the public gallery when the Court convened at
11:00. Behind Baltimore in line was a sightseeing family from
Wauwatosa, Wisconsin, who had postponed their trip home for
one more morning of U.S. history. Later lawyers gathered,
including the *Boston Globe*'s attorney who had his own Pentagon Papers case to worry about. There were well-known faces
in the galleries as well—retired justice Tom Clark, U.S. Senator
John Stennis and iconoclastic journalist I.F. Stone. When the
justices stepped through the red velour draperies to take their
seats in the courtroom, all three hundred seats in the galleries
were filled; more than twice as many disappointed persons had
to be turned away.

Solicitor General Griswold, dressed in the traditional cutaway coat of the government's attorney, sat at the counsel table
with the forty-seven volumes of the Pentagon Papers, in three
unmarked cardboard cartons, underneath. To his side were the
opposing attorneys, Professor Bickel and William R. Glendon,
representing the *Washington Post*. The newspapers' attorneys,
as the newspapers themselves, presented a striking contrast in
styles: Bickel, small, dapper, professorial; Glendon, tall,
slightly disheveled, folksy.

Shortly after he rose to address the Court, Griswold virtually
announced that he gave himself little chance of winning the
votes of the four justices who had not wanted to hear the case
in the first place. For the solicitor general willingly exchanged
sharp remarks with the dean of the libertarians, Justice Hugo
Black. After Black had pressed Griswold on the importance of
the First Amendment, the solicitor general bluntly replied:
"You say that no law [abridging free press] means no law and
that should be obvious. I can only say, Mr. Justice, that to me
it is equally obvious that 'no law' does not mean 'no law' and
I would seek to persuade the Court that is true." On that point,
Griswold could assume that he would receive sympathy from
the other five justices—Burger, Blackmun, Harlan, Stewart and

White. All were on record as rejecting the absolutist view of the First Amendment.

We have a case, said Griswold, of competing constitutional interests, both important but neither absolute. The press, Griswold contended, had never enjoyed unfettered freedom—nor had it sought it. To prove his point, the solicitor general reviewed the nation's copyright laws, which newspapers had always honored. Without those copyright laws, Griswold noted, newspaper exclusives (like the *Times*'s Pentagon series) could be grabbed off by rival journals without fear of legal penalty. Even newspapers, then, could not afford to stand only on the single legal right provided by the First Amendment.

Stewart cut in. Your case does not really depend on any assertion of property rights, does it? No, it does not, replied Griswold. "Your case depends upon the claim, as I understand it, that the disclosure of this information would result in an immediate grave threat to the security of the United States of America," Stewart continued. "Yes, Mr. Justice," answered the solicitor general. It was clear by then that Griswold had spent close to one-fourth of his allotted time arguing a point—that the First Amendment was not absolute—readily conceded by the five justices he needed for a favorable decision. In much the manner that Professor Bickel had gotten off the track with his initial remarks before the Second Circuit, and substantially sapped his effectiveness, Griswold had taken the Court on a detour that did his side no good.

It was not until the close of his initial presentation that Griswold set out his case in the plainest terms. "The heart of our case," he told the Court, "is that the publication of the materials specified in my closed brief will, as I have tried to argue here, materially affect the process of the termination of the war. It will affect the process of recovering prisoners of war. I cannot say that the termination of the war is something that has an immediate effect on the security of the United States. I say that it has such an effect on the security of the United States that it ought to be the basis of an injunction in this case." Griswold was attempting here, and later in rebuttal, to move the Court away from the *Near* v. *Minnesota* narrow standard (troop ship movements and dates) to a more general test of publications that would affect the national security.

But the man who spoke next, Professor Bickel, was trying to steer the Court in just the opposite direction. Given the importance of the First Amendment, said Bickel, the government has a very heavy burden of proof to meet in showing that the national security has been endangered. Bickel then posed his own standard for the government to meet: "the link between the fact of publication and the feared event [must] be direct and immediate and visible." As Bickel was well aware, documents which "materially affect the process of the termination of the war"—Griswold's words—would not meet his standard. The government's proof, said the *Post*'s Glendon, amounted to no more than military options "which I think any high school boy would have no difficulty in either putting together himself or readily understanding." The government's case in the final analysis, Glendon concluded, was one of "broad claims and narrow proof."

Although the major portion of the Court's time was spent listening to the arguments of the three counsels, the most impressive participant in the proceedings was not an advocate, but a single justice, Potter Stewart. His questioning accomplished all that interrogation at oral argument is supposed to. Stewart's queries were incisive, always bringing counsel back to the main issues of the case, forever pushing them to clarify their own thinking—and the Court's in the process.

When the solicitor general complained that the government was forced to prepare its case too hastily, Stewart shot back: "The reason is, of course, as you know, Mr. Solicitor General, that unless the constitutional law as it now exists is changed, a prior restraint of publication by a newspaper is presumptively unconstitutional." Stewart could ruffle the smooth Mr. Bickel as well, even after the Yale professor had delivered his nicely polished legal standard (the connection between publication and the feared event must be direct, immediate and visible). Suppose, said Stewart, that the government could persuade the Court that publication of certain documents in the Pentagon Study would result in the death of one hundred young draftees. The event would be direct, immediate and visible. "What should we do?" asked Stewart. "Mr. Justice, I wish there were a statute that covered it," Bickel replied. No statute, said Stewart. "I am afraid that my inclinations to humanity overcome the somewhat more abstract devotion to the First Amendment in a case of that sort."

When attorney Glendon hesitated in presenting his test for barring publication, Stewart, in effect, told the *Post*'s attorney what he should have said. "The issues in this case then really are factual issues, are they not," Stewart suggested to Glendon. "You agree an injunction could issue despite the First Amendment if it was shown by the government that there was something here the disclosure of which would directly cause a grave, irreparable and immediate danger to the country. You simply say they have shown nothing of the kind." That was precisely what Glendon wanted to show.

The Supreme Court ended the tumultuous controversy over the Pentagon Papers in a three-paragraph opinion supported by six justices (Black, Douglas, Brennan, Marshall, Stewart and White). The majority took notice of an earlier Court decision that confirmed the heavy presumption against the validity of prior restraints and a second, decided earlier that term, which placed the responsibility for meeting that burden squarely on the government. Had the Nixon administration overcome those judicial handicaps? The Court noted that three courts—two

U.S. district courts and the Court of Appeals for the District of Columbia—had not thought so. "We agree."

Those three paragraphs, vapid though they were, contained all that the *New York Times* and the *Washington Post* needed to go forward with publication of the Pentagon Papers. *Times* Publisher Sulzberger's reaction was one of "complete joy and delight" and the *Post*'s Bradlee exclaimed, "It's beautiful." Daniel Ellsberg termed it a "great" decision and Senator J. William Fulbright said, "I could not be more pleased if I were an editor of the *New York Times;* the *Times* has justified the First Amendment." John Mitchell had no comment. Neither did the White House.

The unsigned opinion, unspectacular in itself, was accompanied by passionate concurrences of the individual justices. All nine members of the Court expressed their views on the case, a rare event and one which exposed some of the deep philosophical differences that divided the justices.

At one extreme, as he usually was on First Amendment cases, stood Justice Black, who expressed disappointment that some of his colleagues would entertain exceptions to the First Amendment's protection of the press. In the most resonant words delivered by any member of the Court, Black said: "Paramount among the responsibilities of a free press is the duty to prevent any part of the Government from deceiving the people and sending them off to distant lands to die of foreign fevers and foreign shot and shell. In my view, far from deserving condemnation for their courageous reporting, the *New York Times,* the *Washington Post* and other newspapers should be commended for serving the purpose that the Founding Fathers saw so clearly . . ."

The other members of the libertarian wing of the Court, Douglas, Brennan and Marshall, were not so expansive as Black nor so adamant as their earlier votes not to grant the hearing in the first place had indicated. Though Douglas joined his old compatriot Black in finding "no room for governmental restraint on the press," he nonetheless found it helpful to note that neither the Espionage Act nor the inherent powers of the executive were intended, nor could they justify, prior restraints on the press. Brennan criticized the lower courts' bar to publication in the first place; the government, said Brennan, had raised possibilities, not proof of endangering the national security. Marshall bought Bickel's argument that the Government would have been on firmer ground if Congress had passed a statute to cover the Pentagon Papers situation. Congress had not. Marshall, sounding like the perfect Frankfurtarian, concluded that it was not "for this Court to take on itself the burden of enacting law, especially law that Congress has refused to pass."

At the other end of the judicial spectrum were the three dissenters—the chief justice and Justices Harlan and Blackmun. All three voiced strong sympathies for the Government position that it should have had more time to present its case. The chief justice had not disguised his feelings in the matter, even at oral argument. After the *Times*'s Bickel had noted that the government had not filed suit until a full two days after the newspaper series began, Burger glowered. "Mr. Bickel, aren't you going to allow some time for somebody to really see what this means before they act and some pleadings are drawn, and get lawyers into the courts?" In his dissenting opinion, the chief justice expressed bitter disappointment in the *Times*'s action and seemed, for the moment at least, to forget the special status accorded the press under the First Amendment. "To me, it is hardly believable that a newspaper long regarded as a great institution in American life would fail to perform one of the basic and simple duties of every citizen with respect to the discovery or possession of stolen property or secret government documents. That duty, I had thought—perhaps naively—was to report forthwith, to responsible public officers. This duty rests on taxi drivers, justices and the *New York Times.*"

Justice Blackmun's opinion, like Burger's, was accusatory. Even in his recitation of the facts, Blackmun suggested that something sinister was going on. The *New York Times* "*clandestinely* devoted a period of three months examining the forty-seven volumes that came into its *unauthorized* possession . . ." By the time he reached his conclusions, Blackmun was positively livid: "I hope that damage already has not been done, and if, with the Court's action today, these newspapers proceed to publish the critical documents and there results therefrom 'the death of soldiers, the destruction of alliances, the greatly increased difficulty of negotiation with our enemies, the inability of our diplomats to negotiate' [Blackmun's tests were taken from a lower court judge's dissenting opinion], to which list I might add the factors of prolongation of the war and of further delay in the freeing of United States prisoners, then the Nation's people will know where the responsibility for these sad consequences rests."

Both Burger and Blackmun also joined Justice Harlan's dissent, which, though more carefully drafted and less emotional than theirs, was the most far-reaching endorsement of governmental power of the three. After suggesting that the case had been decided too quickly, leaving many important questions unanswered, Justice Harlan got to the heart of his opinion. The government's position should have been given greater weight because, said Harlan, the question of what endangers the national security is essentially a political judgment better left to the executive branch. In Harlan's view the Court's role should have been limited to: (1) deciding whether the documents properly came within the president's foreign relations power; and (2) insisting that the secretaries of defense and state testify on the impact of the publication of the documents. Once the Court was satisfied that documents touched on the executive's security (on the executive's say-so), Harlan believed that the Court should leave the matter alone.

Between the two polar positions were Justices White and Stewart. They swung the Court to the newspapers' side and, in their concurrences, actually wrote the binding law of the Pentagon Papers cases. White made no effort to hide his hostility toward the newspapers' actions, virtually writing a brief for a future government criminal prosecution of the *Times* and the *Post.* But, for White, an after-publication criminal prosecution was very different from a prior restraint. He rejected Solicitor General Griswold's standard for prior restraint (if the publication presented "grave and irreparable injury to the national security") as too broad. Stewart's opinion complemented White's, since it presented an acceptable judicial standard for prior restraint. The government could hold up publication of an article, said Stewart, only if disclosure of the contents would "result in direct, immediate and irreparable damage to our nation or its people." Together, the White and Stewart opinions defined the rules for future press-government confrontations.

For all the public commentary on the decision and compulsion by the justices themselves to explain what they did and did not mean, the Pentagon Papers ruling did not take the constitutional law much beyond *Near* v. *Minnesota,* the Hughes opinion of 1931. The First Amendment was still sturdy; censorship by government was still frowned upon. But like the Court forty years before, the majority refused to shut the government off from all control of the media. If a future Congress passed a law prohibiting the actions taken by the *Times* and the *Post* in the Pentagon Papers case, the Court that gave the newspapers a victory in 1971 might well reverse itself. And even without the statute, the government might prevail if it could satisfy Stewart's test of "direct, immediate and irreparable damage to our nation or its people."

The Pentagon Papers case closed the 1971 Court term on a

characteristically cautious note. The Court decision did not introduce any sweeping change in the relationship between the federal government and the press. It did not spank the Nixon administration or the *New York Times*. It did not plead with the Congress to do more or ask the press to do less. There was no inspirational moral to be gleaned from the ruling. The majority wrote no more law than it had to. And the Court moved only where the evidence—and those increasingly important pragmatists, Justices White and Stewart—would take it.

CHAPTER NINE

Two More Strict Constructionists

The bad news came in recurrent spasms. On Friday, September 17, 1971, Justice Hugo Black sent word to the president that after thirty-four years of service on the U.S. Supreme Court, a tenure exceeded by only two other justices in the institution's history, his bad health had forced him to resign. Six days later Black's ailing colleague and close friend, Justice John Marshall Harlan, whose own career on the Court spanned sixteen years, submitted his resignation. A day after Harlan's resignation Black, eighty-five, died of inflammation of the arteries and a stroke. Harlan, suffering from bone cancer, died before the year's end.

Black had become an institution within an institution, developing an original constitutional philosophy that was resisted for two decades by the Court majority but finally won the day in the sixties. He was the intellectual architect of the Warren Court revolution, penning its famous *Gideon* decision and inspiring the majority's generous reading of the First Amendment freedoms and its gradual acceptance of his view that the states

were bound to honor the Bill of Rights because of their "incor-
poration" in the Fourteenth Amendment's due process clause.
His spectacular success, like that of the late Justice Louis D.
Brandeis, Harvard's Paul Freund has suggested, was due to the
irresistible combination of "brains, rectitude, singleness of purpose and time."

John Harlan could not have been more different from Black
in roots, philosophy and achievement. And yet, Black, the rural
populist from Alabama, and Harlan, the superbly polished
Wall Street lawyer, had many common talents and goals. Black
did not trust judges to work out their personal solutions to
constitutional problems, so he insisted on a literal reading of the
U.S. Constitution to limit the judge's role. Harlan was equally
apprehensive of judicial ambitions gone astray, but his solution
was to hold the judiciary to a narrow station in the political
system. Harlan patterned his philosophy along the lines of Felix
Frankfurter's judicial restraint. Yet, there was a distinct Harlan
style that clearly distinguished him from his mentor. Frankfurter was as much a judicial preacher as Black, always seeking
an audience, and converts among his colleagues. Harlan was
more deferential, less insistent than Frankfurter. He would
send a fastidiously reasoned memorandum to his brethren asking the same, hard Frankfurtarian questions, but calmly and
with utmost respect.

Black and Harlan opinions were imbued with a special wisdom that came with the authors' high intellect and unwavering
sense of the importance of the institution they served. Now the
two men who had stood for integrity of heart and mind, who
above all others on the Court seemed to assure the public that
the Court remained aloof from the torrents of the day's politics,
were gone. With the Fortas and Carswell affairs still fresh
memories and the president of the United States giving no
indication that his new appointments would be anything more
than politics as usual, the deaths of Black and Harlan could not
have been less timely.

The departure of the Court's two reigning giants naturally prompted editorial writers across the country to urge upon President Nixon successors with similar qualities. White House Press Secretary Ronald Ziegler was quick to reassure. After Black's resignation, Ziegler told the press that a search for "the most qualified man available" would begin immediately. But after Harlan added his resignation to Black's, Patrick J. Buchanan, special assistant to the President, gave a better hint of things to come. The two vacancies, Buchanan suggested, presented an "historic opportunity" for President Nixon to remake the Court in his own political image. With two more appointees to join Chief Justice Burger and Associate Justice Blackmun, he said, "the next Court will be known as the Nixon Court, not as the Burger Court or the Warren Court." And indeed, if the two new appointees proved as faithful to the president's conservative expectations as Burger and Blackmun had so far, the aide's observation would be a good deal more than political puff talk.

The first name to surface, a name mentioned in the same news stories that reported Black's resignation, was Congressman Richard Poff of Virginia. A ten-term congressman from Virginia's southwest panhandle, Poff had always been a favorite of President Nixon. He had served with distinction on the House Judiciary Committee and most recently had played a major role on the commission to revise the federal criminal code. He was young (47 years old) and he was a southerner, two attributes well known to be attractive to the president.

At the mention of his name for the Court, however, Poff ran into trouble. A coalition of civil rights and labor groups, the combination so instrumental in the defeats of the Haynsworth and Carswell nominations, bore in. Poff was branded as an intractable foe of integration, a man who had signed "southern manifestoes" in 1956, one deploring school desegregation and another opposing pending civil rights legislation. It was reported that the congressman had voted against every major civil rights bill to be introduced on the floor of the House of Representatives. The National Organization of Women joined the opposition, scoring Poff for his vote to weaken the proposed equal-rights-to-women amendment to the Constitution.

At the same time, the standing committee on the federal judiciary, the committee of the American Bar Association that passed on the president's Supreme Court nominees, had received Poff's name for investigation. Smarting from criticism of its judgments on Haynsworth and Carswell (the ABA rated both qualified) the committee determined to do a thorough job of investigation and set the highest standards in its history for qualification. Almost immediately, committee members were troubled by Poff's résumé. He did not have the intensive litigative experience that the committee was now demanding for all nominees, except well-known legal scholars. Poff's record showed only four years of the private practice of law, and that as a young attorney in a small rural office in Virginia. Before the committee had completed its investigation, its chairman, Lawrence E. Walsh of New York, phoned Deputy Attorney General Richard G. Kleindienst to tell him of the problem.

A pro-Poff countermovement began to form, joined, with some trepidation, by the liberal *New Republic*. The magazine took a close look at Poff and concluded that he deserved better than the stereotypical southern cast. "Mr. Poff has been a conservative on most issues, including civil rights," noted the *New Republic*. "But he is able and thoughtful and there are indications of depths." Poff's repudiation of his earlier segregationist position was remembered. "I can only say now that segregation is wrong today, it was wrong yesterday, segregation was never right. But it is one of the most lamentable frailties of mankind that when one's wrong is most grievous, his self-justification is most passionate." His civil libertarian positions were duly noted. He refused, for example, to vote for a House motion citing CBS President Dr. Frank Stanton for contempt of Congress for his refusal to hand over tapes of the network's controversial "The Selling of the Pentagon" program. Explaining his vote, Poff said: "The collision here is between the privilege of the press to edit for journalistic purposes and the privilege of the Congress to investigate for legislative purposes. The collision is between press freedom and press restraint . . . I will resolve the doubts in favor of the press. I will prefer the governed. I will choose freedom."

Despite the makings of a formidable public debate on Poff's qualifications, the controversy never really shifted into high gear. The candidate himself cut it short before the ABA had submitted its recommendation, before partisans pro and con could fully marshal their arguments and before the president even had a chance to make his preference official. On October 2, Poff abruptly withdrew his name from consideration to spare himself and his family further anguish. "It appears that the confirmation process would be protracted and controversial," he said.

Shortly after the Poff withdrawal, President Nixon joined U.S. Senator Robert Byrd for a visit to Byrd's home state of West Virginia. Rumors circulated that Byrd, the Senate whip, would be Mr. Nixon's next choice for the Supreme Court. It was soon pointed out that Byrd did not quite measure up to the personal and professional excellence of, say, a Hugo Black or a John Harlan. An organizer of the Ku Klux Klan in his youth, Byrd's record of opposition to civil rights legislation was long and consistent. What was more, Byrd had earned his law degree only in 1963 at American University night school. He had never passed a bar exam. It was unlikely that the American Bar Association committee that had been only lukewarm on the Poff candidacy would show any greater enthusiasm for Byrd, if his name were submitted. ABA committee chairman Walsh, sensing that the bar association's close advisory relationship with the Nixon administration on Court nominees was headed

for trouble, moved to avoid a crisis. He suggested an interview
with the president but received no positive response.

On Tuesday, October 12, President Nixon announced that he
would fill the two Supreme Court vacancies the next week. At
that time, no names had been given to the ABA committee for
investigation. Chairman Walsh called Deputy Attorney General Kleindienst to inquire about the president's plans. He was
told by Kleindienst to begin an intensive investigation of two
candidates, attorney Herschel H. Friday of Little Rock, Arkansas and Judge Mildred Lillie of the California Court of Appeals.
In addition, Kleindienst asked the ABA committee to review,
less intensively, the qualifications of four more candidates:
Senator Byrd, Judge Sylvia Bacon of the District of Columbia
Superior Court, and Judges Charles Clark and Paul Roney of
the U.S. Court of Appeals for the Fifth Circuit. Finally, Walsh
was told to have his committee report on the six candidates
ready in time for the president to send two nominations to the
Senate before Veterans Day, October 22. Walsh was worried
about two things. First, he told Kleindienst that it would be
difficult for the ABA to conduct a proper investigation, which
entailed the evaluation of hundreds of interviews across the
country, in the short time available. Second, Walsh warned that
the combination of a large list of names and short investigation
time would almost guarantee discovery by the media within
forty-eight hours. Kleindienst replied that the time pressure
could not be helped and that premature exposure of the candidates was a risk that the administration was willing to take.

Walsh was right. By the next day, enterprising reporters had
begun cross-country telephone marathons in quest of the names
of the six Court candidates. After calls to scores of lawyers,
judges and scholars throughout the country, the list of six was
public. Unknown to the press, the administration that same day
had instructed the ABA committee to concentrate its efforts
exclusively on Judge Lillie and Mr. Friday.

Before that fact was known, however, the list of six was studied by a bewildered public. Aside from political considerations (four were southerners, two were women), on what basis could Nixon have picked his candidates? Judge Mildred Lillie had gained a modest reputation as the presiding judge of Los Angeles' Domestic Relations Court before her appointment to the state court of appeals. One of her guidelines in moderating domestic disputes: if the wife cried on the witness stand, the marriage could be saved. Her written decisions on the court of appeals seemed no more impressive. Professor Laurence H. Tribe of the Harvard Law School, after reading all of her opinions, concluded that "her reasoning was grossly inadequate, her use of precedent was often misleading and disingenuous and her opinions show her to be well below the qualifications expected of a Supreme Court justice." While Judge Lillie was known as a proponent of law and order, her husband was suspected of being less vigilant in pursuit of the cause. He had been sued twenty two times by creditors in ten years.

President Nixon's other top Court prospect, Herschel Friday, was best known for his persistent defense of the Little Rock School Board's opposition to widespread desegregation. Friday, a bond lawyer and friend of Attorney General Mitchell, was not even the best candidate that the state of Arkansas had to offer, according to Little Rock's *Arkansas Gazette*. Though Friday was a competent attorney, the newspaper was not much impressed with the fact that "much of the legal labor of Herschel Friday over the last dozen years has turned to the purpose of keeping black children out of 'white schools.' " Friday had, in fact, appealed the Little Rock School Board's case more than a dozen times since 1957, which, some fellow lawyers suggested, may have gone beyond the call of duty to his client.

Sylvia Bacon was a thirty-nine-year-old Harvard Law School graduate who, as a Justice Department attorney, had helped draft the controversial D.C. crime bill with its no-knock and preventive detention provisions. The two southern judges,

Charles Clark and Paul Roney of the Fifth Circuit, claimed one
and a half years of judicial experience between them. Senator
Byrd had never even practiced law.

The *Washington Post* cited the six candidates as proof of
President Nixon's "relentless pursuit of mediocrity." One top
official of the American Bar Association reportedly pleaded
with Justice Department officials to add "some people of stature" to the list. Senator Edward M. Kennedy said that the
president had revealed himself "as a radical in the true sense of
the word, a man who seeks to undermine one of the basic and
vital institutions of our nation." Half of Harvard Law School's
seventy-member faculty signed a statement declaring that the
president's action "demeans the Court and risks undermining
public respect for it."

In the meantime, reports on hundreds of interviews on Judge
Lillie and Mr. Friday began to pile up at the Wall Street office
of ABA committee chairman Walsh. Reports from outside
California were of little help on Judge Lillie since almost no one
had heard of her outside her home state. Those who did know
her said Judge Lillie was a decent woman and a hard-working
judge. But time and again members of the California bar described Judge Lillie as "pedestrian." It was a depressingly familiar characterization. As one high-ranking ABA member
ruefully said, "The committee crossed that bridge with Judge
Carswell." Attorney Friday did not do much better. Although
many ABA members knew him (since Friday was a member of
the ABA Board of Governors), few could work up great enthusiasm for his candidacy. "Herschel Friday was not the kind of
guy you could be unpleasant about," said one active ABA
member, "but he just didn't have the distinction we were looking for after Carswell."

On Monday, October 18, Walsh phoned Attorney General
Mitchell to tell him that early indications from the committee's
discussion suggested that neither Judge Lillie nor Friday would

receive the ABA's highest rating. This meant that the committee would either report that it was "not opposed" to the candidates or that it found them "not qualified." In Judge Lillie's case, Walsh told Mitchell, it was likely that the committee would give the lowest rating—"not qualified." Very formally, the attorney general told the ABA chairman to continue deliberations.

After a Tuesday afternoon committee session, Walsh again telephoned the attorney general with still more depressing news. Although no vote had been taken, Walsh said, there was increasing likelihood that Friday as well as Judge Lillie would receive the committee's lowest rating—"not qualified." Mitchell still would not take the ABA off the Lillie and Friday cases. The attorney general did, however, ask Walsh if the committee would be able to issue a prompt report on Lewis F. Powell, Jr., a nationally known attorney from Virginia and a past president of the ABA. Walsh, who knew Powell well, said that he thought the committee could do that and strongly hinted that the Powell report, in all probability, would be highly favorable. Mitchell did not actually ask for the report on Powell. He told Walsh only to keep his committee in session Wednesday until it had sent a final report to the attorney general on Lillie and Friday.

Unknown to Walsh or any member of his committee, Mitchell telephoned Lewis Powell, Jr., that night to offer him one of the vacancies on the Supreme Court. Powell hesitated. At sixty-four, Powell considered himself too old to go on the Court. But that same night, President Nixon placed a call to Powell, personally urging him to accept a Court appointment. Powell asked for twenty-four hours to think it over.

The following day, Wednesday, October 20, the ABA committee convened for an all-day session, again to consider Judge Lillie and Friday, the only candidates, as far as the committee officially knew, that the Nixon administration was seriously considering. The meeting ended at 5 P.M. Walsh reported the committee's conclusions to Mitchell. Judge Lillie was found "not qualified" by eleven committee members, "not opposed" by the twelfth. Friday was found "not qualified" by six committee members, while six others were "not opposed." Since it was the committee's practice to require at least eight votes to report a candidate out other than "not qualified," Walsh held the committee in session to prepare their reports and to see if two members who had voted "not qualified" might shift their votes to "not opposed." The committee resumed discussions on candidate Friday but there were no vote changes.

The *Washington Post* learned of the ABA committee vote on Judge Lillie and Friday on Wednesday evening; the *Post's* Thursday edition carried the story. Tension heightened. In view of the American Bar Association's resounding slap at the administration's prime candidates, Lillie and Friday, would the president risk another public controversy? Or would the president try to get a more favorable rating for two of the other names on the list he sent to the ABA? Finally, would the administration junk its original list and select two fresh candidates? If so, could the president possibly meet his self-imposed deadline of sending his nominations to the Senate before Veterans Day? At noon Thursday, the White House assured the nation that it would know the answers shortly; the president would make a nationally televised announcement on his Supreme Court nominations at 7:30 that night.

Lawrence Walsh of the American Bar Association was particularly curious about the content of the President's announcement. Would the president, Walsh wondered, nominate Lillie and Friday despite his committee's negative ratings or would he simply ignore the ABA altogether and pick two other candidates? In either case, Walsh's ABA committee would not look good. It would either be overruled or ignored. Walsh placed a call to Attorney General Mitchell Thursday afternoon to inquire about the president's intentions. He was told that Mitch-

ell would call him in New York at 5 P.M. Five o'clock passed
with no word from the attorney general. Walsh again called
Mitchell at 6:00 but did not get through to him until 7:20, just
ten minutes before the president was due to speak to the nation.

Mitchell told Walsh that the president would announce
shortly that he would send the names of Lewis Powell, Jr. (who
had accepted Nixon's offer Wednesday night) and Assistant
Attorney General William Rehnquist to the Senate as his nominations for the two Supreme Court vacancies. Mitchell anticipated a positive response from Walsh. He knew, of course,
that Walsh's committee did not approve of Lillie and Friday
and that Walsh, personally, had been enthusiastic about Powell. Investigation would prove that Rehnquist was no mediocrity either.

After the attorney general had told Walsh of the president's
choices, he read a letter addressed to Walsh and ABA President
Leon Jaworski that he would release to the press after the
president's telecast. In the letter, Mitchell briefly reviewed the
role that he had asked Walsh's committee to play in passing on
candidates whom the attorney general would recommend to the
president for Court appointment. Mitchell admitted that both
he and Walsh had been concerned from the outset about the
possibility of premature public disclosure of the choices. "The
events of the past week have made it clear that our concern was
well founded, and I can only conclude that there is no practical
way to avoid unauthorized disclosure of the names submitted
and the advice of your Committee with respect thereto despite
the best efforts of the Committee." Noting that such leaks could
unfairly abuse the candidates' reputations, Mitchell "concluded
that the only fair and proper course is to resume the long-
standing practice of submitting the attorney general's recommendations directly to the president." The ABA had been
ousted from deliberations on Supreme Court nominees.

A high-ranking Justice Department official later suggested

that the sin had not been unavoidable leaks of the ABA's lists but the administration's displeasure with the ABA grading system. The complaint was that the ABA was not rating the administration's candidates on absolute professional standards but comparing their qualifications to other potential candidates. Since Mitchell and the president had bypassed the committee in offering a Court appointment to Powell a day before it had voted on Lillie and Friday (the vote that had been leaked to the press), it seemed that the Nixon administration's gripe was indeed with the ABA committee's conclusions, not its process. High ABA officials have suggested that it was, in fact, the Nixon administration, not the ABA, that leaked the results of the committee's vote, the first such leak in 472 ABA judicial investigations. "It seemed to me," said one ABA committee member, "that the administration had used the leak to divert attention from its own blunder."

Richard Nixon began work on his television speech in Thursday's early morning hours, even before his appointments were a settled question. He taped a draft of his speech and gave it to his valet, Manolo Sanchez, to be delivered to the president's secretary, Rose Mary Woods, for typing. She was instructed to type one copy and return it to the president. The drama that the president so relished began to build throughout Thursday. His secret was so well kept that he had reporters guessing up to air time. In fact, the Associated Press was guessing, wrong as it turned out, only nine minutes before the president's scheduled address when it put on its wires that Nixon's choices were Rehnquist and Judge Arlin Adams of the U.S. Court of Appeals for the Third Circuit. The president, never one to pass up the opportunity for controlled theatre, later said that "I didn't know until the last minute which way I would go."

The speech itself was a masterpiece of calculated suspense. The president first assured his audience that appointments to the Supreme Court were the most important that a president made during his term of office. The White House had received thousands of letters from Americans across the country who wanted to help their president make his choices. Nixon said that many had suggested he appoint a member of Congress, others a woman and still more that the president appoint representatives of religious, racial and nationality groups not then represented on the Court. Nixon then began to build toward the climax of his address.

He would insist on two standards for his nominees. The first would be that his nominees be among the best lawyers in the nation (a new Nixon standard, since the president had previously said he wanted all of his nominees to have judicial experience). Secondly, Nixon said that his appointments to the Supreme Court, an institution which he sportily characterized as "the fastest track in the nation," would be judicial conservatives. A judicial conservative, Nixon explained, would "not twist or bend the Constitution in order to perpetuate his personal, political and social values."

And then, with a methodical cadence, Nixon returned to his familiar political theme: "I believe some Court decisions have gone too far in the past in weakening the peace forces as against the criminal forces in our society . . . I believe the peace forces must not be denied the legal tools they need to protect the innocent from criminal elements . . . I believe we can strengthen the hand of the peace forces without compromising our precious principle that the rights of individuals accused of crimes must always be protected." Ironically, the president had contradicted himself in a matter of a few short paragraphs. A judicial (as opposed to "political") conservative, as the president suggested he was, would not talk in law and order terms, for nothing could be a more obvious imposition of "personal, political and social" values.

By the time the president had finished with the familiar

political litany, liberals were preparing for the worst. They needn't have. The president's two nominees, Lewis Powell, Jr. and William Rehnquist, had impeccable professional qualifications. Both had graduated first in their law school classes, Powell from Washington and Lee, Rehnquist from Stanford. And both earned distinguished reputations in their chosen profession. Powell was a member of Virginia's largest and most prestigious law firm as well as a past president of the ABA, the American College of Trial Lawyers and the American Bar Foundation. Rehnquist was among the select few top law school graduates to be awarded a Supreme Court clerkship (for Justice Robert Jackson). He later became a respected and highly successful lawyer in Phoenix before Nixon appointed him assistant attorney general of the United States.

The president concluded his television speech with a call for reverence for the Supreme Court. The man who had made criticism of the Warren Court a key campaign issue in 1968 said that he had "noted with great distress a growing tendency in the country to criticize the Supreme Court as an institution." The man who as the Republican standard bearer for the presidency had attacked the Supreme Court's *Miranda* and *Escobedo* decisions by name told his television audience that even if one disagrees with Court decisions, "it is our obligation to obey the law whether we like it or not." And the president who that night would call on all Americans to respect the integrity of the Supreme Court would, the following day, remind the public that politics was never far from his mind when thinking of Supreme Court appointments. Nixon told the National Federation of Republican Women that Judge Mildred Lillie should have received a "better break" from the ABA and went on to predict that "there will be a woman on the Court in time." To the Nixon critics' suggestion that the president's Court appointments should be above politics, Attorney General Richard G. Kleindienst has answered: "Under our constitutional form of government, the Supreme Court is the highest political appointment the president can make."

After Richard Nixon's victory at the polls in 1968, Attorney General-designate John Mitchell and his newly appointed Deputy Attorney General Richard Kleindienst began interviews at New York City's Pierre Hotel to fill the top positions of their new Justice Department staff. One of the appointments to be made was that of assistant attorney general, Office of Legal Counsel, whose primary job it would be to draft position papers on the legality of the administration's actions. Since he would be the president's lawyer, the assistant attorney general was expected to find legal support for actions that his client wanted to take. It was an intellectually demanding job and also one that required a high degree of political loyalty to the administration. Kleindienst recommended for the job a friend, lawyer and fellow Arizona Goldwater Republican, William Rehnquist. But Mitchell was not immediately enthusiastic about appointing two men from Arizona to such important jobs in the Justice Department. Kleindienst persisted. With every new name that Mitchell brought up for consideration, his deputy attorney general would again mention Rehnquist and compare the two. Rehnquist's credentials remained superior and ultimately Mitchell agreed to his appointment.

Rehnquist collected four degrees in five years. At Stanford, he won a Phi Beta Kappa key as an undergraduate, earning his B.A. in 1948, a master's in political science in 1949 and his law degree (first in his class and editor of the law review) in 1952. He also received a master's in government from Harvard in 1950. At law school Rehnquist was one of those students whom teachers usually either love or hate. Supremely confident in his own intellectual abilities, Rehnquist persistently demanded the highest intellectual standards from his superiors. He would challenge the positions of his instructors, with probing, precisely formulated queries. One of his law school teachers, John B. Hurlbut, recalled the bristling classroom give-and-take between Rehnquist and himself in which "he tested my stature and sharpened my thinking as an instructor many times."

After law school Rehnquist was selected by Justice Robert Jackson for the much coveted Supreme Court clerkship. Fellow clerks remember Rehnquist as a young man of extraordinarily independent mind. In those days as now, most of the law clerks tended to be of liberal political persuasion, but Rehnquist, who already possessed a highly developed conservative philosophy, refused to buckle under the pressure. He argued with them then and continued the debate years after he had completed his clerkship. "Some of the tenets of the 'liberal' point of view which commanded the sympathy of a majority of the clerks I knew," Rehnquist wrote in 1957, "were extreme solicitude for the claims of Communists and other criminal defendants, expansion of federal power at the expense of state power, great sympathy toward any government regulation of business—in short, the political philosophy now espoused by the Court under Chief Justice Earl Warren."

Rehnquist settled down to practice law in Phoenix—a city, he later said, which attracted people who believed in free enterprise "and by that I mean not just free enterprise in the sense of the right to make a buck but the right to manage your own affairs as free as possible from the interference of government." He was strangely nonaggrandizing for a man of such free enterprise beliefs. Attorney General Kleindienst recalled that members of the city's bar routinely referred cases to Rehnquist not only because he was a highly competent attorney but also because they knew he would not try to win the client away permanently. And although Rehnquist had opportunities to join larger firms (and make more money), he preferred small partnerships. His pleasures centered on his wife and three children: camping, songfests, lively dinner table conversations and the hope, someday, to retire to an apple orchard that he had purchased in the Rockies.

Quiet and unassuming in his private life, Rehnquist was outspoken and assertive in the public forum. He did not like the trend of the Warren Court's rulings and said so in a 1958 article in the *American Bar Association Journal* shortly after the Court had issued its series of rulings upholding the civil liberties of many Americans, including some Communists. "A decision of any court based on a combination of charity and ideological sympathy at the expense of generally applicable rules of law is regrettable no matter whence it comes," wrote Rehnquist, "but what could be tolerated as a warmhearted aberration in a local trial judge becomes nothing less than a constitutional transgression when enunciated by the highest court of the land."

By 1964 Rehnquist had become an active member of the Young Republicans and, with Kleindienst and others, succeeded in leading the organization into the Goldwater fold. At the same time he was attentive to local political issues. Rehnquist alone among Phoenix residents appeared before the city council to challenge a proposed public accommodations measure that would have barred segregated facilities in public places. "I would like to speak in opposition to the proposed ordinance," said Rehnquist, "because I believe that the values that it sacrifices are greater than the values which it gives. I take it that we are no less the land of the free than we are the land of the equal. . . . There have been zoning ordinances and that sort of thing but I venture to say that there has never been this sort of an assault on the institution [of private property] where you are told, not what you can build on your property, but who can come on your property."

Despite Rehnquist's plea, the public accommodations ordinance easily passed into law. Still, Rehnquist determinedly pressed his argument in a letter to the *Arizona Republic* newspaper. "The ordinance summarily does away with the historic right of the owner of a drugstore, lunch counter or theater to choose his own customers. By a wave of the legislative wand, hitherto private businesses are made public facilities which are open to all persons regardless of the owner's wishes. . . . Unable to correct the source of the indignity to the Negro, it [the ordinance] redresses the situation by placing a separate indignity on the proprietor. It is as barren of accomplishment in what it gives to the Negro as in what it takes from the proprietor. . . . It is, I believe, impossible to justify the sacrifice of even a portion of our historic individual freedom for a purpose such as this."

Three years later Rehnquist was at it again, taking what was an unpopular position against government-imposed desegregation. This time his target was Phoenix's superintendent of schools, who had declared that we "are and must be concerned with achieving an integrated society" and had proposed an ambitious program for the Phoenix public high schools to achieve that objective. Rehnquist retorted: "We are no more dedicated to an 'integrated' society than we are to a 'segregated' society . . . we are instead dedicated to a free society, in which each man is equal before the law, but in which each man is accorded a maximum amount of freedom of choice in his individual activities. . . . The schools' job is to educate children. They should not be saddled with a task of fostering social change which may well lessen their ability to perform their primary job."

In stating his positions, Rehnquist was never equivocal, never evasive. His forthrightness had impressed his teachers and fellow law clerks, some of whom spoke of his courage in the face of strong opposition. But as his philosophical positions spilled over into sensitive political areas, like race relations, his uncompromising views were not admired as courageous so much as criticized as bull-headed or, worse, bigoted. Those working for civil rights causes sometimes interpreted Rehn-

quist's rigid philosophical conservatism as outright racial prejudice. It was a false and unfortunate interpretation but one that
Rehnquist did little to discourage.

When he went to work in John Mitchell's Justice Department, Rehnquist took what could best be termed as an "activist" view of his duties as assistant attorney general. It was
Rehnquist's opinion that he was not hired simply for his legal
competence as an attorney but, just as importantly, because
John Mitchell recognized that he was politically and philosophically attuned to the goals of the Nixon administration. In terms
of his Justice Department work, Rehnquist suggested that his
tasks might be different from those of his predecessor under
Attorney General Ramsey Clark. Rehnquist characterized
Clark as "an outspoken advocate of the civil liberties of the
individual and the rights of the criminal defendant." In contrast, said Rehnquist, John Mitchell "chooses to place more
emphasis on the right of society to apprehend and punish those
guilty of crime." That new emphasis on law and order at the
Justice Department suited the new assistant attorney general
just fine.

Rehnquist was the administration's chief advocate for the
tough District of Columbia crime bill, and a very effective one
at that. In supporting the bill's pretrial detention provision,
Rehnquist acknowledged the citizen's right to freedom from
unwarranted official detention. "But another aspect of this notion of freedom" said Rehnquist, "is surely the right to be free
from robberies, rapes and other assaults." When critics of pretrial detention insisted that at the very least the government
which detains a suspect in jail before trial must assure him a
speedy trial, Rehnquist was ready with counterproposals. If the
defendant was to benefit from an accelerated trial schedule,
Rehnquist suggested, then other measures to help law enforcement officials ought to be considered as well. The possibilities,

for Rehnquist, included support for a nonunanimous jury verdict and a sharp curtailing of federal court intervention in state criminal trials where prisoners claimed their constitutional rights had been violated. "A system of criminal justice which insists that defendants be brought to trial within a mandatory time limit of, for example, sixty days," Rehnquist asserted, "but then permits a convicted defendant to spend the next ten or twenty years litigating the validity of the procedures used in his trial, is a contradiction in terms."

Assistant Attorney General Rehnquist took special aim at some of the Warren Court's most sweeping criminal law decisions. He questioned those decisions that prohibited the introduction at trial of evidence seized without a search warrant, confessions given without the *Miranda* warnings and suspect identifications made in line-ups without the presence of a lawyer. Rehnquist spoke admiringly of the early English common law, where the sole purpose of the criminal trial was to determine guilt or innocence. Peripheral issues, such as whether the evidence was legally or illegally obtained, were decided at other proceedings. Rehnquist maintained that recent Supreme Court decisions had been so confusing as to what should be excluded from trials and what should not that police officers could be breaking the constitutional law without really knowing it. The judgments demanded of police officers were so difficult, said Rehnquist, that it might be better—if the question were to come up for original decision—to follow the English practice in which the severity of the crime was considered when deciding whether evidence should be excluded. The assistant attorney general suggested a possible solution to at least one of the problems posed: overrule the *Miranda* decision.

Rehnquist again risked the wrath of civil libertarians in his strong defense of the Justice Department's surveillance policies. He clashed publicly with U.S. Senator Sam Ervin during Ervin's subcommittee hearings investigating government methods for collecting data on private citizens. Faced with heated criticism of the administration's surveillance network, Rehnquist asserted that "the First Amendment does not prohibit even foolish or unauthorized information gathering by the government." If that wasn't enough to raise the massive eyebrows of the senior senator from North Carolina, Rehnquist calmly told Ervin that if the government wished to snoop on any American citizen, including the senator, it could do so without fear of constitutional violation. Rehnquist was not saying that widespread surveillance was laudable or even necessary in all instances; he was only making the point, as the government's chief constitutional law advocate, that nothing in the Constitution prevented it.

Reckless behavior by government officials did not bother Rehnquist nearly so much as reckless conduct by private citizens. Civil disobedience, even if it was nonviolent, could not be tolerated if it interfered with government operations, Rehnquist maintained. When District of Columbia police arrested thousands of May Day demonstrators in 1971 and held most of them in compounds for long hours without providing lawyers or the charges against them, the assistant attorney general defended the police action. The capital was in a state of qualified martial law, said Rehnquist, because the city was threatened with violence. Under those circumstances, Rehnquist contended, the police were justified in skipping over a few of the normal procedures that guaranteed the constitutional rights of the accused.

Rehnquist's advocacy was not confined to law and order causes. When the Carswell nomination was floundering, Rehnquist went to the attack against Carswell's detractors. In a letter to the *Washington Post,* which had published editorials bitterly critical of the nominee, Rehnquist charged that the *Post* was saying one thing (that Carswell was hostile to civil rights litigants) but meaning something very different (that Carswell did not share the *Post*'s editors' overall activist constitutional philosophy). "In fairness," Rehnquist concluded, "you ought to state all of the consequences that your position logically brings in its train: not merely further expansion of constitutional recognition of civil rights but further expansion of the constitutional rights of criminal defendants, of pornographers and of demonstrators. Such a declaration would make up in candor what it lacks in marketability."

After the president ordered American troops into Cambodia in 1970, Rehnquist again was by his commander-in-chief's side, amid growing public controversy over Nixon's action. In a debate with Dean Robert B. McKay of the New York University Law School over the constitutionality of the president's action, Rehnquist posed three questions: (1) could U.S. troops lawfully fight a foreign power without a congressional declaration of war? (2) did the president's constitutional powers give "him more than just a seat of honor in a reviewing stand?" (3) did the president's constitutional power as commander-in-chief, absent congressional authorization, cover Nixon's Cambodia action?

Rehnquist answered all three of his questions affirmatively, backing his positions with skillful historical and legal analysis. He asserted that U.S. presidents had made war numerous times without congressional declaration, beginning with hostilities with France in 1798 and including President Polk's ordering of American soldiers to the Mexican border to protect U.S. annexation of Texas and President Truman's decision to send U.S. forces to Korea. None of the actions, Rehnquist maintained, had the firm congressional endorsement that Congress's Gulf of Tonkin resolution gave President Nixon. That resolution offered support for Nixon's Cambodia action, said Rehnquist, because it authorized the president "to take all necessary measures to repel any armed attack against forces of the United States and to prevent further aggression."

Before responding to Rehnquist's arguments, Dean McKay, a respected constitutional scholar, paid the assistant attorney general a high compliment. "I have of late often differed with our president," McKay began, "but I must agree with his conclusion that when the action is hot, the rhetoric must remain cool, and I express to you now my admiration for his deputy, Mr. Rehnquist, who has kept the rhetoric very cool indeed. I find to my pleasure that he and I read the same Constitution, in general even the same clauses. We read the same history, and in large part, we come up with the same interpretation."

Rehnquist was so highly regarded at the Justice Department that it was widely assumed that he would soon be awarded a federal judicial appointment and, if Republican political fortunes held up, eventually land on the Supreme Court. Weighing against a Rehnquist judicial appointment were his youth and his obvious value to the administration in the Justice Department. Still, the attorney general was keeping an eye open for federal judicial vacancies, and when it was rumored that Chief Judge David Bazelon of the U.S. Court of Appeals for the District of Columbia might retire in 1971, high officials at the Justice Department were considering Rehnquist as a replacement. But Bazelon did not resign.

The first official word that William Rehnquist received about a judicial appointment came shortly before the president announced his intention to nominate the assistant attorney general to the Supreme Court. Only a few days earlier, Rehnquist had dutifully defended Judge Mildred Lillie's judicial record and, when rumors later developed that he might be considered for the Court, Rehnquist neatly squelched the gossip and at the same time contributed a snippet of humor to an otherwise humorless week. You've got the wrong man, deadpanned Rehnquist. "I'm not a woman, I'm not a southerner and I'm not mediocre." When Attorney General Mitchell informed

Rehnquist that he was indeed the president's choice, the justice-designate was incredulous.

Once the initial feeling of relief wore off that Nixon had not nominated Judge Lillie or Herschel Friday, the president's critics realized that there might have been a great deal to be said in support of Senator Hruska's mediocrity. Rehnquist was what many libertarians had long feared: a smart conservative who, unlike a mediocrity, could possibly win other justices to his point of view.

Reaction to the Rehnquist appointment split predictably along philosophical lines. Those who had admired the work of the Warren Court and believed in the expansion of individual constitutional rights were appalled. John Frank, the former clerk to Justice Black, said that Rehnquist was "the intellectual heart of the right wing." The *New York Times* labeled the nominee a "radical rightist." Senator Barry Goldwater, on the other hand, said that Rehnquist "is unquestionably one of the most brilliant legal craftsmen in America."

At Rehnquist's confirmation hearings, the liberal members of the Senate Judiciary Committee, notably Senators Birch Bayh, Edward Kennedy and John V. Tunney, attacked his conservative positions. Rehnquist's views on government surveillance, wiretapping and preventive detention were closely questioned; his defense of the May Day arrests, the Cambodian invasion and the administration's antibusing stand criticized. Civil rights advocates accused him of being a segregationist and a member of the John Birch Society. When Rehnquist later responded to the Birch charge by signing an affadavit that "he is not now, nor has he at any time in the past, been a member of the John Birch Society," Joseph Rauh, Jr., attorney for the Leadership Conference on Civil Rights, demanded more. "That affadavit is the weakest denial I have ever heard. It says he wasn't a member. What about all the relationships that are possible short of that? I am absolutely flabbergasted that a man who is trying to get on the Supreme Court of the United States should send up an affadavit so limited in its denial of relationships." The attack smacked of a desperate era a generation past and caused Senator Kennedy to calm Rauh down. Rauh's suggestion, said Kennedy, was "completely unwarranted and completely uncalled for."

Throughout the two-day grilling, Rehnquist retained his composure. He strongly defended his law and order positions but never allowed his liberal adversaries to push him into untenable positions. He said, for example, that his defense of government surveillance had never gone further than the position taken by the Supreme Court. When he was asked if he could conceive of a situation where government surveillance might chill the First Amendment rights of private citizens, Rehnquist replied that such a situation was conceivable and should not be tolerated. He did not approve of criminal trials being won by defendants on technicalities but admitted that some illegal police practices, such as the unwarranted ransacking of Dolree Mapp's Cleveland apartment was more than a technicality. And he confessed error in opposing the public accommodations ordinance in 1964, attributing his new attitude, in part, to "having become acquainted with more members of minority groups" and having "come to appreciate the importance of the legal recognition of rights such as this." At the same time, the nominee refused to budge on his antibusing stand, contending that "transporting long distances is undesirable for whatever purpose."

The Senate Judiciary Committee liberals were never able to do the damage to Rehnquist that they did to Haynsworth and Carswell. But one of Rehnquist's toughest adversaries, Senator Bayh, remained convinced of the rightness of his attack long after Rehnquist had been confirmed by the Senate. "Philosophically, Rehnquist's feet are planted on ice as far as social justice is concerned," said Bayh. "It has nothing to do with ethics or intellect. Rehnquist uses his intellect to look at the facts from the wrong philosophical view. Law is an inexact science; a justice will always weigh values and Rehnquist will give more weight to the side of property than to people. I think Rehnquist is a G. Harrold Carswell with a magna cum laude. I hope he proves me wrong."

After Rehnquist's confirmation there was the usual hopeful talk among civil libertarians that men change once they go to the Supreme Court. In Rehnquist's case there was the particularly relevant precedent of Justice Jackson, who, as attorney general, held views on executive power very different from those he later expressed on the Court. As President Roosevelt's attorney general in 1941, Jackson had justified the president's seizure of a strike-bound aircraft plant, although FDR had no statutory authorization for his action. But in 1952, Justice Jackson voted with the Court majority that ruled that President Truman was wrong to have seized the nation's struck steel mills during the Korean conflict without congressional approval. Faced with his own earlier arguments as attorney general, Justice Jackson declared: "A judge cannot accept self-serving press statements of the attorney for one of the interested parties [in the aircraft plant seizure] as authority in answering a constitutional question, even if the advocate was himself . . . I should not bind present judicial judgment by earlier partisan advocacy."

Would Rehnquist cease to be an advocate for government causes on the Court? A high-ranking Justice Department official thought it was a possibility. Rehnquist, "though astoundingly conservative in his approach," said the official, was always able to reevaluate his positions. Professor Alexander Bickel of Yale, who clerked with Rehnquist at the Supreme Court, was less sure. According to Bickel, Rehnquist would more likely serve as the Court's resident conservative ideologue, a "man with a first-rate independent intellect who would keep the other justices' toes to the fire." Rehnquist may have given the best prognosis of his future Court behavior when he wrote in 1959: "It is high time that those critical of the present Court [the Warren Court] recognized with the late Charles Evans Hughes that for one hundred seventy-five years the Constitution has been what the judges say it is. If greater judicial restraint is desired, or a different interpretation of the phrase " 'due process of law' or 'equal protection of the laws,' then men sympathetic to such desires must sit upon the High Court."

Lewis Powell, Jr., had always ranked near the top of Attorney General Mitchell's list of Supreme Court candidates. In 1969 Powell was informed of that fact and politely sent word back to the administration that he would prefer to have his name removed from consideration. Powell gave as his main reason his age (then sixty-two) but his resistance had as much to do with professional preference as self-confessed obsolescence. Powell had always thought of himself as a lawyer and had never really aspired to anything else, including a judgeship. For a lifetime, Powell had found gamesmanship, whether in athletics or in the courtroom, exhilarating. As a lawyer, he had the freedom to compete on his terms, to say and do what he wanted to. As a judge, he would enjoy no such freedom. Besides, the practice of law had allowed Powell to achieve virtually everything a man in his profession could desire: professional success, a modest fortune and national prominence.

But the president of the United States has a talent for getting his way. So when President Nixon personally telephoned Powell on October 19, 1971, to ask him to reconsider his earlier decision, Powell wavered. Within twenty-four hours, he had told Nixon that he would accept the Court appointment. When confronted with his own and Powell's argument that men younger than sixty-four should sit on the Court, the president retorted: "Ten years of Powell is worth thirty years of anyone else."

Powell had long been an American history buff and could credit genealogy as much as standard textbooks for his love of the subject. The first Powell in America arrived in 1609 as one of the early Jamestown colonists. Another served as an officer in Washington's army during the American Revolution and, to this day, the Powells retain membership in the Society of Cincinnati, an organization open to descendants of officers of the Revolutionary War.

When the nation split, the Powells of Virginia naturally fought with the Confederacy. Powell's view of the Civil War has been influenced by loving memories of his maternal grandfather, who fought and lost an arm at Fredericksburg. But Powell's parents always taught the boy that the war had turned out best for both the South and the nation. Never parochial in his views, Powell supported a strong U.S. role in the world community. When Europe was being devastated by Hitler, for example, Powell urged U.S. involvement on the side of the Allies, long before Congress actually declared war.

Born in Suffolk, Virginia, in 1907, Powell's schooling was received at a fine southern university (Washington and Lee) as well as a "national" law school (Harvard). At Washington and Lee, Powell won top academic honors and, though his father urged him to take his law degree at Harvard, he chose to remain at his undergraduate alma mater. He graduated first in his class from Washington and Lee's law school, then belatedly took his father's advice, earning a master's degree in jurisprudence at the Harvard Law School. At Harvard, Powell studied under Roscoe Pound and Felix Frankfurter, whose philosophy of judicial restraint strongly influenced Powell's own notion of the proper role of the courts in the federal system.

As a child, Powell had known that he wanted to practice law

(his history books suggested that the nation's great policy-makers were either military men or lawyers). So, after graduation from Harvard, Powell pursued his life's ambition, joining Richmond's and the state of Virginia's most prestigious law firm. Individuals and corporations from other states who had legal problems in Virginia frequently sought the counsel of Powell or his associates. Powell, as a result, never had the sense of being a local or even a Virginia lawyer. His reputation as an outstanding, cosmopolitan attorney was, in large part, responsible for Powell's success as a leader of the national bar. He also served as director of more than a dozen corporations, including the New York-based Philip Morris, Inc.

Throughout his career, Powell blended political conservatism with conciliation to achieve leadership in the Richmond community as well as the bar. Typical was his position as chairman of the Richmond School Board from 1953 to 1961. His term came during a period of massive resistance to the Court's school desegregation mandate from many southern communities. Rather than obey the Court, many southern school districts closed their schools. Powell and the other four members of the school board vowed to keep the segregated Richmond public schools open despite demands from rabid segregationists to close them down. It seems now that Powell and his colleagues took a rather modest leadership position. But in those troubled times, moderation was not an enviable position. Powell was accused by irate segregationists of being suspiciously soft on segregation, even though Richmond's schools remained almost completely segregated throughout his term on the school board. Impatient civil rights advocates, on the other hand, did not wholly admire the Powell go-slow position either.

As president of the American Bar Association, Powell admitted that he was basically opposed to federal intervention in the legal profession. He specifically voiced reservations about the federal poverty program's plans for government attorneys to bring suits on behalf of the poor. But once it was clear to Powell that local bar associations could not adequately handle the legal problems of the poor and clearer still that the legal services program was going forward with or without ABA support, Powell put the prestige of his office behind the federal policy.

If there has been a single philosophical theme to Powell's generally pragmatic approach to society's problems, it is that all change must come within a carefully structured legal process. For Powell, there has never been an excuse for civil disobedience, though he has long regretted the abuses heaped upon American blacks. In speaking of that abuse, Powell admitted that "the entire legal process, from the police and sheriff to the citizens who serve on juries, has too often applied a double standard of justice." But he still refused to condone the civil rights sit-ins of the sixties or applaud the leadership of Martin Luther King, Jr. Powell, in fact, criticized both.

When Powell sensed threats to the rule of law, he sometimes abandoned his conciliatory stance. Always a vocal anti-Communist crusader, Powell returned from a visit to the Soviet Union in 1958 so concerned about Communism that he introduced a course in the Richmond schools teaching its dangers. With the rise of a new radicalism in the sixties, Powell tended to lump the New Left with the old left of the fifties. In defending the Nixon administration's policy of wiretapping suspected domestic subversives, familiar catch-phrases of a earlier day crept into the Powell vocabulary. The charge that the administration was suppressing civil liberties, said Powell, was "standard leftist propaganda." He blamed "the radical left, with wide support from the customary camp followers" with "propagandizing the case of the Berrigans." Powell saw an ominous leftist conspiracy bent on discrediting the administration: "The radical left, strongly led and with a growing base of support, is plotting violence and revolution. Its leaders visit and collaborate with foreign Communist enemies. Freedom," Powell warned, "can be lost as irrevocably from revolution as from foreign attack."

Powell's unbending devotion to the rule of law sometimes led him to unpredictable conclusions. At the height of the attack on the Warren Court in the early sixties, an attack often headed by members of the organized bar, Powell defended the liberal Court majority. He openly criticized the "Court of the Union" proposal made at the annual American Bar Association convention which, if passed into law, would have given the chief justices of the state supreme courts a final say on the constitutionality of the U.S. Supreme Court's decisions. The proposal, said Powell, was nothing more than an ill-conceived court-packing plan. "Many of the decisions of the Supreme Court which are criticized today," Powell said, "are likely, in the perspective of history, to be viewed as significant milestones in the ageless struggle to protect the individual from arbitrary or oppressive government." Those were strong words and all the more impressive because the man who wrote them had often taken issue with Warren Court decisions and had singled out its *Escobedo* and *Miranda* decisions for specific criticism.

Powell prepared for his Senate confirmation hearings with the care of a lawyer going to trial. One of his smartest decisions was to allow press interviews before he appeared in front of the Senate Judiciary Committee. Powell felt it was important that a private attorney nominated to the Court be known to the public. The interviews benefited Powell as much as the public, since the nominee could answer questions on his finances and racial views, sure to come up at the Senate hearings, without the harrassment of committee members or hostility of witnesses opposing his nomination. He admitted to newsmen that his financial holdings might pose some potential conflict of interest problems and pledged to do whatever was necessary to avoid those problems. He acknowledged membership in two segregated private clubs in Richmond but noted that he rarely attended the clubs and, when he did, it was only to play tennis. At the same time, Powell pointed out, he was a member of two other private clubs in New York City in which the membership was integrated. With those two potentially explosive issues of ethics and race out in the open and largely diffused, Powell's hearings promised to be considerably friendlier than those of the president's other nominees from the South, Haynsworth and Carswell, and indeed more so than those of his fellow nominee, William Rehnquist.

The hearings sometimes seemed less an interrogation than a competition among witnesses to outdo each other in complimenting Powell. Law deans and professors, bar association presidents and federal judges effusively praised the qualities of the nominee. Powell had "exceptional strength of intellect," said Dean Phil C. Neal of the University of Chicago Law School. He had devoted himself selflessly to civic causes, offered Bernard G. Segal, former president of the ABA. He possessed "wisdom and judgment," said Senior Judge J. Edward Lumbard of the U.S. Court of Appeals for the Second Circuit. Senator Bayh, chief nemesis of President Nixon's other southern nominees, recalled his work with Powell when the nominee was ABA president, saying "I have certainly felt that that experience has been a fine one for me." Powell received the highest rating of the staid ABA as well as the endorsement of the Virginia chapter of the NAACP.

Most impressive of all was a letter written by Urban Law Institute director, Jean Camper Cahn, a very bright black attorney who had worked with Powell on the legal services aspect of the poverty program. After noting Powell's key role in support of the program, Mrs. Cahn paid eloquent personal tribute to the Court nominee: "I am drawn inescapably to the sense that Lewis Powell is, above all, humane; that he has a capacity to empathize, to respond to the plight of a single human being to a degree that transcends ideologies of fixed positions. And it is that ultimate capacity to respond with humanity to individualized instances of injustice and hurt that is the best and only guarantee I would take that his conscience and his very soul will wrestle with every case until he can live in peace with a decision that embodies a sense of decency and fair play and common sense."

With testimonials accumulating by the dozens, the hearings were little more than a cakewalk for Powell. To be sure, the liberal members of the Senate Judiciary Committee (Bayh, Kennedy and Tunney, particularly) asked all the right questions. Did Powell strongly believe in the Bill of Rights? Was there a reasonable limit to the government's power in sensitive areas of individual liberty such as wiretapping? Should not government be prevented from "chilling" the First Amendment freedom of speech of citizens who disagreed with administration policy? But, somehow, the senators asked the questions, seeming to know that Powell would answer them properly.

Why had he criticized the Warren Court's *Escobedo* and *Miranda* decisions as a member of the President's Commission on Crime? Powell recalled riding with police in Richmond as part of his Commission investigation. "It is pretty awkward, really," Powell told the committee, "when you are on the scene and a crime has been committed and you have one suspect or one fellow who you know was involved and not to be able to interrogate him to try to put your hands on who his confederates were." There was no posturing on Powell's part, no tough law and order phrases. It just seemed to the nominee at the time of those Warren Court decisions that, in addition to making the policeman's legitimate work more difficult, the loss of confessions (and guilty pleas in court) would further burden already overcrowded courts. Having given his reasons of opposition,

Powell then offered two moderating points. He had heard about studies (but not yet read them) that showed that his greatest fears of the consequences of the Court's confession decisions were unfounded. He also emphasized that his main disagreement with the *Escobedo* decision was not the specific ruling (that the suspect was denied his constitutional rights because he was *prevented* from seeing his lawyer before interrogation) but its broad scope (that police must *guarantee* that a lawyer is available to every suspect before interrogation).

As anticipated, committee members questioned Powell on his uncharacteristically shrill remarks about radicals on the left and the government's need for wiretapping. The nominee first admitted that he had made a mistake in expressing his views in a newspaper article in which, he said, he could not deal with the nuances of the issues presented. He then proceeded to shade the broad black and white statements of the article, beginning with his views on wiretapping. The issue was a close one, Powell said, with legitimate arguments on both sides. "You should have no concern about my opposing indiscriminate use of wiretapping," Powell assured the committee. "I remember very well Mr. Justice Holmes's shorthand way of disposing of it. He said: 'Wiretapping is dirty business.' Of course, it is dirty business. The public interest, on the other hand, is to try to protect the innocent people from business that is equally dirty and in many instances dirtier."

In support of the mass arrests in Washington on May Day, Powell had written that "the alternative to making mass arrests was to surrender the government to insurrectionaries." Three months later at his confirmation hearings, Powell weighed his words more carefully: "I think the public authorities had a responsibility to keep the bridges and streets open. I think they had a responsibility to accomplish that with a minimum of force. I think they had a responsibility to try to accomplish it without injury to or arrest of innocent people."

Powell confirmed his reputation as a proceduralist, a man with a steady faith that justice would be done so long as the legal process itself functioned within well-defined rules. Asked about the role of the Supreme Court, Powell summarized his views in a six-point outline. Five of the six points defined procedural limits on the Court's authority: respect for the prerogatives of the executive and legislative branches; respect for the states; judicial restraint meaning, in most cases, "avoiding a decision on constitutional grounds where other grounds are available"; respect for precedent; avoidance of imposing political and economic views on a judgment. Only on the last point did Powell mention a positive substantive duty of the Court: to protect the individual liberties guaranteed in the Bill of Rights and the Fourteenth Amendment.

Despite hearing Powell's essentially conservative views, his more liberal interrogators appeared satisfied with the single day's work. They had asked the high, hard ones, the questions that would have given men of less substance than Lewis Powell, Jr., some very bad moments. The nominee had responded with candor and high intelligence. Powell was no less satisfied than the committee. Before leaving the committee room, Powell thanked the senators "for this very generous opportunity to appear before you." Powell found the discussion "stimulating," the questions "relevant and fair," the entire proceeding "a great pleasure and privilege." The fifteen-member committee unanimously recommended Powell's nomination to the Supreme Court. The Senate followed the committee's recommendation, voting Powell's confirmation by an 89 to 1 vote. About the only high-ranking government official who did not respond euphorically to the Powell nomination was a member of the Justice Department who had backed both Judge Lillie and Herschel Friday and, in any case, thought Rehnquist would be a far superior justice to Powell. "I just don't buy the 'great man' theory," he said.

After President Nixon's latest Court nominees, Rehnquist and Powell, were confirmed by the Senate, the "Nixon Court" label suddenly became more than the hopeful forecast of a White House aide or a derisive put-down by the president's critics. The Nixon Court was, indeed, very close to a numerical reality since the President had the extraordinary political fortune of being able to appoint four members to the Court in his first three years in office. If his latest two appointees approached the conservative voting records of Chief Justice Burger and Associate Justice Blackmun, then there would surely be an effective and highly visible Nixon bloc on the Court.

Although some anxious conservatives would not be satisfied until the president had made that fifth and decisive appointment to the Court, many careful observers of the Court's folkways assumed that the president had already effectively accomplished his task. The reason was that, in addition to the four Nixon appointees, two holdovers from the Warren Court, White and Stewart, had often dissented from the most sweeping libertarian rulings of the old majority. Although neither could be counted on to vote the "conservative" line as consistently as Burger or Blackmun or, undoubtedly, Justice-designate Rehnquist, both White and Stewart were known as cautious jurists, men who were never comfortable with a judicial sermon or edict. If either White or Stewart decided to go back on a Warren Court trend or, more likely, not to carry one forward, the vote would make the Nixon Court majority.

Precisely how the justices would arrange themselves on the intricate constitutional issues that would pass to the Court for judgment was open to the most uncertain speculation. Some libertarians feared that the effect of the new Court appointees would be no less than that of a new Republican administration taking over from a Democratic one in the executive branch. A thorough housecleaning would take place with all the old dogma from the Warren Court era thrown into the trash basket.

Others pointed out that the judgment was too rash, that in fact the Court had been moving more cautiously for several years and that Justice Black, at least on many questions of criminal law, had moved with the changing public tide. There was general agreement, nonetheless, that the new Court would have faint resemblance to the activist Warren Court of old.

CHAPTER TEN

Law and Order Mood

In the early months of 1972, millions of voters across the country received a letter from Maurice H. Stans, chairman of the Finance Committee for the Reelection of the President, suggesting several important reasons why they should contribute to the Nixon reelection campaign. First, said Stans, the president had made good on his promise to withdraw U.S. troops from Vietnam and to "set us on the path to peace" in Southeast Asia. Second only to the Nixon Vietnam policy, Stans listed the president's role in bringing back "law and order to America." The courts, wrote Stans, "are once more concerned about the rights of law-abiding citizens as well as accused law breakers." Singled out for special attention were the four Nixon appointees to the Supreme Court—Chief Justice Burger, Justices Blackmun, Powell and Rehnquist—"who can be expected to give a strict interpretation of the Constitution, and protect the interests of the average law-abiding American." In a similar letter of solicitation a few months later, Stans maintained that the four Nixon appointees "have shifted the balance away from protection of the criminal to the protection of law-abiding citizens."

Describing judicial decisions in purely political terms is always hazardous. But Stans did have a legitimate point. The four Nixon appointees had usually taken the prosecutor's position in criminal cases and their votes in all areas, remarkably cohesive, had "shifted the balance" on the Court. Of the 70 cases in which all nine justices participated during the 1972 term, the Nixon appointees voted together in 53. Moreover, they joined in one opinion in 45 of those 53 decisions.

Time and again, the Nixon bloc demonstrated its willingness to rule with the police and prosecutor in criminal cases. The corollary, of course, was that the conservative justices were less generous in interpreting the constitutional rights of the accused. By the end of the term, one could almost posit an algebraic equation to explain the Court's performance in the criminal field: $4N$ (four Nixon appointees) $+ X$ (the unknown being either Justices White or Stewart) $= LAO$ (law and order or, in other words, decisions that favor the police or prosecutor rather than the criminal suspect).

The three Warren Court liberal holdovers, Douglas, Brennan and Marshall, fought the conservative trend with diminishing success. The split decisions were matched, according to widespread rumors, by behind-the-scenes divisions as well. Justice Douglas was said to have been so infuriated by what he considered Chief Justice Burger's highhandedness—Burger reportedly had assigned an important majority opinion although he had not voted with the winning side—that he threatened publicly to expose the chief's conduct. For his part, Burger complained that it was extremely difficult to get through the Court's overloaded calendar when "one of the brethren packs up and leaves town early and then tries to conduct his business back and forth across four thousand miles or however far it is out there." The chief justice did not mention any names, but the only justice to leave the nation's capital before the end of the Court term was Douglas, who for years had mailed the final edits of his opinions from his vacation retreat in Gooseprairie, Washington.

On rare occasions, Burger and his fellow Nixon appointees crossed philosophical lines to join Douglas and his liberal colleagues. All nine members of the Burger Court voted, for example, to extend the Warren Court's famous *Gideon* decision. The *Gideon* decision had been limited to guaranteeing poor defendants a lawyer in serious criminal cases. The Burger Court was asked to do more after Jon Richard Argersinger was convicted of carrying a concealed weapon and sentenced to three months in the Leon County, Florida, jail and a $500 fine. Argersinger was poor, like Gideon, and was not represented by a lawyer. But unlike Gideon, Argersinger's offense was a misdemeanor; he did not come under the Warren Court's constitutional umbrella. In a sweeping ruling, the kind familiar during the Warren Court era, the Burger Court held in *Argersinger* v. *Hamlin* that no person could be jailed for a petty offense, unless he had been furnished free legal counsel or waived that right.

When the *Gideon* ruling was announced in 1963, many lawyers fretted that the Court's mandate would simply overwhelm the legal profession and the courts. Where would lawyers be found to represent the 350,000 felony defendants every year? And even if bar associations could supply the lawyers, could the courts possibly cope with the sure-to-increase caseloads of contested suits? If the legal profession was upset by *Gideon*, it was likely to be apoplectic over *Argersinger*. Compared to the 350,-000 potential law suits under *Gideon*, *Argersinger* would affect defendants charged with an estimated four to five million petty offenses annually who could now demand a lawyer. The extraordinary new responsibilities placed on the legal profession worried Justices Powell and Rehnquist, who recorded their

pessimistic views in a concurring Court opinion. But Chief
Justice Burger assured his colleagues and the bar that "the
dynamics of the profession have a way of rising to the burdens
placed on it."

On close analysis, it was not all that surprising that the Nixon
appointees agreed to extend the *Gideon* ruling. For one thing,
right to counsel for the poor as well as the rich was such an
elemental concept of justice that there was very little room for
debate. For that reason, the Warren Court's ruling was one of
its most popular among lawyers and laymen alike. Just as important as the concept of justice embodied in *Gideon,* particularly to the pragmatists on the Burger Court, was the fact that
the legal profession soon found that it could meet the new
demands of *Gideon.* In a word, *Gideon* worked. And so, said
the Burger Court, could *Argersinger.*

The frequently polarized Burger Court also held together
long enough to rule on a legal issue that had gone unresolved
through six presidential administrations: could the Justice Department listen in on conversations of suspected subversives
without first obtaining a court warrant? Presidents, beginning
with Franklin Roosevelt, were not so curious about the answer
as to risk a confrontation with civil libertarians in open court.
Instead, they simply carried out the policy on the sly. In 1940,
FDR secretly instructed his attorney general, Robert Jackson,
to wiretap suspected Nazi agents without asking a court's permission. By 1946 the Justice Department had expanded its
warrantless wiretapping operations to include suspected
domestic subversives and major underworld figures.

In 1967 the Warren Court began to curb the Justice Department's unsupervised snooping policy, holding that wiretapping
must not violate the Fourth Amendment's prohibition against
unreasonable searches. Congress responded the next year by
making wiretapping legal so long as law enforcement officials
had first obtained a court warrant. Still, neither the Court nor

Congress had made clear whether warrantless wiretapping in national security cases, where the secrecy of government operations had special value, was unreasonable. Attorney General Mitchell then decided to test his claim that the Justice Department did not need a judge's permission to listen in on conversations of domestic radicals.

Mitchell's opportunity came after Lawrence Robert ("Pun") Plamondon and two other members of the leftist White Panthers organization were charged with conspiracy to destroy offices of the Central Intelligence Agency in Ann Arbor, Michigan, in 1968. The Justice Department admitted that it had conducted warrantless wiretaps but said that in such cases involving alleged domestic subversives a warrant was not necessary. The government first argued that the President's "inherent" constitutional authority to protect the nation entitled the executive branch to wiretap without judicial approval in national security cases. Later, the Justice Department modified its claim to say that its wiretapping in such security cases was reasonable and, therefore, not a violation of the Fourth Amendment.

Before the Court heard arguments in the wiretapping case, Justices Black and Harlan resigned, giving President Nixon his third and fourth "law and order" justices. Ironically, the president's chances of obtaining a favorable ruling on the wiretapping issue appeared to diminish. The primary reason was that Justice Rehnquist, who had worked on the Justice Department brief in the case, would have to disqualify himself. That left the Nixon administration with one less certain vote (Black did not consider government wiretapping a violation of the Fourth Amendment; Harlan's judicial restraint was well known.) Justice Powell, however, seemed firmly in the administration's corner. Only a few months before going on the Court, Powell had written an article that supported government wiretapping, calling the furor over Justice Department wiretapping "a tempest in a teapot" and contending that only bona fide criminals had anything to fear from the Nixon administration's policies.

On June 19, 1972, the Court stunned the entire legal community, civil libertarians and law and order advocates alike, with its decision in the White Panther case. By a unanimous 8–0 vote (Justice Rehnquist did not take part), the Court declared unconstitutional the government's practice of wiretapping in domestic subversive cases without a warrant. The Court carefully avoided judgment in foreign espionage cases and, further, virtually invited Congress to set standards in the wiretapping field. Despite those familiar markings of a conservative Court, Justice Powell's opinion underscored the value of civil liberties in a free society: "History abundantly documents the tendency of government—however benevolent and benign its motives—to view with suspicion those who most fervently dispute its policies. Fourth Amendment protections become the more necessary when the targets of official surveillance may be those suspected of unorthodoxy in their political beliefs. The danger to political dissent is acute where the Government attempts to act under so vague a concept as the power to protect 'domestic security'. . . . The price of lawful public dissent must not be a dread of subjection to an unchecked surveillance power. Nor must the fear of unauthorized official eavesdropping deter vigorous citizen dissent and discussion of Government action in private conversation. For private dissent, no less than open public discourse, is essential to our free society."

The White House had no comment on the Court's wiretapping decision, which represented a sharp rebuke to administration policy. But it was a defeat the president could take in good spirits since, on the whole, Nixon's four appointees had given strong indication that they were backing the president's "peace forces as against the criminal forces in society." The justice who fit in most comfortably with the new law and order trend was

William Rehnquist. By his earlier writings, actions as assistant attorney general and answers before the Senate Judiciary Committee, Rehnquist established himself as a strong ally of law enforcement authorities. The talk that Rehnquist might change his views on the Court was put to rest almost as soon as he took his place on the bench. Rehnquist carried an immutable conservative philosophy into judicial conference and exited with that conservatism completely intact.

In his first opinion, Rehnquist alone dissented from the Court's ruling on the claim by a Buddhist convict in a Texas prison that he had been denied access to the prison chapel and punished for distributing religious literature in violation of his constitutional rights. The Court majority issued a brief opinion saying that the prisoner was entitled to a hearing in federal court on the constitutional question. In his dissent, Rehnquist suggested that prisoners were not entitled to the same constitutional guarantees accorded other Americans. He further complained that courts were already unnecessarily deluged with legal petitions from "writ writers" in jail who spent most of their time concocting baseless claims.

The next day Justice Rehnquist wrote his first majority opinion, upholding the Florida murder conviction of a man accused of the brutal killing of a woman traveling companion. In a written statement at the trial, a third traveler, a man, identified the defendant as the killer. The defendant was not allowed to crossexamine his accusor and that, he claimed, violated his constitutional right to confront a witness against him.

A 1968 Warren Court decision had held that a defendant must be able to confront all witnesses against him or have his conviction thrown out. But the newest and youngest member of the Court had no trouble distinguishing this case from the Warren Court precedent. Unlike the 1968 case, said Rehnquist, the error made in the Florida trial was "harmless," because there was overwhelming evidence of the defendant's guilt from both his confession and the independent evidence gathered by police. Rehnquist said that the Court was only required to reverse the conviction if the tainted evidence (here, the male companion's statement) substantially contributed to the conviction. Rehnquist concluded that the defendant would have been convicted with or without the improperly admitted evidence. "The defendant is entitled to a fair trial," wrote Rehnquist, quoting from a 1953 Court decision, "but not a perfect one."

Justice Rehnquist zealously favored the government's side of a legal question even, his critics argued, when he was duty-bound to stay out of the case. Assistant Attorney General Rehnquist had defended the Army's domestic surveillance policy; Justice Rehnquist joined a Court majority that threw out an American Civil Liberties Union suit challenging that policy. ACLU attorneys were so outraged by Rehnquist's failure to disqualify himself that they immediately filed for a new hearing in the case, claiming Rehnquist's participation had poisoned the decision. If he was disturbed by his critics, Rehnquist didn't show it. He also voted in a case involving a grand jury investigation of the Pentagon Papers leak, although he had earlier performed minor duties for the Justice Department in its Pentagon Papers suit. And though Assistant Attorney General Rehnquist had spoken out against a newsman's asserted right not to appear before a grand jury, as a member of the Court Rehnquist rejected three newsmen's claim to that privilege. In each of the three decisions, the Court divided 5–4, with Justice Rehnquist casting the decisive vote in favor of the government.*

Rehnquist's philosophical toughness was not totally unex-

*In October 1972, Rehnquist issued a memorandum specifically rejecting the argument that he should have disqualified himself in the Army surveillance case. Central to Rehnquist's argument was his contention that a man who takes a position on an issue before his appointment should not be disqualified from judging later. "Proof that a justice's mind at the time he joined the Court was a complete *tabula rasa* [clean slate] in the area of constitutional adjudication would be evidence of a lack of qualification, not lack of bias," Rehnquist wrote.

pected, though unusual for such a new justice. Justice Powell, on the other hand, came to the Court with different background and expectations. He had been a pragmatist in private practice, a weigher of competing values, an appraiser of the effects of decisions before the decisions were made. On the Court, Powell began to translate that lawyer's caution into carefully reasoned legal judgments. Always an admirer of the late Justice Harlan, Powell in his first opinions seemed to emulate his predecessor. The opinions were deliberate and well reasoned and, like Harlan's, they usually left law enforcement officials alone whenever constitutionally possible.

On a single day Justice Powell delivered two of his—and the Court's—most important opinions of the 1972 term, both strengthening the prosecution's hand in criminal cases. The first focused on a century-old prosecutor's problem: how to force a reluctant witness to talk to a grand jury without violating the constitutional right prohibiting self-incrimination. Congress first thought it had found a way out of the dilemma when it enacted a statute granting a witness immunity from any prosecution based on his compelled testimony. But in 1896 the Supreme Court ruled that the immunity grant could be valid only if it protected the witness from prosecutions of all crimes which he had talked about before the grand jury (even if his actual testimony was not used). Federal and state legislation conforming with the Court's ruling followed. By 1970, however, Congress and twenty-four states had passed laws loosening the old standards by permitting the government to prosecute a witness for a crime that he had discussed before a grand jury so long as the police could prove they had developed their evidence independently of the defendant's forced testimony. Supporters of the new laws argued that there was no reason why a witness who had been forced to testify before a grand jury should be rewarded with total amnesty. The Burger Court agreed.

To grant a reluctant witness complete immunity from prosecution, said Justice Powell for the majority, gave the witness more than he deserved—or that the Constitution required. The government should not be allowed to renege on its promise not to use a witness's testimony against him. But that pact was firm, Powell reasoned, so long as the witness's testimony, or the leads developed from it, was barred from later prosecutions. Under those rules, Powell concluded, the witness would find himself in the same position vis-à-vis the prosecution after his grand jury appearance as before.

In dissent, Justice Marshall suggested that the Burger Court majority was rather too trusting of government officials. Marshall feared that police might use leads developed from a witness's testimony to prosecute him later—and simply not say so. He was skeptical of Justice Powell's assurances that the government would have the burden of showing that its evidence was gathered independently. "Though the Court puts the burden of proof on the Government," wrote Marshall, "the Government will have no difficulty in meeting its burden by mere assertion if the witness produces no contrary evidence."

The Powell-Marshall dialogue underscored a basic difference in approach between the Warren and Burger Court majorities. For the liberal justices of the Warren Court, the government's good intentions were never taken for granted. They had to be proved and the Warren Court majority was not easily persuaded. The Burger Court majority, in contrast, consistently expressed confidence in the high intentions of government officials.

Since the Middle Ages, the single institution in English common law standing between a man accused of a crime and a state intent on punishing him was the petit jury. Composed of twelve members, the jury could only find a man guilty by a unanimous vote. Any disagreement and the accused went free. When the Sixth Amendment was drafted guaranteeing trial by jury, the jury was still made up of twelve persons who could only judge a man guilty of a crime by unanimous vote. Over the years, a few states began to experiment with the jury concept. Concerned both with inefficiency and a rising crime rate, they reduced the jury membership to less than twelve and required less than a unanimous vote for a guilty verdict. In 1970, the Burger Court gave its imprimatur to the first experiment, ruling that the jury number of twelve was an "historical accident" which U.S. courts were not bound to honor.

Split jury verdicts were challenged in the Supreme Court two years later when convicted men in Louisiana and Oregon (where 9–3 and 10–2 guilty verdicts were allowed) argued that they had not been proved guilty beyond a reasonable doubt since a minority of jurors wanted to acquit them. They also charged that split verdicts undercut a basic purpose of a jury trial—to enable a defendant to be judged by a panel of his peers —since two or three of his peers were excluded from the decision. Behind the specific complaints was the knowledge that split verdicts favored majority rule and the suspicion that the majority tended to vote for conviction. That suspicion was backed by studies of law professors in Oregon and Louisiana showing that split verdict systems produced more convictions than unanimous verdict systems. In their massive study *The American Jury,* Professors Harry Kalven, Jr. and Hans Zeisel of the University of Chicago came to a similar conclusion. In hung jury cases, Kalven and Zeisel found that the majority favored the prosecution more than three times as much as the defense.

The defense's challenge to the split verdict system must fail, the four Nixon appointees and Justice White decided. Recalling the Court's 1970 decision sanctioning less than twelve-member juries, Justice White reasoned that a heavy majority voting for conviction in a split verdict system was not significantly different from a unanimous vote by a smaller jury. To his dissenting colleagues, concerned that split verdicts would effectively exclude minorities from the final decision, White said that the Constitution guaranteed minorities the right to sit on a jury and be heard. But it did not give them "the right to block convictions," White concluded. Justice Powell, the swing vote in the decision, said that split verdicts should be permitted in state trials, where experimentation was allowed, but maintained that in federal trials unanimous verdicts were required.

Powell's careful federal-state dichotomy was altogether too precious for the dissenters. "In my opinion," wrote Justice Brennan, "the right of all groups in this Nation to participate in the criminal process means the right to have their voices heard. A unanimous verdict vindicates that right. Majority verdicts could destroy it." Justice Douglas was even blunter. He accused the majority of succumbing to the nation's "law and order mood" and he concluded that "the vast restructuring of American law which is entailed in today's decisions is for political, not for judicial reasons."

With the emergence of the conservative Court majority during the 1971 term, opposing justices began debating the meaning of the new results. The majority said that it was not overruling Warren Court decisions, but only refusing to expand them. Thus, Chief Justice Burger saw no need to overrule the *Miranda* decision when the majority ruled in *Harris v. New York* that confessions given without the *Miranda* warnings could be used in court for some purposes. The *Miranda* decision had not covered the situation presented in the *Harris* case, said Burger. To apply the *Miranda* decision to the later case, the chief justice maintained, would give the old Warren Court ruling new meaning. Not so, said a dissenting Justice Brennan. What the Burger Court was doing was overruling *Miranda* but just not saying so. The semantic debate resumed during the 1972 term when the Burger Court majority ruled that the Warren Court's guarantee of a lawyer for suspects at identification proceedings did not cover every identification situation. The majority was not overruling the earlier Warren Court ruling, it said, just refusing to extend it.

Before the Warren Court ruling, it had not been unheard of for police to put their prime suspect in a line-up in which he was sure to be conspicuous. If he was short, he might be surrounded by six-footers; if he was black, his line-up companions might all be white. The unscrupulous ways in which police could get their identification unfairly were numerous and, because of this fear, the Warren Court insisted that an attorney be present with every suspect at the line-up. Although the Warren Court rule was cumbersome and not always practical —the lawyer really had nothing to do but stand around—it did seem to guarantee a higher standard of fairness than was previously demanded.

That right to counsel was challenged, following the conviction of two Chicago men for robbery. The men had been stopped by police and asked for identification two days after a man named Willie Shard had reported a stolen wallet. One of the suspects presented three travelers' checks and a social security card, all with Shard's name on them. The other suspect also showed police papers identifying Shard as the owner. The first suspect later explained that the travelers' checks were actually play money, but then changed his story. He had won them in a crap game, he said. Both men were taken to the police station. In a squad room with only themselves and two Chicago policemen, the two suspects were identified by Shard as the men who stole his wallet. After their conviction, the men appealed on the grounds that they had been denied their constitutional rights to counsel at the time they were identified in the police squad room.

Those facts were written into Justice Potter Stewart's majority opinion in *Kirby* v. *Illinois,* supported by the four

Nixon appointees, which held that the earlier Warren Court decision, guaranteeing a lawyer at the identification stage, did not apply to the case before the Court. The main reason, said Stewart, was that the law enforcement authorities had not reached "a critical stage of the prosecution" when the two men were identified. Indictment, said Stewart, marked the beginning of the criminal prosecution and the suspect's right to counsel at identification proceedings. In the earlier Warren Court decision, the suspect had already been indicted when he was identified without counsel; in the Chicago case, Stewart noted, the men had been arrested but not indicted.

The Stewart distinction (the arrest is not a critical stage for the prosecution but the indictment is) was attacked as artificial by Justice Brennan and liberal constitutional scholars. They suggested the Burger Court majority consciously blinded itself to the spirit behind the Warren Court ruling. The Warren Court meant to protect suspects at identification proceedings and it did not matter whether those proceedings took place before or after an indictment. It would have been better if the Court had simply overruled the earlier Warren Court decision, maintained Professor Yale Kamisar of the Michigan Law School. Then, said Kamisar, at least the Court would have been "intellectually honest."

The nine justices were so overwhelmed by work in 1972 that, for the first time in the institution's history, it looked as if the chief justice might not be able to gavel the Court's regular session to a close until July. Actually, the Court beat the July heat by two days, closing the term on June 29 with 689 pages of opinions.

On that final day of the Court's term, the conservative bloc of four Nixon appointees continued to dwell on the law and order theme that had been the hallmark of the session. On two significant constitutional issues, the Nixon four were joined by

Justice White to extend the long arm of the law even further. Both decisions broadened the license of grand juries and prosecutors to question witnesses during their investigation. What made the cases unusual and significant from a constitutional point of view were the particular witnesses beckoned to the grand jury. In the first instance, a Boston grand jury inquiring into the leak and subsequent publication of portions of the Pentagon Papers wanted to ask some questions of aides to U.S. Senator Mike Gravel and, possibly, the senator himself. The second case involved three newsmen, including Earl Caldwell of the *New York Times*. Caldwell had refused to testify before a grand jury about confidential information and sources he had developed in covering the Black Panther Party in San Francisco.

What Senator Gravel and Earl Caldwell had in common was a constitutional claim that they were protected from answering the questions of the Boston and San Francisco grand juries. The senator, who had first read portions of the Pentagon Papers at a midnight session of a congressional subcommittee and later arranged for their publication, said that he and his aides were protected by Article I, Section 6 of the U.S. Constitution. That section provided that no congressman could be questioned on any legislative speech or debate outside the halls of Congress. The *Times's* Caldwell, Paul Branzburg of the *Louisville Courier Journal* and Paul Pappas, a Boston-area television cameraman-reporter, all haled before grand juries who were officially curious about some of their stories and sources, claimed that the First Amendment's protection of the press shielded them from such investigations.

The former deputy attorney general, Justice White, wrote the majority opinion in both cases, giving powerful testimony to his belief in the importance of criminal investigations by grand juries. That importance was so great, in White's mind, that the competing constitutional claims by Gravel and the newsmen had to fail. In the Gravel case, White posed a stiff test for congressional immunity: the conduct could only be immune if it was an integral part of the legislative process. He did not consider the senator and his aides' part in obtaining the Pentagon Papers or later publishing them within his definition. The grand jury, therefore, was free to move ahead with its inquiry, including questions to the senator's aides on how his office was able to obtain the Papers. The four dissenters were left wondering why the conservative majority's balancing process was weighted so consistently in favor of law enforcement authorities.

The question was not answered in the newsmen's case, where Justice White, for the five-man majority, again found the government's interest in investigating crime compelling. "We cannot seriously entertain the notion that the First Amendment protects a newsman's agreement to conceal the criminal conduct of his source," wrote White, "on the theory that it is better to write about crime than to do something about it." Once he had put his values in order, White began to question the basic assumption of the newsmen's case. White was not at all sure that, as the press claimed, news sources would dry up once grand juries were free to question a reporter on his confidential notes and friends. The claim was speculative, said White, and could in no way supersede the public's interest in prosecuting crimes reported to the press. White noted that Congress and state legislatures were still free to grant the privilege to reporters, something the Supreme Court had never been willing to do by constitutional interpretation. In response, the usually controlled Justice Stewart delivered a biting attack on the majority opinion. The Court's holding, said Stewart, "invites state and federal authorities to undermine the historic independence of the press by attempting to annex the journalistic profession as an investigative arm of government."

If the announcement of the Gravel and Caldwell decisions

had been the only order of business that last day of the Court
term, the two holdings undoubtedly would have monopolized
headlines across the country and occupied law review editors
for months and years to come. But that same day the Court
issued a third decision which settled, at least for the present
time, an issue that had been gnawing at the American psyche
for more than a century: should the death penalty be abolished?

Hudson walked to the wooden chair in carpet slippers
and sat down quietly. His two guards fastened leather
straps around his waist, chest, legs and arms and over his
eyes and mouth, catching him between breaths. . . . Now
the metal cap with its electrode and thick, coiled cord was
placed over Hudson's head. The ground was put on his
right calf, bared by a slit in the khaki slacks. Maybe any
man looks small in the electric chair, but Hudson looked
absolutely harmless. At 9:59 the executioner, an ordinary-
looking man with gray hair and a gray three-button suit,
slowly turned a large wheel on the wall behind the prisoner. Ten small glass panes in the wall lighted gradually.
There was a zzzt sound, and Hudson jerked back in the
chair. The wheel was slowly turned around further, and
the panes dimmed and went out. Further, and they began
lighting again; further still, they were bright, another zzzt,
then around again. As I watched the turns, glancing at my
watch, recording the time of each jolt, I could almost feel
the wheel go round, and I braced for the next zzzt: 9:59
one, two; 10:00, three, four; 10:01, five, six; 10:02, seven,
eight. The executioner signaled "Enough," and shut off
the power. The power line was disconnected and discharged, the straps removed, the man's shirt opened.
Three doctors listened with a stethoscope, then, at 10:04,
one pronounced the ritual words: "This man is dead."

When Barry Satlow, a United Press International reporter, witnessed the execution of Ralph James Hudson, at the Trenton State (New Jersey) Prison in 1963, 39 countries no longer imposed the death penalty. The abolition movement began in 1798 in the tiny principality of Liechtenstein. Although the U.S. government in 1963 had made no move to follow Liechtenstein's 165-year-old lead, nine states had either abolished or severely limited the application of the death penalty. And in 1963 the issue of abolition was raised by Justice Goldberg of the U.S. Supreme Court, who, in a dissent from the majority's decision not to review lower court rulings in two rape cases, suggested that the Court determine whether the death penalty for rape was a violation of the U.S. Constitution.

Those lawyers and scholars looking for legal grounds to abolish the death penalty saw their opportunity in Goldberg's opinion. Although Justice Goldberg had not mentioned racial discrimination as the possible ground for the constitutional challenge, Professor Anthony Amsterdam, then at the University of Pennsylvania Law School, and other abolitionists thought that the discrimination issue would be their most compelling legal argument. Statistics did nothing to discourage their thinking: half of the murderers and approximately 90 per cent of the convicted rapists executed in the United States since 1930 had been black. Moreover, only fifteen states retained the death penalty for the crime of rape and all fifteen were either southern or border states.

In 1964 Jack Greenberg, director-counsel of the NAACP Legal Defense Fund, asked Amsterdam and Marvin Wolfgang, a criminologist from the University of Pennsylvania, to undertake a broadly based survey into the sentencing patterns of southern juries from 1945 to 1965. To assist the two professors, the Legal Defense Fund dispatched law students to southern states in the summer of 1965 to read trial transcripts and interview officials about the practices and procedures of juries in rape cases. From the collected data, Wolfgang concluded that only two factors could explain the high proportion of blacks sentenced to death for rape: the defendant's race (black) and the victim's race (white). Although the Wolfgang study did not persuade a single court to declare the death penalty unconstitutional, the claim, along with others put forth by LDF lawyers, caused courts to issue stays of execution while the constitutional issues were unresolved. As a result, by the end of 1967, the LDF had imposed a de facto moratorium on executions in the U.S.

In 1968 the Supreme Court began tightening the judicial standards under which it would allow a man to be put to death. That year, the Court said that prosecutors could no longer automatically dismiss prospective jurors in capital cases who voiced reservations about the imposition of the death penalty. For dismissal in the future, prosecutors would have to show that the prospective juror would not vote the death penalty under *any* circumstance. Since the decision applied retroactively, prisoners on death row and their lawyers pressed courts with the same claim: that prosecutors in their trials had wrongly dismissed prospective jurors with scruples against capital punishment.

By 1970, abolitionists were ready to press their case a step further. In defending William Maxwell, Professor Amsterdam attacked the Arkansas's jury procedures as unconstitutional. If the Amsterdam argument prevailed, the death penalty in the United States would have been close to extinction, since almost every state provided for just the procedures in capital cases that Amsterdam said were unconstitutional.

The Court sidestepped the issue in the Arkansas case by reversing the conviction on a technicality. But the next term Justice Harlan appeared to put the abolitionists' procedural arguments permanently to rest with his decision in *McGautha v. California*. If the procedures in death penalty cases were to be changed, Harlan suggested in *McGautha*, legislatures should do it. And so the only constitutional argument that stood between the more than six hundred condemned men and women on the nation's death row and their assigned fate was that capital punishment was "cruel and unusual punishment" forbidden by the Eighth Amendment. The Legal Defense Fund sent its attorneys back to the courts for what they thought could be the last legal attempt to outlaw the death penalty.

Unexpectedly, in February 1972 the highest court in California gave the abolitionists encouragement, ruling that the death penalty violated the "cruel or unusual punishment" provision of the California constitution. The majority held that the execution and "the dehumanizing effects of the lengthy imprisonment prior to execution" are "impermissibly cruel" and that the infrequency of the punishment made it constitutionally unusual. It concluded that the death penalty was "unnecessary to any legitimate goal of the state and is incompatible with the dignity of man and the judicial process."

The California decision spared the lives of 102 men and 5 women awaiting execution in the state's prisons, including two of the most famous convicted murderers of all times, Sirhan Sirhan and Charles Manson. California Governor Ronald Reagan characterized the decision as "a case of the courts setting themselves up above the people and the legislature." That elevation, said Reagan, made "a mockery of the constitutional process." What made the court decision all the more infuriating for Reagan was the fact that one of his appointees, Chief Justice Donald R. Wright, whom Reagan had labeled a "law and order" jurist, wrote the majority opinion. After the court's decision, Reagan called on the legislature to draft a state constitutional amendment to restore capital punishment.

Reagan was by no means alone in his resistance to abolition of the penalty. While there had been an effective movement in some states (eight had abolished or restricted the death penalty since 1962), the sentiment was far from unanimous. To the contrary, if public opinion polls were to be believed, the abolitionists had actually lost ground. In 1965 public opinion was evenly divided between pro- and antideath penalty forces. By 1972, however, a public opinion poll recorded 51 per cent in favor of retaining the penalty, 40 per cent opposed and 9 per cent undecided. And those favoring the penalty had friends in high places. Both Attorney General Mitchell and President Nixon supported its retention. By the time the "cruel and unusual" issue was before the U.S. Supreme Court, the president had placed four "law and order" justices on the Court. With the vote of either swing man, Stewart or White, the death penalty would be preserved.

Those in favor of the penalty focused on two arguments, both having had great philosophical appeal to Stewart and White in the past. First, no one could persuasively argue that either the framers of the Constitution or any Supreme Court in history had seriously considered the death penalty to be a violation of the Eighth Amendment. If the justices were to outlaw the penalty, they could not justify their action on the basis of the intentions of the framers or previous Court decisions. Secondly, proponents of the penalty said the decision before the Court required a political judgment, one in which the judge had no special expertise. As a result, they argued, the decision had appropriately been left to the executive and legislative branches of the government.

Abolitionists answered that the Court, first of all, must deal with "cruel and unusual punishment" as perceived in the 1970s, not the 1870s or the 1770s. Concepts of justice change in time, the abolitionists argued, and the unusual cruelty of one group of civilized men putting a fellow human being to death for a crime was patently wrong in the advanced civilization of the twentieth century. It simply was not credible, in a world where so many governments had found the death penalty abhorrent, for the United States to continue the practice.

Those challenging the penalty presented another and, it turned out, crucial argument for attacking capital punishment. The penalty, applied so infrequently and with such haphazard inconsistency, reflected a basic irrationality in the judicial system. And random selection for death was no more the business of legislatures, the abolitionists contended, than it was of judges.

To almost everyone's surprise, that final point—the sheer arbitrariness in the application of the penalty—won both Stewart and White and, therefore, the Court for the abolitionists. But before the Court had finished with the death penalty issue, every justice had recorded his views in opinions that ran the spectrum of philosophical possibilities.

For Justice Brennan, the key question was whether "a punishment comports with human dignity." He concluded that "death, quite simply, does not." Marshall joined Brennan in the absolutist position, welcoming the United States to the community of nations "which celebrate their regard for civilization and humanity by shunning capital punishment." The third vote for abolition came from Justice Douglas, who dwelled on the unfairness of the penalty, which, he said, was applied unevenly and most often to minority groups.

Typically, neither White nor Stewart, who wrote the pivotal opinions, rested their decisions on moral grounds. Of major importance to White was the fact that the death penalty did not accomplish a prime goal of the criminal law—deterrence. He concluded that the death penalty "is so seldom invoked that it ceases to be the credible threat essential to influence the conduct of others." Stewart's opinion had more of the scent of moral indignation but, like White, he chose to focus on the law's procedural inadequacies rather than the larger philosophical concepts. Said Stewart: "These sentences are cruel and unusual in the same way that being struck by lightning is cruel and unusual . . . the petitioners are among a capriciously selected random handful upon whom the sentence of death had in fact been imposed. I simply conclude that the Eighth and Fourteenth Amendments cannot tolerate the infliction of a sentence of death under legal systems that permit this unique penalty to be so wantonly and so freakishly imposed."

The nuances of the Stewart and White opinions were lost on the six hundred men and women on death row whose executions were effectively stayed by the Court's ruling. In Georgia's state prison at Reidsville, where twenty-two men were condemned to death, announcement of the Court's decision sparked a demonstration of "clapping and yelling like crazy." One of the clappers and yellers, Lucius Jackson, Jr., a petitioner in the Court case, exulted: "I've been thinking about death for a long time; now I can think about life." At Florida's state prison farm at Raiford the reaction was no less exuberant, with shouts of "Right on, Mr. Justices." Another sentenced to die, Marylin Dobrolenski, celebrated with quiet tears in her cell in Pennsylvania.

"I think that there will no longer be any more capital punishment in America," said the Legal Defense Fund's Jack Greenburg. Others were not so sure. It was clear from all four dissenting opinions by Nixon appointees that they thought the Court had made a serious mistake. Justices Powell and Rehnquist condemned the Court's intervention as a blatant usurpation of legislative powers. In a more personal appeal, Justice Blackmun reiterated his long-held position that, were he a legislator, he would vote to outlaw the death penalty. But in Blackmun's view, judges, unlike legislators, had no business making such value judgments.

Chief Justice Burger may have written the most prophetic opinion of all. He took care to note that the majority had not actually outlawed capital punishment, but only rejected the procedures then applicable in death penalty cases. Burger then gave legislatures some suggestions on how they might retain the death penalty and still obey the majority's ruling. Lawmakers could draft new laws, said Burger, that set specific, rational standards for applying the death penalty. If that proved impossible, Burger said, the death penalty might be made mandatory for certain egregious crimes. Although the Chief Justice did not support such mandatory sentencing, he mentioned it as a means of eliminating the standards argument altogether.

The chief justice's words were encouraging enough to set a number of law and order politicians into action. The day of the decision Representative Louis C. Wyman of New Hampshire introduced a constitutional amendment into the House of Representatives that would allow the death penalty for murder and treason in federal cases. That night, President Nixon, remarking that he had not read all of the opinions from the Court but that he had read the chief justice's, wished out loud that the Congress would retain the death penalty for the crimes of kidnapping and airplane hijacking. Within twenty-four hours of the Court's decision, legislators and other officials in at least five states had announced that they would press for new state laws to retain the death penalty. Even without legislative action, a number of constitutional scholars suspected that the abolitionists' victory might be short-lived. Majority opinions of 5–4 were not the sturdiest of precedents. The Nixon bloc minority would become the majority with one more vote, a vote that could easily materialize if the president won reelection and the opportunity to appoint a fifth justice. "The final outcome [of the death penalty issue]," said Michigan's Yale Kamisar, "will be decided by the next presidential election more than the commas and semicolons and footnotes of the [Court's] decision."

CHAPTER ELEVEN

A New Balance

"Mr. President, do you consider the Supreme Court now to be in balance, or do you think it needs another dose of strict constructionism if that occasion should arise?" The question, asked at a White House news conference the last day of the 1972 Supreme Court term, was greeted with smirks and smiles around the room. Even the president allowed himself the slightest grin. "I feel at the present time," Nixon answered, "that the Court is as balanced as I have had an opportunity to make it."

The president had every reason to be pleased with the Court and to share his pleasure with the American public. As the Republican presidential candidate in 1968, Nixon had campaigned on a law and order platform. Throughout the campaign, there was the thinly veiled threat that, if elected, Nixon would throw out the rascals who had caused all the trouble—the politicians and judges who had backed the "criminal forces." The new president had made good on his promise. He had replaced Attorney General Ramsey Clark, a liberal, with tough John Mitchell. More important, he had put four of his choices on the Supreme Court, and those appointments had translated into four dependable conservative votes on law and order issues.

The Court's new balance in the criminal law area was only the most conspicuous shift in the Court's constitutional direction. The Supreme Court, which had started the desegregation revolution in 1954 and adamantly stood by its decision for the better part of two decades, suddenly seemed a little tired of the whole subject. Even the first principle of the Warren Court, school desegregation, was not as safe as it used to be. The four Nixon appointees underscored that fact when they recorded the first dissents from a Supreme Court holding on school discrimination since the *Brown* decision of 1954. The people of Emporia, Virginia, where schools were predominantly white, wanted to secede from the Greensville County school system, which was largely black. The five Warren Court holdovers blocked the secession. The effect of the move, said the majority, would be to discourage desegregation and, therefore, could not be permitted. The four Nixon appointees, dissenting, said the majority was demanding too much of southern school systems. "The goal," Chief Justice Burger contended, "is to dismantle dual school systems rather than to reproduce in each classroom a microscopic reflection of the racial proportions of a given geographical area." So long as there was no provable racist intent, the Nixon bloc was willing to let local schools boards settle their desegregation problems without the help of the High Court.

While racist-motivated school plans would still have problems passing the Burger Court's inspection, more devious actions that accomplished segregated results, such as the closing of public swimming pools, could get by. And though there would be no outright barring of black children at the schoolhouse door, six justices were willing to let their parents be shut out of private clubs. That judgment was made after K. Leroy

Irvis, a black Pennsylvania state legislator, was denied guest privileges at Harrisburg's Moose Lodge because of the color of his skin. Irvis challenged his exclusion from the private club as a violation of his constitutional rights.

For the Burger Court, the case turned on the question of whether the state liquor license to the club, which required the club to submit its financial records and physical facilities to the liquor board's inspection, constituted "state action." If so, then the club would have to abide by the Fourteenth Amendment's equal protection clause. If not, the Moose Lodge could have its racist constitution and honor it daily. Justice Rehnquist, for the majority, freed the Moose to do as it pleased. An interpretation of "state action" that would cover the Moose, said Rehnquist, would "utterly emasculate the distinction between private as distinguished from state conduct."

The signals emitted from the Court were no more encouraging for the poor as a class than for the blacks who made up a large segment of that class. The Warren Court had given the Fourteenth Amendment's equal protection clause its most expansive reading in American history, helping the poor to cut down discriminatory barriers to low-income housing projects, voter registration and welfare payments. The Burger Court was not so generous in its interpretation. Instead of knocking down statute after state statute for what the Warren Court found to be a violation of equal protection, the Burger Court loosened the constitutional standard and, in the process, preserved the state laws. For the new majority, the state had only to show that its legislators had been rational in passing laws, no matter how discriminatory those laws might be.

Under the Burger Court, the State of Maryland could set maximum limits on welfare payments and Texas could be more generous with the aged than with young families on welfare. In the Texas case, Justice Rehnquist's majority opinion was almost contemptuous of the petitioners' argument that the state should not be allowed to pay families with dependent children (predominantly black and Mexican-American) less than aged and disabled (predominantly white) welfare recipients. Rehnquist labeled it a "naked statistical argument" that could not qualify under the Fourteenth Amendment's equal protection clause. The state of Texas, said Rehnquist, might well have decided that young welfare recipients were better able to make their way with less funds than the aged. But whatever the reason, Rehnquist said, it was not for the Court to be second-guessing state officials on the proper distribution of limited welfare funds.

In another area of Warren Court strength, civil liberties, the new majority again showed itself to be less steadfast. The Warren Court majority believed that the First Amendment freedoms that opened the political process to dissent from all quarters deserved special consideration. Even for those less purist in their constitutional interpretations than Justice Black, that meant, at the very least, that when free speech competed with other constitutional rights, the First Amendment rights would take constitutional priority. In the words of Justice Brennan, the Warren Court was committed to the principle that debate on public issues should be "uninhibited, robust and wide-open."

The First Amendment did not enjoy that same exalted position under the Burger Court. Freedom of the press, for example, was carefully measured against the government's interest in national security in the Pentagon Papers case and later, in the Caldwell case, the executive branch's right to investigate criminal actions. In a third decision, the Burger Court suggested that the First Amendment protections had been lowered (or competing constitutional values elevated) in the minds of the majority.

The case began on November 14, 1968, when five young anti-Vietnam war protesters attempted to distribute protest leaflets at the Lloyd Center shopping mall in Portland, Oregon. The fifty-acre mall was attractive to promoters of causes, since its sixty stores and offices delivered huge crowds of customers to proselytizers. The Salvation Army was permitted its Christmas solicitations, the American Legion its poppy sales and presidential candidates their political harangues. But the shopping center authorities said no to the five antiwar advocates, fearing that their printed message would make the customers uncomfortable and the mall untidy.

On request, the antiwar protesters left the mall but insisted that the shopping center authorities join them in court later. They said that their First Amendment rights had been violated and cited Supreme Court precedents in their favor dating back to 1946. In protecting a Jehovah's Witness's right to proselytize in a company town that year, the Court had said that "the more an owner, for his advantage, opens up his property for use by the public in general, the more do rights become circumscribed by the statutory and constitutional rights of those who use it." Later, the Warren Court gave First Amendment protection to labor picketers in a private shopping center, ruling that the center was the "functional equivalent" of a public business district.

Despite those precedents favoring free speech rights, the Burger Court coolly matched the interests of the antiwar protesters against those of the shopping center owners. Unlike the earlier labor picketers, who were protesting the practices of a store in the shopping center, the Burger Court said that the war protesters could effectively make their point elsewhere. "It would be an unwarranted infringement of property rights," Justice Powell wrote, "to require them to yield to the exercise of First Amendment rights under circumstances where adequate alternative avenues of communication exist. Such an accommodation would diminish property rights without significantly enhancing the asserted right of free speech."

The U.S. Supreme Court, under Chief Justice Warren Burger, was no longer the nation's ombudsman. Not only were the justices less anxious to solve America's most pressing problems, but they were even reluctant to identify them for others to work on. There were no sequels to the broad manifestos of the Warren Court's race, reapportionment and civil liberties decisions. Nor would the Burger Court run with the new causes of the seventies.

Ecologists learned the hard way when the Sierra Club challenged Walt Disney Productions' plans to build a $35 million complex of motels, restaurants, swimming pools, ski lifts and parking lots in Sequoia National Forest. The project would so adversely change the area's aesthetics and ecology, the Sierra Club contended, that it must be stopped. Apparently so convinced of the justness of their cause, the conservation club's attorneys did not even bother to show how the Disney complex would specifically injure the members of the Sierra Club who had brought the suit.

The Sierra Club and ecologists everywhere were promptly given a sharp lesson in judicial procedure by the Burger Court majority. Justice Stewart, writing for the Court, scolded Sierra Club attorneys for trying to gain passage to the Court without taking the necessary preliminary legal steps. To have a legitimate lawsuit, Stewart said, a lawyer must show that his client has been specifically and individually injured. Otherwise, the Court would soon find itself reviewing the complaints of every individual or organization disturbed by someone else who did not share his value preferences. The Sierra Club's suit was thrown out.

The Court's reluctance to make headlines was again shown when a majority refused to enter the battle between civil libertarians, including Senator Ervin, and the Nixon administration over the Army's widespread data-gathering and surveillance system of private citizens. The American Civil Liberties Union had put the Army's policy to a court test. The ACLU charged that the Army's action violated the First Amendment rights of citizens whose speech (and criticism of government) would be inhibited by the knowledge of military surveillance. The U.S. Court of Appeals for the District of Columbia ordered the Army to trial to defend its policy. The decision was consistent with the activist judicial philosophy of the appellate court's chief judge, David Bazelon. Checking up on the practices of other public institutions, Bazelon had said at a 1971 lecture at NYU, was "the most important function of courts in a democratic society." Bazelon declared that the courts had an obligation "to see to it that the other institutions are in fact doing what they are supposed to do."

The Burger Court thought otherwise. The four Nixon appointees and Justice White rejected the ACLU's claim because, they said, there was no proof that the Army's action had caused specific harm to those claiming injury. "The allegations of a subjective 'chill' [of First Amendment rights] are not an adequate substitute for a claim of specific, present objective harm," wrote Chief Justice Burger. "Stripped of its essentials, what respondents [ACLU] appear to be seeking is a broad-scale investigation," which Burger suggested would inevitably place the courts in the position of the investigators. "Carried to its logical end," wrote Burger, "this approach would have the federal courts as virtually continuing monitors of the wisdom and soundness of executive action." It was a role that the court of appeals' Bazelon invited and one that Burger, and four of his colleagues, rejected.

But that was not the end of the losing battle waged by judicial activists, such as Bazelon, against the counselors of restraint on the Supreme Court. The Army surveillance case, in fact, was not even the most dramatic confrontation in 1972 between Bazelon and Burger and their differing philosophies. Shortly after the justices had packed for summer vacation, Burger hastily summoned them back for a special session to review a decision handed down by Bazelon's court. Douglas flew in from Houston, Powell came from Richmond and Justice Brennan took part in the Court's deliberations by telephone from his vacation retreat in Nantucket.

The quintessential political question had been posed: should the courts settle a dispute between rival political factions at the Democratic National Convention in Miami Beach? It all started in June when Senator George McGovern completed his incredible chain of victories by taking the winner-take-all California primary and the state's 271 delegates to the Democratic convention. Old pros and new in the Democratic Party agreed that the California victory virtually wrapped up the nomination for McGovern. But they had not counted on the determination of McGovern's rivals, who were able to convince their people on the party's credentials committee to make a last, desperate attempt to deny McGovern the nomination. It happened when the stop-McGovern faction on the committee stripped the South Dakota senator of 151 California delegates on the theory that the state's winner-take-all primary violated the party's own reform rules. Senator Hubert H. Humphrey, who stood to gain most from the credentials committee decision, dispensed with the usual high-blown rhetoric and, between broad grins, told reporters that his chances had improved. "I'm not going to say any more," remarked Humphrey, saying more. "I've got the votes." McGovern was not so taciturn. He told a news conference that the credentials committee vote was "an incredible, cynical, rotten, political steal" and vowed to challenge the committee's decision in court.

McGovern received no satisfaction from a U.S. district court judge who refused to overturn the credentials committee's decision in the California case. But on the second try, before a three-judge panel in the D.C. Court of Appeals, McGovern was victorious. Chief Judge Bazelon and his colleague, Judge

George E. MacKinnon, ordered the reinstatement of the 151 delegates committed to McGovern. Noting that the credentials committee had ignored both the California law and the implicit understanding of the party's presidential candidates, who had campaigned with full knowledge of the winner-take-all consequences of the primary, Bazelon and MacKinnon concluded: "Because we are convinced that the process of electing the president of the United States is not, and cannot be, placed outside the rule of law, we set aside the arbitrary and unconstitutional action of the Democratic Party."

The ruling would have practically handed the Democratic Party's nomination to McGovern—had it stood up. It did not. In its special summer session, the Supreme Court decided to send the whole credentials controversy back to the Democrats in Miami Beach. Among the "grave doubts" expressed by the Burger Court about the court of appeals opinion were the total lack of precedent for the appellate decision and the failure of the lower court to consider "the large public interest in allowing the political process to function free of judicial supervision."

Had the Burger Court followed immediately on the heels of the Vinson Court of the early fifties, there would be no cries of outrage from civil rights and civil liberties lawyers. For, if anything be true, it is that the Burger Court's overall record on the issues that most touch libertarians is more impressive than the Vinson Court's. In the criminal law field the Vinson Court granted states far greater license to patrol their own territories than the Burger Court. The Burger Court's decision insuring a lawyer to the poor in state misdemeanor cases, for example, would not have been likely during the Vinson regime. Nor could Justice Douglas have found four colleagues on the Vinson Court to rule that the death penalty was cruel and unusual punishment. They were available on the Burger Court. Would a Vinson Court, so timid during the McCarthy era, have had the courage to demand that the Justice Department seek a court warrant before listening to the conversations of suspected domestic subversives? Not likely.

Neither the Vinson Court nor the Burger Court showed much enthusiasm for jumping too far ahead of the electorate's thinking in the field of race relations. But neither backtracked. On another Fourteenth Amendment issue, however, Justice Black's argument that the Vinson Court enter the reapportionment controversy was soundly put down by Justice Frankfurter and the conservative majority. To be sure, the Burger Court has allowed variations from the one man–one vote reapportionment principle, but it has not seriously questioned the Court's right to be involved in the controversy.

Measured by Vinson Court standards, then, the Burger Court record is impressively libertarian. The trouble is that the Burger Court will not be matched up with the Vinson Court, but rather with its immediate predecessor, the Warren Court. And in the civil rights and liberties fields, the Warren Court was the most innovative in the history of the nation. It introduced sweeping reforms into the nation's social and political life, vastly changing the nation's values and expectations. The justices, not the president or the Congress or the state leaders, defined the new perimeters of citizenship in the fifties and sixties. The noncitizens and second-class citizens of the past stood taller because of the Warren Court. The black and the poor and the political radical and even the least pitied of all Americans, the criminal suspect, were provided with new protections and new hopes as well.

As governments in developing nations have discovered, rising expectations of the people can be dangerous. For once the march toward a better life has begun, slacking brings resentment. The prime beneficiaries of the Warren Court revolution —the blacks, the poor, the political dissidents and the criminal suspects—are no different. Former Justice Arthur Goldberg has described the phenomenon in the civil liberties field. "The cries of repression," Goldberg has written, "are the result, at least in part, of a long sustained expectation. Any disappointment of the expectation, any step backward, is subject to a multiplier effect—its symbolic value and the import of the message it communicates will heavily outweigh the corresponding reactions to an equal step forward."

That rising expectation has allowed civil libertarians to concede the favorable decisions of the Burger Court (wiretapping, capital punishment) and still find the overall performance of the Court unsatisfactory, even repressive. Any cutback on the Warren Court criminal decisions—and there have been several—has brought immediate attacks from liberal scholars and lawyers. By the same token, a Burger Court that has held to the Warren Court's desegregation mandate is no hero to blacks or civil rights organizations. The Court has been accused, not of backtracking on civil rights, but of not going forward, which, in their minds, is almost as bad. The Warren Court welcomed the poor to the courtroom. Now the new Court is less hospitable and the poor are disappointed. The new interest groups of the sixties instinctively translated their grievances into lawsuits. With the emergence of the Burger Court, that enthusiasm already shows signs of waning.

In addition to settling the immediate disputes before it, the Warren Court performed a vital role in what philosopher Alexander Meiklejohn termed "our national teaching." Meiklejohn wrote: "And to us who labor at that task of educating Americans it becomes, year by year, more evident that the Supreme Court has a large part to play in our national teaching. That court is commissioned to interpret to us our purposes, our own meanings. To a self-governing community it must make clear what, in actual practice, self-governing is. And its teaching has peculiar importance because it interprets principles of fact and of value, not merely in the abstract, but also in their bearing upon the concrete, immediate problems which are, at any given moment, puzzling and dividing us. But it is just those problems with which any vital system of education is concerned. And for that reason, the court holds a unique place in the cultivating of our national intelligence. Other institutions may be direct in their teaching influence. But no other institution is more deeply decisive in its effect upon our understanding of ourselves and our government."

At times, the Warren Court seemed so immersed in its pedagogical role that it let the specific cases before it slip into the background. The justices were guilty, as their critics charged, of functioning as the nation's Platonic guardians. They were not content merely to interpret the laws of the land. They wanted to teach the nation its deepest purposes and meanings. And it is that special role that the Burger Court neither serves nor covets.

EPILOGUE

In his own way, every U.S. President has tried to mold the Supreme Court in his own political image. Washington stacked the Court with dedicated Federalists, Lincoln appointed men with strong pro-Union views and Franklin Roosevelt named New Deal loyalists. No president in history has outdone Richard Nixon. With four appointments in his first term alone, Nixon has already delivered on his promise to blunt the judicial revolution of the Warren Court. The new conservative majority has cut back on the rights of criminal suspects, largely ignored the constitutional demands of the poor and held firmly but narrowly to the desegregation line that the Warren Court drew in 1954. The Court has been transformed from a tribunal of unprecedented legal daring to one of modest aims and self-limiting accomplishments. It is no longer a bold, innovative institution and has abandoned, for the moment at least, the role of keeper of the nation's conscience.

Richard Nixon, then, has succeeded in dissolving a Warren Court that was the nation's premier symbol for progressive leadership for more than a decade. Ironically, he could not have performed that extraordinary feat without the help of the Court itself. When the Warren Court majority confronted a problem that the other branches of government either could not or would not rectify, the Justices often filled the breach. Using the

Fourteenth Amendment as its major instrument of change, the Warren Court wiped away legal barriers of discrimination, eliminated rural bias in the state legislatures and virtually wrote a new constitutional code of criminal justice. By the late sixties, those sweeping Warren Court decisions had alienated large and influential segments of the electorate.

As Republican presidential candidate in 1968, Richard Nixon sensed that the Warren Court was politically vulnerable. At a time when most Americans were locking their doors and minds in reaction to a rising crime rate and freer social and political order, the Warren Court proceeded on its activist way, expanding the rights of criminal defendants, political radicals and even pornography peddlers. In many Americans' eyes, the Warren Court not only favored a radical fringe of society, but had almost become a part of it. So when a Warren Court demanded that the nation continue to meet its lofty libertarian standards, it was greeted increasingly with complaints and attacks.

Like Nixon himself, the majority did not want reform so much as a return to the old ways. A forward looking Warren Court represented the past; a backward looking Richard Nixon represented the future. The call was for managers, not leaders, men who would solve problems without delivering sermons. And so Nixon made the Warren Court a political issue in the 1968 campaign, concentrating most of his fire on the Court's decisions expanding the rights of criminal suspects. Although Nixon entered the White House in 1969 with the thinnest of victory margins, he was determined to follow through on his campaign rhetoric.

Only one day after taking office, Nixon met with his new attorney general, John Mitchell, to discuss the new Administration's law and order policies. "I said that I would take personal command in this area," Nixon later recalled. "In urban affairs I have a lot of experts—Finch, Romney, Moynihan—and I'll learn. But in this area I know something myself." With Attorney General Mitchell replacing Ramsey Clark, the President not only effected a cosmetic change in the federal law enforcement agency but rearranged its prosecutorial priorities as well. There would be less attention given to the rights of criminal defendants and more to the prerogatives of the police and prosecutors. But to make those new priorities stick, the Justices Department would need cooperation at the top, that is, in the U.S. Supreme Court.

The President's first four successful Court appointees were men with well known law and order views. Chief Justice Warren Burger had been criticizing Warren Court criminal decisions for years and, in his opinions on the U.S. Court of Appeals for the District of Columbia, had earned the reputation of a law and order judge. Justice Harry Blackmun was a quieter Warren Burger, conservative in the criminal field and uncomfortable with sweeping judicial rulings in other legal areas as well. As John Mitchell's Assistant Attorney General, William Rehnquist not only supported the Justice Department's tough new law and order policies but became the Department's chief advocate on Capitol Hill. Before his Court appointment, Lewis Powell, Jr. had publicly defended the Nixon Administration's wire-tapping policy and had long been on record as a critic of the Warren Court's *Miranda* decision.

Quite aside from their specific positions on the criminal law, the four Nixon appointees held very different views from the old Warren Court majority on the proper role of the Supreme Court. Where the Warren Court majority was innovative, the new Justices urged restraint. Where the Warren Court did not hesitate to upset state laws that ran contrary to its broadly conceived egalitarianism, the new members avoided that uncomfortable confrontation whenever possible. The emerging conservative majority (the four Nixon appointees plus Justices Stewart or White) refused to extend Warren Court decisions and, in some cases, consciously backpedaled from the spirit of the Warren Court's rulings.

Two days before the 1972 presidential election, Nixon vowed to continue his policy of appointing conservative judges to the Court, if the voters returned him to office. The nation and the Court needed men like Burger, Blackmun, Rehnquist and Powell, the President told the *Washington Star-News'* Garnett Horner, judges Nixon characterized as "not reactionary judges but men who are constitutional conservatives." The President then indulged in a bit of political prognostication. "I feel very strongly that this country wants and this election will demonstrate that the American people want and the American people will thrive upon a new feeling of responsibility, a new feeling of self-discipline, rather than go back to the thoughts of the sixties that it was government's job every time there was a problem, to make people more and more dependent upon it to give way to their whims."

That election analysts might question the President's preelection interpretation of voter preferences was hardly important on the evening of November 8, 1972. Regardless of the reasons, Richard Nixon's reelection victory was an extraordinary personal and political triumph. He won more than 60 per cent of the popular vote, swept 49 states and dealt Senator George McGovern the worst defeat ever suffered by a Democratic presidential candidate. The victory not only stood as an indisputable affirmation of Nixon's first term performance but, in a sense, a strong endorsement of the Court he had so effectively remodeled. Those "thoughts of the sixties" that the President had predicted would be rejected in 1972 had often been identified (inaccurately) with the Warren Court. That was the institution that many Americans believed had licensed permissiveness in the courtroom and literature.

The President has already been so successful in dealing with the Court on his terms, almost anything he does in his second four years in office will almost seem anti-climactical. If Nixon has additional opportunities to appoint members to the Court in the next four years, he undoubtedly will keep to his formula of the first term. His appointees will again boast conservative positions—tough on law and order issues, deferential to the other branches of government in policy-making areas and generally modest in their aspirations for the Court.

That was what the public ordered in 1968 and the message was louder and clearer in 1972. Americans still wanted to cool off from the turbulent sixties. Those who offered bold new initiatives, like George McGovern, were doomed to the footnotes of history. The nation's majority simply did not want sudden change of any kind. No instant end to the Vietnam War or fast tax reform or dramatic social experiment. The American people wanted stability above all else and that meant caution everywhere, including on the Supreme Court. It was a time, the ballots indicated, for a Burger, not a Warren, Court.

Where will a Burger Court with additional Nixon appointees take the law and the nation? Much, of course, depends on unknown factors, including how many Court vacancies occur in the next four years and where. If the President is able to name even two appointees, and they replace activists on the Court (Douglas, Brennan or Marshall), then a "Nixon" Court will be a reality for many years after its creator's stay in the White House.

Beyond the numbers, the names of the appointees will be crucial. If the President chooses appointees of Justice Rehnquist's tough philosophical fiber, the Court could move in a yet uncharted direction. For Rehnquist is an activist, every bit as tenacious as William Douglas. The difference is that where Douglas is a liberal activist, Rehnquist goes just the other way. With a majority of Rehnquists on the Court, it is at least conceivable that the Court could return to the pre-1937 days when its major interest was the protection of private property, not human rights.

But such a Court majority is unlikely, primarily because Justice Rehnquist's views are to the right of both President Nixon and the national majority. Neither the President nor the nation as a whole appears ready to erase the hard fought victories in the civil rights and liberties fields of the last three decades. The President, therefore, will probably choose appointees with views closer to the current American mainstream. Appointees like Justice Lewis Powell, Jr. With a conservative instinct but pragmatic temperament, Powell has a far higher regard for the actions of law enforcement authorities (even when they stifle individual liberties) than did the Warren Court majority. And yet, if he spots a flagrant abuse of the public trust, Powell is willing, as he did in the domestic wiretapping case, to call a halt to the practice. In other fields, Powell has acted with emulative caution. He is extremely reluctant to limit the freedom of action of state legislatures and the Congress. But there is no reason, based on Powell's record so far, to think that the restraint that Powell wants for the Court will move to the point of absolute restriction on judicial action.

A majority of Nixon appointees on the Court will surely produce some surprises, just as the President did in his first four years in office. But the pattern, nonetheless, is clear enough. There will be little attempt to accomplish by judicial decision what the electorate is reluctant to do by ballot. Decisions like *Brown* v. *Board of Education* and *Baker* v. *Carr* may be relics of a bygone judicial day. For the Burger Court, unlike its predecessor, has no appetite for the sweeping judicial mandate. Already moving toward a philosophical position of judicial restraint, Burger Court changes in the future will be measured in terms of degree, not direction. With more of President Nixon's "constitutional conservatives," the Court is likely to hold to its cautious rulings with a tenacity and conviction reminiscent of the days of the early fifties when Justice Felix Frankfurter dominated the Court. In short, the Court will move slowly and

deliberately, like Chief Justice Burger's favorite symbol for the
law, the tortoise.

The impact of the new Court on the nation will be enormous.
For one thing, lower courts in both the state and federal systems
will have to take notice of the new Court's posture and act
accordingly. That means that conservative state and federal
judges, once intimidated by the activist rulings of the Warren
Court, will become more forthright in their decisions now that
they no longer have to fear reversals from the High Court. At
the same time, activist courts, like the D.C. Court of Appeals,
will break new judicial ground at the high risk of reversal by
the Burger Court. The Burger Court has already shown the
D.C. Court of Appeals [in the Army surveillance and Democratic Credentials Committee cases] that it will not hesitate to
throw out rulings it finds overly ambitious.

In addition to its effect on judges, the Burger Court will be
telegraphing a new message to citizens throughout the country.
For civil libertarians, the message will not be welcome, for the
Burger Court promises no special consideration for individual
liberties when they collide with government interests. Civil
rights attorneys insisting on new advances for blacks may find
the judicial going rough as well. And for the new interest
groups, such as environmentalists, the new Court direction
suggests that they may have to look elsewhere for relief.

The Burger Court has begun to shift the balance of governmental power away from the courtroom, where it often resided
during the Warren Court years, and toward the executive man-
sions and legislative halls. Except in the criminal area, the
individual rights won under the Warren Court still stand. But
the Burger Court will not be anxious to create new ones. In fact,
if there are to be further innovations, many aggrieved Americans and new interest groups will have to look in another
direction, most often to their elected representatives. Given the
prevailing conservative mood of America in the early seventies,
that channel for change is not promising.

SOURCE NOTES

Much of the material for this book was collected in confidential interviews which makes a complete accounting of my sources impossible. Where I have borrowed extensively from publications, either for direct quotation or background, I have given credit in the following selected bibliographical narrative. Persons interviewed, who did not request anonymity, are listed after the narrative.

For general history on the U.S. Supreme Court, I turned first to Charles Warren's two volumes, *The Supreme Court in United States History*. Robert G. McCloskey's book, *The American Supreme Court*, provided a more pointed summary of the Court's history and his *The Modern Supreme Court* covered a period untouched by the Warren volumes. Carl Brent Swisher's *The Supreme Court in Modern Role* was also instructive for more recent Court history as was Alpheus T. Mason's *The Supreme Court from Taft to Warren*. Leo Pfeffer's *This Honorable Court* and Fred Rodell's *Nine Men* offered highly readable summaries of the Court's work and will be of particular interest to the layman. For the relationship between the President and the Court, I found Robert Scigliano's *The Supreme Court and the Presidency* essential. Joseph P. Harris' *Advice and Consent of the Senate* was my key reference in studying the Senate's role in passing on a president's Court appointees. Charles L. Black, Jr.'s discussion of the Senate's advice and consent function can be found in the Yale Law Journal, volume 79, page 657.

Archibald Cox's *The Warren Court: Constitutional Decisions As an Instrument of Reform* and *The Warren Court,* a collection of essays edited by Richard H. Sayler, Barry B. Boyer and Robert E. Gooding, Jr., provided excellent, generally favorable, appraisals of the Warren Court's work. A provocative and more critical analysis was offered in *The Supreme Court and the Idea of Progress* by Alexander M. Bickel. An insider's thoughtful view of the Court was given by former Justice Arthur J. Goldberg's *Equal Justice: The Supreme Court in the Warren Era.* *The Warren Court and its Critics* by Clifford M. Lytle told who the Court's enemies were and why. *The Making of Justice: the Supreme Court in Action* by James E. Clayton provided a vivid account of one term of the Warren Court and was especially valuable for the discussion of the Kennedy Administration's deliberations on Court candidates. For a history of post-World War II America, I found Eric F. Goldman's *The Crucial Decade and After, 1945–60* particularly informative.

The oral argument of *Brown v. Board of Education* and excellent prefatory remarks were contained in *Argument,* edited by Leon Friedman. Alfred H. Kelly's chapter on the *Brown* decision in *Quarrels That Have Shaped the Constitution,* edited by John A. Garraty, provided excellent background material. Anthony Lewis' *Gideon's Trumpet* gave a superb account of *Gideon v. Wainwright.* Fred P. Graham's *The Self Inflicted Wound* offered a fair and thorough study of the Warren Court decisions in the criminal field.

John D. Weaver's *Warren, the Man, the Court, the Era* was helpful for anecdotal material on Earl Warren's early years. Anthony Lewis' profile on Chief Justice Warren in *The Justices of the United States Supreme Court, 1789–1969,* edited by Leon

Friedman and Fred Israel, provided important material on Warren as a judge as did his interview with the former Chief Justice in the *New York Times Magazine,* October 19, 1969. Valuable background material on the appointment of Warren's successor, Warren Burger, was found in Julius Duscha's *New York Times Magazine* article on the new chief justice, October 5, 1969. Alpheus Mason's profile on William Howard Taft in *The Justices of the United States Supreme Court, 1789–1969* was excellent.

John P. Frank's *The Warren Court* provided important biographical material on Justices Harlan and White. Jerold H. Israel's profile of Justice Stewart in *The Justices of the United States Supreme Court, 1789–1969* was valuable, particularly Israel's analysis of Stewart's judicial philosophy. The best biographical material Justice White was written by the Justice himself in an article in *Sports Illustrated,* December 10, 1962. The record of the Senate Judiciary Committee's hearings on Clement Haynsworth, Jr., G. Harrold Carswell, Lewis Powell, Jr. and William Rehnquist supplied important material on those four nominees. The report by the American Bar Association's Standing Committee on the Federal Judiciary, October 31, 1971, provided important details of the dialogue between the ABA and the Nixon Administration before the Powell and Rehnquist appointments.

For an understanding of Richard Nixon, I found Garry Wills' *Nixon Agonistes* and Theodore H. White's *The Making of the President 1968* particularly instructive. *Nixon in the White House: The Frustration of Power* by Rowland Evans, Jr. and Robert O. Novak was helpful for the study of the first two years of the Nixon presidency. Robert Shogan's *A Question of Judgment* gave a careful account of the rise and fall of Justice Abe Fortas. I relied heavily on material in Sanford Ungar's *The Papers & the Papers* for behind-the-scenes activities at the *New York Times* and *Washington Post* in the Pentagon Papers case.

For Daniel Ellsberg's thinking on U.S. policy in Vietnam, I consulted material in Ellsberg's book, *Papers on the War.* Barry Satlow's account of the execution of Ralph James Hudson was found in *Juris Doctor,* November 1971. Alexander Meiklejohn's views on the role of the Court as teacher were presented in his book *Free Speech and Its Relation to Self-government.*

Among those persons interviewed for this book:

Birch Bayh, U.S. Senator; David L. Bazelon, chief judge, U.S. Court of Appeals for the District of Columbia; Alexander M. Bickel, Chancellor Kent Professor of Law and Legal History, Yale University; Charles L. Black, Jr., Henry R. Luce Professor of Jurisprudence, Yale University; Benjamin C. Bradlee, executive editor, the *Washington Post;* Patrick J. Buchanan, special assistant to the President; Leroy Clark, professor of law, New York University; Tom C. Clark, Associate Justice of the U.S. Supreme Court, retired; John Hart Ely, professor of law, Yale University; Abraham S. Goldstein, dean of the Yale Law School; James C. Goodale, vice president and general counsel, the *New York Times;* Jack Greenberg, director-counsel, NAACP Legal Defense Fund;

Erwin N. Griswold, U.S. Solicitor General; Richard G. Kleindienst, U.S. Attorney General; Burke Marshall, deputy dean of the Yale Law School; Michael Meltsner, professor of law, Columbia University; Lewis F. Powell, Jr., Associate Justice of the U.S. Supreme Court; A.M. Rosenthal, managing editor, the *New York Times;* Albert J. Rosenthal, professor of law, Columbia University; John Sears, former deputy counsel to the President; Potter Stewart, Associate Justice of the U.S. Supreme Court; John G. Tower, U.S. Senator; J. Skelly Wright, judge, U.S. Court of Appeals for the District of Columbia.

ACKNOWLEDGMENTS

This book could not have been completed without the help of a number of people: Carey Winfrey, a friend and fellow journalist, who suggested the idea for the book; Wendy Weil, my agent, who steered me through the publishing world labyrinth; my superiors at *Time* who granted me the leave of absence to write the book; Elie Abel, dean of the Columbia Graduate School of Journalism, who found office space for me; Alexander M. Bickel, Chancellor Kent Professor of Law and Legal History at Yale, Abraham S. Goldstein, dean of the Yale Law School, and Albert J. Rosenthal, professor of law at Columbia, who took time away from their busy schedules to read parts of the manuscript and offer invaluable suggestions for its improvement; Erika Sánchez, a *Time* colleague, who researched much of the manuscript under deadline pressure; my wife, Marcia, the ideal editor, who provided the perfect blend of criticism and compassion and, finally, my children, David and Lauren, who at crucial times dragged me away from "THE BOOK" to play.

INDEX